Praise for

THE TWILIGHT OF BOHEMIA

"Who would have thought that a book about artist housing in Lower Manhattan would be impossible to put down? The force and beauty and clarity of Peter Trachtenberg's writing is what makes *The Twilight of Bohemia* a page-turner about so much more than the characters we meet and the lost world of New York City that it so vividly evokes."

—FRANCINE PROSE
author of *1974: A Personal History*

"*The Twilight of Bohemia* is both succinct and sprawling. It's a melancholy love story about a painter friend who offed himself in a utopian housing project in Manhattan that everyone knows about and no one understands. So Peter ferrets out the details of Westbeth, a completely original enclave for artists in New York, spilling gossip about the building's residents like Diane Arbus, like Merce Cunningham, and himself—a pattern of episodes as puzzling, glamourous and wrenching as an artist's life is—one falls down and the others continuing, like Peter, to say what his friendship was, still trembling."

—EILEEN MYLES
author of *Afterglow (a Dog Memoir)*

"This fascinating recovery of a time and place has been magnificently researched and written with verve, wit, and compassion. It represents a standard for how urban history should be done. Westbeth's history is conveyed frankly, both its promise and its stumbles along the way."

—PHILLIP LOPATE
author of *A Year and a Day: An Experiment in Essays*

"Reading *The Twilight of Bohemia*, I had the feeling that its subject—a complex of buildings—had been condensed into book form through some Borgesian literary-alchemical process. This work is elegiac, intimate, and wry. Trachtenberg tells interlacing tales of an architectural entity, artists who have lived as neighbors for fifty years, an art world that now only exists in New York City's rear-view mirror, and a friendship that began in youth and ended with suicide in Westbeth. But the book is also a true historical document, detailed and precise. And completely crucial."

—NELLY REIFLER
author of *Elect H. Mouse State Judge: A Novel*

"With tenderness and mischievous humor, *The Twilight of Bohemia* spins through a carousel of the grimy, effulgent high notes and heartbreaks of New York City's glorious weirdos. This account of the utopian promise and indignities of the country's first publicly funded artist housing project, Westbeth, is a love letter: to trying to strike it big, to the grit of getting by, to the pitfalls of soaring imagination, and to friendship. Trachtenberg's deft hand tallies the tragic dimensions of extraordinary dreams under ordinary capitalism."

—TRACY O'NEILL
author of *Woman of Interest: A Memoir*

"Westbeth is the *other* great twentieth century New York City artist community, without the brand-dominance of the Chelsea Hotel, but arguably more important. This raw, beautiful book is part eulogy. But it's also a celebration—of the spirit that makes the City a global arts hub and, crucially, what it takes to support and sustain that spirit."

—WILL HERMES
author of *Lou Reed: The King of New York*

"Beautiful! How often have you read a great book and thought, 'Why can't I live there? Why can't I live that story?' Those are the questions I asked myself as I reluctantly finished Peter Trachtenberg's *The Twilight of Bohemia*.

Trachtenberg has artfully, tenderly, and wisely recreated New York City's legendary Westbeth artists' community through the stories of dozens of artists who lived there, himself included. The result is a messy tale of love and loss anchored in the equally messy act of creation. It is the story of an oasis in a mad world (though the madness sometimes sneaks in the door alongside the residents!). It is a story that left this reader hungering for more."

—MARY GABRIEL
author of *Ninth Street Women: Lee Krasner, Elaine de Kooning, Grace Hartigan, Joan Mitchell, and Helen Frankenthaler: Five Painters and the Movement That Changed Modern Art*

"Peter Trachtenberg's *The Twilight of Bohemia* is a deeply moving book and is unlike anything I have read before. An uncanny blend of elegy for a lost friend and history of New York at what might well be its peak of cultural relevance and vitality, Trachtenberg's warm voice sweeps us through the corridors of an actual housing development for actual artists, where we confront genius and ridiculousness in almost equal measure, and, along the way, are reminded of the fragility of art and the people who create it."

—SCOTT SPENCER
author of *An Ocean Without a Shore*

"*The Twilight of Bohemia* is freaking fantastic. I'm a visual artist and I think and see in painting terms, so to me, the book has a deep accomplished chiaroscuro, containing all the elements of Westbeth's history along with the entire art world in the seventies, balanced with the heartbreak of Gay Butch Milius holding the whole composition together, resulting in a very fine portrait."

—EDITH VONNEGUT
painter and illustrator

"Peter Trachtenberg has, with sharpest eye and keenest empathy, retrieved a piece of a lost time. His *The Twilight of Bohemia* captures Westbeth — the 70s-era dream of an artists' utopia on the Lower West Side. He was there and he brings the lens in close on his fellow artists. Their lives are aspiring, hardscrabble, and sometimes — as with Diane Arbus — tragic. The stories light up a fragile and self-enclosed world. History survives in such acts of attentive witness — would that all our lives be one day told with such care."

—SVEN BIRKERTS
author of *The Miró Worm and the Mysteries of Writing: Essays*

"Peter Trachtenberg is a brilliant observer of humanity. *The Twilight of Bohemia* is vivid and compelling. We experience the [Westbeth] community at large as well as the intimate experiences of individual artists, including the author's own creative journey and a life-changing friendship. I was completely transfixed and transported and in awe of the trip."

—JILL MCCORKLE
author of *Old Crimes: and Other Stories*

"As New York City becomes increasingly inhospitable to all but the wealthiest residents, *The Twilight of Bohemia* takes us inside the rare Manhattan building that continues to nurture a grassroots creative community against all odds. Peter Trachtenberg has given the Westbeth the artful and compassionate biography it has long deserved."

—JESSE RIFKIN
author of *This Must Be the Place: Music, Community, and Vanished Spaces in New York City*

THE TWILIGHT OF BOHEMIA

THE TWILIGHT
OF BOHEMIA

Westbeth and the Last Artists in New York

PETER TRACHTENBERG

BOSTON
BLACK SPARROW PRESS

Published in 2025 by
BLACK SPARROW PRESS
Boston, Massachusetts

LIBRARY OF CONGRESS CONTROL NUMBER 2022951486
Names: Trachtenberg, Peter, 1953- author.
Title: The Twilight of Bohemia : Westbeth and the last artists in New York
    / Peter Trachtenberg.
Description: Boston : Godine, 2025. | Includes bibliographical references.
Identifiers: LCCN 2023051094 (print) | LCCN 2023051095 (ebook) | ISBN
    9781574232516 (hardback) | ISBN 9781574232523 (ebook)
Subjects: LCSH: Artists–New York (State)–New York–Biography. | Westbeth
    Artists' Housing (New York, N.Y.) | Arts and society–New York
    (State)–New York–History–20th century. | Arts and society–New York
    (State)–New York–History–21st century. | New York (N.Y.)–Social life
    and customs–20th century. | New York (N.Y.)–Social life and
    customs–21st century.
Classification: LCC NX511.N4 T73 2024 (print) | LCC NX511.N4 (ebook) |
    DDC 700.92/2747–dc23/eng/20240311
LC record available at https://lccn.loc.gov/2023051094
LC ebook record available at https://lccn.loc.gov/2023051095

First Printing, 2025
Printed in the United States of America

For Mary

I am everyday people.

—SLY STONE

CONTENTS

Preface

THIS BOOK IS A HISTORY of five decades in the life of Westbeth, a subsidized artists' community in New York City. It's one of only a few such communities in the United States and the only one created and sustained by a partnership between the federal government and a private foundation.

The story is told primarily from the perspectives of seven long-term tenants, though other artists pass through: the photographer Diane Arbus, the conceptual and performance artist Lorraine O'Grady, the visual documentarian Hans Haacke. Some of these people are now deceased, among them the painter and novelist Gay Milius, who was my friend and landlord. He took his life in his apartment in 2006.

The story is told chronologically, decade by decade. Westbeth is home to almost four hundred artists—more, if one counts their dependents. It's the equivalent of a village: it is a village. As with any village, the community has legends, folklore, hauntings. These occupy some of the shorter interludes between the long chapters. And because from the very beginning I wanted this book to cast light on the circumstances of artists elsewhere in the city, I've also devoted two interludes to the testimony of creators from outside the building. The conditions they faced—the constant search for affordable space and sometimes the need to patch one together from scavenged materials, the underpaid and often humiliating day jobs that drained their energy and time—are the conditions that called Westbeth into being. They're the conditions many of the tenants remember from their earlier lives. Westbeth was their refuge from them.

THE TWILIGHT OF BOHEMIA

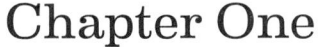

Chapter One

AFFORDABILITY OF RENTAL HOUSING
IN NEW YORK CITY, 1960-2021

YEAR	RENT-TO-INCOME RATIO
1960	19%
1965	20%
1968	21%
1970	20%
1975	21%
1978	28%
1981	27%
1984	29%
1987	29%
1991	28.5%
1993	30.0%
1996	30.0%
1999	29.4%
2000	35.6%
2012	32.2%
2015	32.0%
2021	32.25%

SOMETIME BETWEEN JANUARY 17 AND 18, 2006, probably late at night, a middle-aged white man named Gay Edward Milius III took his life in his loft apartment on the thirteenth floor of Westbeth, a vast neoclassical building—actually a complex of buildings—occupying a square block in the neighborhood that was once called the Far West Village but is now better known as the Meatpacking District. The oldest of its structures dated from before the Civil War, when an extra avenue still ran along the Hudson River. The rest had gone up during the Gilded Age. In the decades that followed, the complex had become a temple of American science and technology, whose hierophants found ways to project the human voice across vast distances and built prototypes of the television and digital computer and developed the radar systems that guided bombers during the Second World War. In the 1960s it had been transformed into a showpiece of the Great Society that sought to end poverty in America. Forty years later, though, the Great Society was just a politicians' sour joke. No one still believed in a great society.

Milius wasn't the first person in Westbeth to die by their own hand. In 1971 alone there'd been three suicides, the most notorious being that of the photographer Diane Arbus, who slashed her wrists in her bathtub on July 26, a little more than a year after the complex, which had been converted from disused labs and offices of the Bell Telephone Company into subsidized housing, opened to residential tenants; the first apartments rented for as little as $110 a month. Westbeth may have owed some of its history of suicides, and its haunted vibe in general, to the fact that its 384 living spaces were occupied almost exclusively by artists—painters, sculptors, poets, playwrights, actors, dancers, composers, musicians. You know what they say about the artistic temperament. Decades later, many kids in the building still called it "Westdeath," or alternatively, "Deathbeth."

Milius, a painter, flea-market picker, and aspiring novelist who'd lived in Westbeth since its opening in 1970, was known to other residents mostly for his aloofness and the large, well-behaved dogs that rode up and down with him in the elevators. He lived in the A building, whose front door opened onto the no-man's-land of West Street and the chthonic rumble of the West Side Highway, and if he came in through the main entrance on Bethune, wanting to pick up his mail or drop off his rent check in the management office, he had to take an elevator up to the third, sixth, or ninth floor, then walk down a long, endlessly zigzagging hallway to a second elevator that brought him the rest of the way to thirteen. His neighbor Murray Bruce recalled Milius's habit of locking himself out of his loft, knocking on the Bruces' door, and then climbing out one of their windows to inch along the narrow ledge thirteen stories above the street until he could step through an open window (he always kept one open) into his own apartment. "You'd see him and say, 'Wait a minute, what are you doing?'" More than a decade later, Bruce still looked aghast. "You're *outside* the building!" What struck him was not just his neighbor's physical daring but his calm, which was so at odds with his usual irritable nervousness. Bruce always knew Milius had locked himself out from the loud cursing in the hallway, the angry, despondent cursing of someone who suspects that whatever has happened is his own fault.

On the night he died, Milius stepped out a different window that opened onto the roof outside his painting studio and attached a length of rubber hose to the propane tank of a gas grill his subtenant kept there for summer barbecuing. He ran the hose back into his apartment. Once inside, he slipped a white plastic garbage bag over his head and fed the end of the hose through a hole he'd cut level with his mouth; he'd gone to the trouble of edging the hole with duct tape to keep the hose in place. With the same thoroughness, he tucked the open end of the bag into the neck of his sweater; as a young man he'd been a meticulous, if eccentric, dresser, and in the last hours of his life the habit returned. I don't know if he'd already opened the valve of the gas tank or if he waited till he'd rigged the trash-bag mask, which was both menacing, like the one Michael Myers wears in *Halloween*, and a little pathetic. The second expedient would have meant climbing back out onto the roof, which must have been ten degrees colder than the street and lashed by the wind off the Hudson, and groping his way over to the gas tank. With the garbage bag over his head, he might easily have blundered over the edge of the roof and plummeted to his death. It would have been the kind of irony Milius appreciated.

Either way, he succeeded in opening the stopcock. The gas would quickly have made him woozy. He lay down on a sofa in the apartment's sitting area facing a row of double-hung windows that extended almost all the way up to the eighteen-foot ceiling. The bag may have been thin enough to allow him a last, occluded look at the night sky and the darker skyline of Weehawken across the river, but when he was found on the morning of January 19, his body was turned the other way, facing the back of the sofa like someone trying to grab a few more minutes' sleep before he's forced to face the unwelcome day.

HE WAS BRILLIANT AND GENEROUS and very kind. When I first met Gay in the mid-seventies he was painting like the pre-Raphaelites, but he went on to paint like the crime scene photographer Weegee would have if Weegee had painted and if his interest in the urban lurid had coexisted with a secret, swooning Romanticism. He'd built his Westbeth loft space from the subfloors up, stacking its constituent platforms like the pieces of a giant Jenga set and cutting a winking crescent moon into the bathroom door. When his friend Edie divorced her first husband and was drinking too much, he used to come over every day to wash her dishes for her. After my mother died, he laid out food and liquor for the shiva and stayed till I was ready to leave, at which point he began to scold me for singing "Amazing Grace" to her on her deathbed. He told me, "You killed your poor mother by singing a Christian hymn!" He was also an asshole. Mostly he meant no harm: he was just incapable of keeping a thought to himself, however hurtful to others. His assholishness was an expression of his suffering, like somebody else's cry of pain. Even the people he was an asshole to seemed to realize that, since most of them forgave him. This includes his first wife, Molly, whom he left for Karen, who became his second.

Gay Milius was my best friend for thirty years; I doubt there'll be another. This is why I keep trying to figure out why he killed himself. I can't forget that one of the times he spoke of suicide, I told him that anybody has the right to kill himself. I still believe that. I just hope he didn't take it as permission. Artists—I'm speaking of creators across the art forms—are suggestible people. They have to be to visualize something where there is nothing, or the bland, aggressive meaninglessness that is worse than nothing. Unlike buyers of chelated mineral supplements or crypto investors or adherents of crackpot religions or thralls of political demagogues, they don't succumb to external suggestion, only to their own. They hypnotize themselves. Sometimes the hypnosis coexists with a realistic sense of their work and its place in the world, which allows them to become—I don't know what other word to use—*successful*. Sometimes, though, the hypnosis is all-enveloping and unwavering, you could say delusional. Artists to whom that happens rarely do well. Coming out of such a hypnotic state can be highly dangerous because when one awakens there is no one to blame (for the lost years, the lost income, the lost friendships, the lost love) but oneself. There's no one to punish but oneself.

This is also the story of Gay's Westbeth neighbors, a few who knew him or knew of him and others on whom his death registered only as a disturbance on the top floor of the A building. Because of its location, the thirteenth floor had none of the casual foot traffic that was common elsewhere in the complex, and in the early hours of January 19 nobody noticed the super and maintenance men rushing upstairs, or later, following at a more stately pace, the detectives from the Sixth Precinct. Down on the lower floors, Jack Dowling knew nothing about the suicide, and the poet Edward Field only heard about it weeks later and in passing. "The thirteenth floor was a mysterious other world," recalls Field, who's won some of the most prestigious awards in American poetry. At this writing he's a hundred years old. "We don't understand the world of the thirteenth floor." The collagist Joan Hall, who lived on nine, didn't remember the event. It's impossible to say what her neighbor Barton Lidicé Beneš knew about it, since by the time I began researching this story he'd been dead seven years, though his ashes enjoy a kind of afterlife in a full-size replica of his old apartment, which is now exhibited in a museum in Grand Forks, North Dakota. The playwright and visual artist Christina Maile remembered that someone on the thirteenth floor had killed himself but didn't recognize the name Gay Milius. Well, who can be expected to know the names of all her neighbors, especially when there are more than 383 of them?

All these people had other things calling for their attention. Dowling, a painter and short-story writer, was enjoying the success of the Westbeth Gallery's 2005 holiday show, the eighth he'd curated since first being elected chair of the building's Visual Arts Committee in 1997. It was a feat not just of aesthetic composition but of personal diplomacy, since the contributing artists were also neighbors and connected by the currents of loyalty, rivalry, and spite peculiar to people who live side by side for a long time. One year, a painter refused to share a wall with a printmaker because the printmaker had once had an affair with the painter's husband. Edward Field was writing and caring for his partner, Neil Derrick. Derrick was blind, and they were a familiar sight in the West Village, two handsome elderly men gliding through the streets with one man's hand resting lightly on the other's shoulder. Black-Eyed Susan, the revered actor who'd been the diva and muse of Charles Ludlam's Ridiculous Theatrical Company, was in lengthy rehearsals for Stephanie Fleischmann's phantasmagoric multimedia production *Red Fly/Blue Bottle*, which owed its title to Wittgenstein's dictum that the purpose of philosophy is to show the fly the way out of the bottle. Barton Beneš was arranging objects from his many collections—he kept them in apothecary cabinets whose drawers were variously labeled CRIME, NAPKINS/TISSUES, MEDICAL, POLITICS, CELEBRITIES, and DEATH—inside one of the multicompartmented boxes that had become his signature medium; they were like larger versions of Joseph Cornell's boxes, their strangeness offset by a veneer of drollery. The hand-painted cards on which the artist mounted their individual components looked like invitations to children's birthday parties, the kind I remember going to as a little kid in the sixties: WE'RE CELEBRATING! Christina Maile, who'd moved into Westbeth as a playwright in 1970 and in the intervening years worked as a carpenter and landscape architect, was now creating bright, iconographic prints that reflected her mixed African Caribbean and indigenous Malaysian ancestry in their exuberance of color and pattern and their theme of vulnerable, uprooted bodies situated in landscapes that were at best oblivious and sometimes actively malign.

Some of Westbeth's tenants were internationally recognized. At a time when TV cameras had to be rolled on wheels and television showed little more than newscasts, quiz shows, and *Bewitched*, Nam June Paik had understood that the technology could be both the instrument and the subject of a new art form. He used video cameras to record and assemble disparate images into installations that might have been the realized forms of Borges's Aleph, a point where all other points on earth are visible at once. He'd also turned television sets into sculpture, furniture, garden fixtures, and, in one case, a notably cumbersome bra that his collaborator Charlotte Moorman wore while playing the cello. (On another occasion, she'd played the instrument topless at Carnegie Hall during the second act of Paik's 1967 *Opera Sextronique*; the performance was interrupted by police who trooped onstage and arrested them both.)

Hans Haacke used different media to create artworks that functioned as visual essays that traced the dependencies and complicities between the art world and corporate buyers, donors, and systems. In 1970 his entry in a show of younger artists at the Museum of Modern Art had been a poll that asked museumgoers, "Would the fact that Governor Rockefeller has not denounced President Nixon's Indochina policy be a reason for you not to vote for him in November?" Haacke hadn't disclosed the question until just before the show's opening, which was probably a smart move, since David Rockefeller, the chairman of MoMA's board, was also the governor's brother. Sixty-eight percent of the poll's respondents (tallied by a count of the slips they deposited in one of two Plexiglas boxes) voted Yes. A year later at the Guggenheim, Haacke displayed a series of photographs with text that documented the real estate empire of one of New York's most vulturine slumlords—or rather, he would have displayed it if the show hadn't been canceled at the last minute by the Guggenheim's director, who for good measure fired the curator who'd supported it. The director condemned the piece, *Shapolsky et al., Manhattan Real Estate Holdings, a Real-Time Social System, as of May 1, 1971*, as "an alien substance that had entered the art museum organism." This may have inadvertently proved Haacke's point.

In photo collages, critical essays, and performances, Lorraine O'Grady was conducting a visionary multimodal inquiry into the status of Black women in art and the art world: the few, narrow spaces where they were admitted, the many from which they were shut out. The inquiry was scathing, mystical, polemical. It was also playful. In response to someone's pronouncement that "avant-garde art doesn't have anything to do with Black people," she'd staged an intervention at the 1983 African American Day Parade in Harlem during which she'd ridden a float up Adam Clayton Powell, Jr. Boulevard holding up an oversized gilt frame to the neighborhood's streets and apartment buildings; outlined in this manner, the surroundings revealed a ghostly resemblance to the squares and palazzi of Canaletto's Venice. White-clad assistants circulated through the crowds holding up smaller frames and inviting anyone who wished to pose as a living work of art. O'Grady collaged old photos of her mother and aunts onto one of a New England mansion where they might have worked as ladies' maids when they came over from Jamaica and made a fleet of warships tumble out of a Black woman's crotch. The piece was called *Lilith Sends Out the Destroyers*, after Adam's apocryphal first wife, who declared herself his equal. "To name ourselves rather than be named we must first see ourselves," O'Grady wrote in her landmark essay "Olympia's Maid: Reclaiming Black Female Subjectivity." "For some of us this will not be easy. So long unmirrored in our true selves, we may have forgotten how we look."

Most of Westbeth's tenants, including the geniuses, were situated in the middle class, sometimes the very lower middle class. Along with making art, they were performing the daily chores and rituals that occupy all but the wealthiest or very poorest New Yorkers: shopping for groceries at the D'Agostino's on Greenwich Street and trundling them home in the folding wheeled carts that are a rarity in almost any other American city, where people do their shopping by car. They cooked meals for their families or their partners or just themselves. They went over their phone bills. They bought tickets for shows. They walked children to school. They took the subway on Fourteenth Street to jobs as teachers, cab drivers, and art movers; someone in the building was said to be a psychoanalyst. They shopped for books at the Strand or art supplies at Pearl Paint. They practiced their instruments, they did stretches and voice exercises. They uncovered their work from the day before and looked at it with pride, despair, or curiosity, just wanting to see what was there. They phoned their agents. They applied for grants that were always too small.

Still, they had one of the most coveted resources in New York City: comfortable and relatively—sometimes genuinely—spacious apartments whose rents were a fraction of those for comparable ones in virtually every neighborhood in the city.

In 2006 the average rent in the metropolitan area was $2,400 a month. Rents in Westbeth ranged from about $650 for a studio to $1,100 for a three-bedroom, which the building, through its Admissions or In-House Moves Committee, reserved for families with two or more children. (By 2024 the average rent for an apartment on the Lower West Side had gone up to $6,989.00 while that for a studio in Westbeth was under $1,000; a three-bedroom was only $1,400.) This is one reason the complex had a ten-year waiting list (at this writing the list is fifteen years long, and closed.) Some of the studios were small and awkwardly proportioned. When renovating the old industrial spaces in the late sixties, the architect Richard Meier and construction manager Dixon Bain were forced to work within the confines of both the existing structure and the budget put up jointly by the National Council on the Arts, the forerunner of the NEA, and the J. M. Kaplan Fund. Some apartments were shimmed into corners or wedged between stairwells and elevator shafts. People on the lower stories often complained that their spaces were dark and noisy. There was an ongoing problem with lead, which would necessitate an expensive and intrusive abatement process a decade later. But even the least desirable spaces were solidly constructed, some of that solidity—the thick concrete walls and double-hung steel windows—a vestige of the building's industrial origins. And, unlike virtually every other residential dwelling in the city, from tenements to luxury high-rises, this one had as its primary purpose creating conditions that allowed the tenants to do their chosen work in comfort. Black-Eyed Susan, who moved into Westbeth in 1980, put it the most simply: "It saved me." Christina Maile called it "a modern-day utopia," but added a caveat: "Any utopia takes a lot of effort."

By 2006 the Meatpacking District had become a home to creative workers who were markedly more successful than most of Westbeth's residents—or, put another way, more famous and better rewarded. Laurie Anderson lived in a glass tower on Perry Street, in an apartment she shared with Lou Reed, who forty years before had recorded the song that might have been the future anthem of every leather bar and sex club on Washington Street, until those bars and clubs shut down during the AIDS years; actually, though, the DJs' sets had run mostly to disco and house, not "Venus in Furs." You used to see the couple crossing West Street into Hudson River Park walking their rat terrier Lolabelle. On West Eleventh Street, Julian Schnabel was building himself a Pepto Bismol–pink Venetian palazzo on top of an old perfume factory that had been built over some older horse stables; he might have chosen the site expressly for its parfait layering of crudeness and refinement, which was so suggestive of his work. He was partly offsetting the project's cost by selling the upper stories as luxury condos. When the Palazzo Chupi was finished, one observer would describe it as "an exploded Malibu Barbie house." Schnabel might have enjoyed the description if it hadn't depressed the condos' prices.

But there are only so many Schnabels or Reeds or Andersons. In 2006, it had been a long time since the Meatpacking District or the Far West Village, if you preferred, was a neighborhood of artists. What had happened there was the same thing that had happened earlier in SoHo and Tribeca, and would later happen across the East River in Williamsburg and Bushwick: after settling in and improving louche, neglected spaces that nobody cared to live in, artists were driven out by hedge fund managers and tech magnates who suddenly did care to live there; some of the latter saw themselves as artists in their own right, artists who worked in money or algorithms. At the unassumingly named Jeffrey department store, a gleaming blade of luxury that had slid into the neighborhood in 1999 and helped jimmy it open, the merchandise included Christian Louboutins at prices ranging from $395 to $6,000 for "super-platform" high-heeled pumps encrusted with thousands of crystals. More frugal shoppers could make do with Manolo Blahniks, which topped out at $1,095. (Jeffrey folded in 2020 but today there are *two* Louboutin stores selling shoes and leather goods barely four blocks from Westbeth.) Back in the late eighties and early nineties, Westbeth artists, especially the older ones, had been kept inside their apartments by the menace of the street, the sixteen-year-olds who strutted along the piers with Rugers sticking out of the waists of their baggy jeans, the witchy crack-whores who'd just as soon stab someone as give them a blow job. By 2006, they had to contend with the street's heartless opulence: from Washington to Hudson and from Charles to Fourteenth, it was filled with amenities the artists couldn't afford, meant for strangers who made their surreal incomes in businesses that sounded like jokes to them, though maybe the joke was on those artists, who quaintly painted on easels like artists a hundred years before and had never heard of Myspace, let alone Facebook.

Most of Westbeth's tenants were older: that is, they were old. (Is there any other adjective whose intensive form paradoxically softens it?) More than 60 percent were over sixty. They'd moved into the building quivering with the energy of the young, the kind that makes deer explode from the brush in front of oncoming cars, and filled with youth's confidence and horniness. (In Westbeth's fiftieth-anniversary exhibition in 2021, a startling number of the photos of those early tenants show them naked; in one, a woman whose partner had started a magazine called *Titslapper* appears to be demonstrating the title as in a game of charades.) Their art was the art of young people in an era before the glut of MFA programs. Hans Haacke had shown them that with the right degree of épater-ing, they too might create something that would be canceled at the Guggenheim. Some of the tenants had remained bomb-throwers. Others had shifted their focus. They became less interested in what they could arouse in an audience than in what they could elicit from their materials or subject matter. The ones who had children became absorbed by the problem of their upbringing. During all this, certain things were happening to their bodies and to the life force that resided in those bodies. They grew slower and more brittle and, as a result, fragile. They fell and broke hips. Some had bad hearts. Along with comfortable, affordable apartments, the building provided them with an array of services made possible by solicitous government agencies and nonprofits: social workers, movie nights, vision and hearing testing, improv workshops, and senior yoga classes. Westbeth is a rare instance of what sociologists call a Naturally Occurring Retirement Community, or NORC. Most New Yorkers their age didn't have it half so good. But Westbeth's artists had grown old in a city calibrated to the speed and hummingbird attention span of youth, and they were of limited means in a city that worshipped money.

Of course, for a long time very few people became artists thinking it would make them rich. The word *bohemian* may be popularly associated with disorderly lives of sensual and romantic excess, but originally it simply meant living to make art, as in the aria in Puccini's *Tosca*: "Vissi d'arte"—"I lived for art." By that standard, the residents of Westbeth were bohemians. The primary criterion by which they'd been awarded their apartments wasn't the quality of their work but their commitment to their art form; residents stressed this point. Roger Braimon, the harried, sweet-natured print and textile artist who served as president of the Westbeth Artists Residents Council (WARC), explained, "It was never about aesthetics because everybody has their opinion, it was about being a professional or dedicated to your craft." This was measured by the frequency and currency with which applicants showed or published or had work performed. The screening committees made a considered effort to exclude attorneys who painted on weekends and realtors who every so often took a role in a community theater production. Most of the residents had jobs—they had to have them—but they were usually the kinds of jobs that brought in money without drawing too strenuously on the imagination. (I'd make an exception for Christina Maile, who as a landscape architect for the New York City Parks Department created small oases of wildness amid a desert of monetization.) The apartments were the artists' reward for devoting their lives to making something that seems to have been essential in every society in recorded history, since even the poorest and most marginal of those societies produced art. Another reading might be that the apartments were a consolation prize for people who had squandered their prime earning years pursuing a chimera. Judged by the minuscule percentage of state and federal budgets allocated to the arts, the United States may be the only nation that thinks of the arts as useless except as generators of employment and taxable revenue. Some of that may be because the arts are valueless, both in the moral sense and because their monetary value is slippery and Heisenbergian, resistant to being fixed.

In the eighties this began to change.

"It used to be that when art was made, people would be unsure of its value until—slowly, through all kinds of critical discourse and debate—the art would acquire cultural significance," the critic Donald Kuspit once told Janet Malcolm. "And *only then* would people arrive with money and say, 'I want that.' Now—and I think this started with Pop Art—there's money waiting like a big blotter to blot up art, so that the slightest bit of inkiness is sponged up." This was in 1986. The change has only accelerated since then. By some reckonings it culminated in the $84.5 million that went to blot up a Francis Bacon triptych in 2020. Or maybe the high point came the following year when $69 million absorbed a purely digital artwork entitled *Everydays: The First 5000 Days* by an artist calling himself Beeple; sure, it was less money, but who'd ever heard of Beeple or laid out such a vast sum for art that didn't even exist in physical space? (The buyer turned out not to be a collector but a cryptocurrency speculator going by the pseudonym MetaKovan.) What was true for visual art was true on a smaller scale for writing, even the disappointing stepchild of literary writing: the $2-plus million paid for a first novel based on the Manson family murders, the $1.2 million that went for a collection whose title story dwelt on a sexual experience that fell into the murky zone between the unpleasant and the traumatic.

Plainly, $84 million paintings or $1 million manuscripts aren't the norm. But then neither are $40 million football contracts, and that doesn't stop kids from risking brain damage trying to make varsity. Could one hear of the spectacular sums that went to blot up a Bacon or a Beeple — or earlier, a Jeff Koons or a Cecily Brown (I'm envisioning a mixed-media piece consisting of a roll of paper towels in which each sheet is an over-sized $10,000 dollar bill: it's called *The Quicker Picker-Upper*) — without coming, even unconsciously, to think of those sums as rewards for the work of art and its creators, maybe even a creator like oneself? And not to receive those sums, not even to come within several zeroes of them, might be viewed by some people as failure.

Maybe Milius saw it as failure.

After a much-anticipated 1981 SoHo gallery show that didn't get reviewed or net major sales, the wonderful, lurid, quizzically romantic paintings of Gay's thirties gave way to elaborately executed jokes; one depicted an empty frame with price tags hanging from it. And eventually even the jokes stopped, and he became more interested in scuba diving and collecting not art but *stuff*: Depression glass, clam baskets, old brass diving helmets. His first marriage broke up. He backed into a second one, complaining comically that he'd been bullied into it until the complaints stopped being funny and you began to see the bitterness they sprang from. He left the city. He started a novel, a picaresque set in the antiquing and collecting world of the Eastern Shore of Virginia. It was endlessly inventive, with wild snarls of plot and joke piled on top of joke like a stack of crockery in a Dr. Seuss illustration, waiting to be whisked neatly away or sent crashing to the floor. It was a novel that could have been published in the seventies, but by now it was the first decade of the two-thousands, and the publishers were putting out flimsy, swiftly plotted Masonic thrillers. It's hard not to view yourself as a failure when you see nothing that remotely reflects your way of being in the world and when your uniqueness isn't treasured but ignored.

Gay's artistic loneliness was made worse by poverty. He had no money and no job. He would have been homeless if his friends hadn't kept paying the rent on his loft and gone hungry if they hadn't bought him groceries. In his suicide note, he wrote, "My book is on disks and the computer. Anyone who wants can finish it and have it . . . Probably not worth the effort."

It has to be said that Gay suffered from mental illness and probably substance abuse disorder as well. He might have committed suicide if he'd been a bookkeeper; he just would have had more money. Nor can I say what drove any of his predecessors in Westbeth to take their lives. I know what they say about the artistic temperament, but in point of fact suicide rates are higher among fishing and hunting workers, machinists, and welders. Anyone who lasts even a few years as a creator has to be resilient. I once heard this from a young visual artist named Nicolina, who at the time lived not in Westbeth but in Bushwick, under the tracks of the elevated train, in a formerly derelict loft that she'd renovated more or less singlehandedly and subdivided into rooms that she rented out to cover her housing costs. When she'd first come to New York years before, she'd scrabbled out a living waiting tables, but the work left her too drained to make art. She did a thought experiment. "I imagined myself as an old woman looking back on my life and wondering what if I'd done what I really wanted to do, which was to be an artist. I recognized that if I tried and failed that I could live with that as an old woman. But if I never tried, I would feel it was a tragedy. So then I was left with no choice but to try.

Because I was super scared about it, I was like I'd better just give this thing everything I have. Like a backflip. You don't hesitate with a backflip."

Every artist who lived in Westbeth had made some version of that backflip. None, as far as I could tell, had landed on a soft pile of money. But they had landed in their apartments and a community that didn't view them as idlers or freaks. Of course, lots of artists have chaotic, self-indulgent personalities, and because the ones in Westbeth were freed from the disciplining exigency of having to pay typical New York rents, they often behaved chaotically and self-indulgently, especially during the chaotic, self-indulgent seventies and eighties. They had affairs. They did drugs. They quarreled violently and pounded on each other's doors at three in the morning. Only a few of them achieved fame. Obscurity drove others to bitterness, especially when all around them old friends and enemies were getting NEAs or solo shows at the Holly Solomon Gallery or a premiere at the Brooklyn Academy of Music. And because art—whether in the form of paintings, sculptures, plays, novels, dance pieces, or symphonies—has no commonly accepted standard of perfection, they were always failing. The ones who were serious knew this.

It's a terrible thing to have a dream that you can neither fulfill nor let go of.

Interlude: Becoming Contemporary

WESTBETH'S VISUAL ARTISTS SOMETIMES SPEAK of it as home to the last of the easel painters. There were more of these in the seventies, when Joe Lewis first came to the building to study with the lyrical expressionist Anne Tabachnick. Although he liked Westbeth ("The building was very cool. I was probably nineteen, twenty years old, and there were a lot of kids my age there. Everything was in the hallways. There was always something going on, you could always hear music") and later performed in the art gallery, he never applied for an apartment. "I had too many things to do, places to go, people to see to be thinking in those terms. And I probably wouldn't [have been] able to provide the information that they needed. I wasn't interested in documenting stuff. In fact, most of the stuff I have until about 1990 is because other people took pictures of it and sent them to me."

The protocols of the art world were changing, and so was the very notion of what art was, and who could make it. Lewis was one of the cofounders of Fashion Moda, a space that from 1978 to 1993 served as a platform for exchanges and collaborations among downtown artists, graffiti writers, and residents of its South Bronx neighborhood. It helped mainstream the art careers of Fab 5 Freddy, Futura 2000, Lady Pink, and Lee Quiñones, among others. Although their names were on most of the subway cars in New York, it was Fashion Moda that made them celebrities. "At that time [1990], you were considered a whiz-kid if you were an artist with a solo show before you were fifty-five. There was only half the number of galleries, really, and there were a lot fewer museums, but there were a lot of people in town making art—you know, in Manhattan—because people felt you had to go to Manhattan to be a real artist, so people from all over the world came to Manhattan. In the late seventies, it was seriously economically depressed, so there were cheap spaces. It was perfect for our situation. You could do a little jive job, pay your rent, and focus on making work.

"I did a little urban entrepreneurship. I was in the restaurant industry. I did everything in the restaurant except be the maître d', the bartender, or the executive chef. I was in construction, and I did Sheetrock. I did tiling and I did painting. I took odd jobs, some retail, and I did some writing. Occasionally, I sold a little piece, but that was it. And let me also say I lived in New York, in this hovel where you could put three, four, or five twin beds together: that was about the size of the space I lived in on Mott Street, between Spring and Prince. It was in the rear of the building on the ground floor. There was no insulation in the basement. It was so cold in the winter that I went away once and had this half gallon of wine in the place. I was away for a week, and when I came back, that wine was frozen. *It was frozen!* And I turn on the oven, all four burners of my little White Rose stove, and left that baby on for, like, two days, and you can still see your breath. I think it was ninety bucks a month, and I was always four months behind in the rent. I spent more time in landlord-tenant court than I probably did in all my classes in college. *See, see, look, see this rat here! That's why I'm not paying.* I didn't have the money.

"I'm one of two dark spots in the downtown Manhattan art scene: there may be three dark spots, but I'm one of them. And because of my background, and because my father knew that there was another kind of art world besides this one in downtown Manhattan that was, you know, with Black people, Stefan [Eins] and I both realized that there was more art than what was happening downtown. And so Stefan goes up to the South Bronx, and he sees a couple of places, and he rents this place, which was a burnt-out store, and we put on a new front and a little bit of a roof, borrowed some electricity from the city on occasion, and opened Fashion Moda.

"Now, I'm working in this space, and artists are coming and doing these things which I had yet to learn, experience, or reference. I said, *What are these people doing?* Like putting a spot on the wall? I'm saying, *What the fuck is this!?* But I knew because of studying the history of art, I remembered that everything new is always thought of as bullshit, and then a hundred years later, it becomes academic. And that time kick gets smaller and smaller and smaller as we move into today. Like graffiti's ascension, for example: it took over fifteen years to get accepted as a legitimate art form. So I knew that, and then I also figured that if a person is doing this shit, there has to be something to it, right? If this person is putting all that time into painting a red circle on the wall, it has to mean something, even if I don't understand it. So it took me from 1975 to 1979 to become a contemporary art person."

Lewis wasn't the first artist to understand that the world we inhabit is predominantly a world of images, which have crowded out the wild and manufactured things that were the subjects of art for thousands of years before. He and the artists with whom he worked made images their subject matter and raw materials. They did this with varying attitudes, from the blank verisimilitude of Andy Warhol's soup can to the dread and rage of Lewis's own *Underground Railroad* series, in which the silhouettes of confined bodies—for example, the bodies packed into the undercarriage of a freightliner smuggling them across the Southern border—recalled the bodies packed into the holds of slave ships three hundred years before. "Looking into the future is not difficult," Lewis wrote. "The problem is acceptance; accepting that lives can change due to actions done in the here and now. At times it's just an errant word or aroma that lifts the curtain, because the present, as our future, is nothing more than multiple images; not just any images but the ordered relocation of our past."

The work is a kind of repurposing, and repurposing was the prevailing aesthetic of Fashion Moda, whose name itself was a repurposing and abbreviation of the sign on its storefront: Fashion 装 Moda МОДА—the word *fashion* rendered in English, Mandarin, Spanish, and Russian. Much of the art that was shown there repurposed images that were floating in the atmosphere, on TV screens, in comic books, and on public health posters, recombined them, irradiated them with new meaning. And because the South Bronx was a poor neighborhood, much of the art also used repurposed (found and sometimes appropriated) materials, e.g., a subway car or the used refrigerator boxes from which Jane Dickson built a maze that visiting artists enjoyed tagging and the neighborhood's children loved playing in.

Of course, Westbeth itself was repurposed, a hybrid atelier/apartment building quarried out of a gargantuan complex of offices and research labs.

The beauty of repurposing is that it restores value to things that have been devalued and often discarded. That might include devalued art forms. "There were definitely a lot of easel painters in that building," Lewis says. "That was when art was considered *art*, when the building came on line. Maybe [they weren't] the most distinguished painters. I always wonder about that. I was involved in Baltimore trying to set up artists' work-live spaces, and they set up all these prerequisites. And people would paint something, but does it matter whether or not they are really contributing to the field or they're just making *plein air* paintings?

"The question is, when was the last time a painting created a revolution? But there was a painting recently that did start a revolution. It was Dana Schutz's painting of Emmett Till. When that guy stood in front of that painting, that caused a whole lot of stuff to jump down. [When Schutz's *Open Casket* was shown at the 2017 Whitney Biennial, the African American artist Parker Bright stood in front of it for several hours, blocking it from view; he was wearing a T-shirt with the slogan "Black Death Spectacle" on the back. Later the writer and artist Hannah Black called for the painting to be removed from the show and, on top of that, destroyed.] That happens a lot but not at the level of that particular intervention in the museum space. And the funny thing is, I was looking at that painting. If someone put that painting in their portfolio to get in [to my university], they wouldn't get in. Cause it's a shitty painting. But that's the crazy thing about art. You can make the most godawful stuff, but one day you can walk into the studio and do something transformative, and everything else is forgotten. And everything you did before becomes better than it was."

Chapter Two

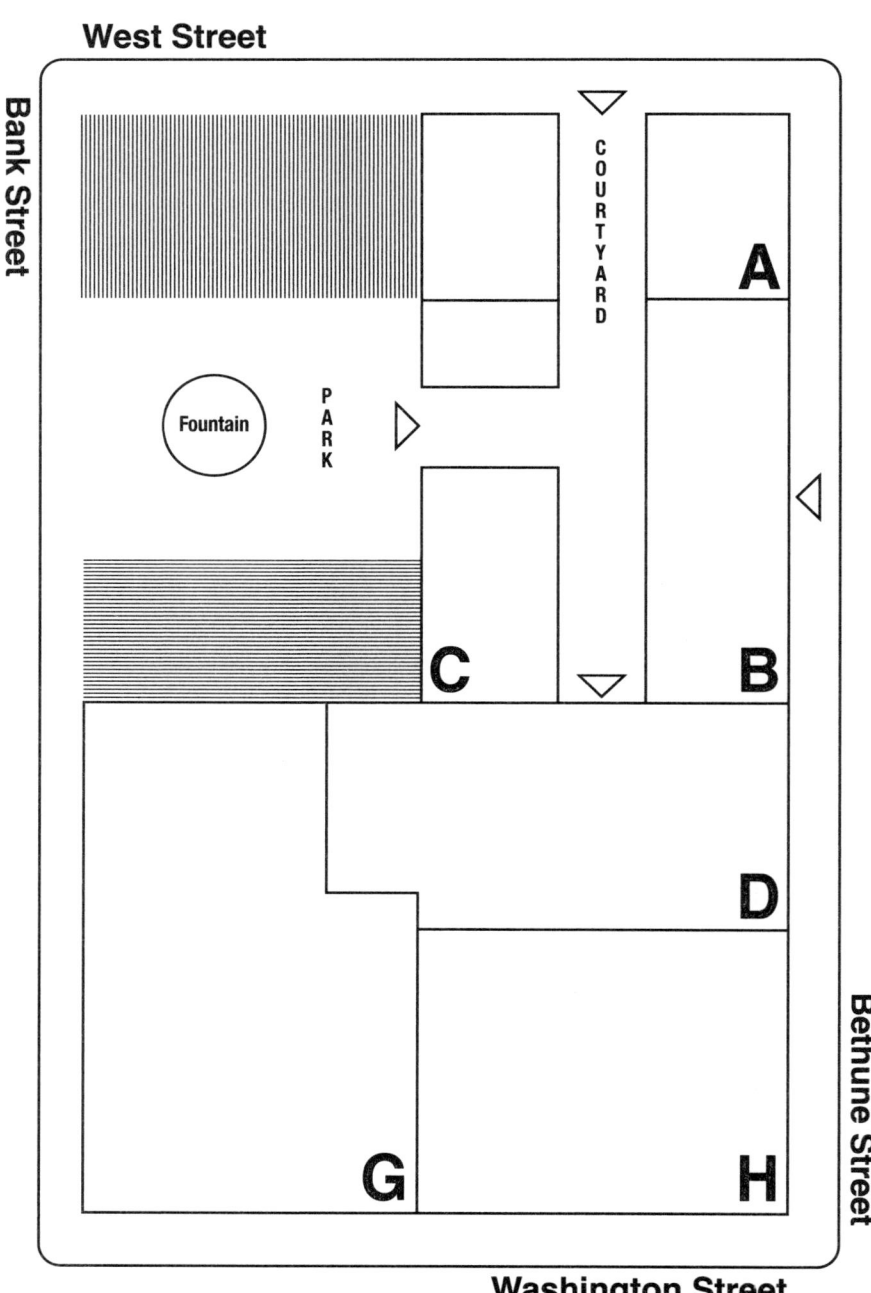

West Street

Bank Street

Bethune Street

Washington Street

Fountain

PARK

COURTYARD

A

B

C

D

G

H

THEY USED TO SPEAK OF shopping malls as being "anchored" by certain stores, usually large, high-volume national outlets like Sears and Target and Old Navy. At the beginning of the twentieth century, the New York City block bounded by Bethune and Bank Streets on the north and south and Washington and West Streets on the east and west was anchored by two industrial buildings. The first of these was the four-story Hook's Steam-Powered Factory Building at 445–453 West Street, built in 1860 in the Italianate vernacular style and boasting "power to the extent of 100 horses." The second, at 455–465 West Street, 149 Bank Street, and 732–734 Washington Street, was the Western Electric Company's ten- and thirteen-story office and factory building for the manufacture of telephone- and telegraph-related equipment used by the Bell system, of which Western Electric was a subsidiary. The building was designed by Cyrus L. W. Eidlitz and constructed by Marc Eidlitz and Son between 1896 and 1903 at a cost of $1.136 million. The modest neoclassical exterior was clad in buff-colored brick and terra cotta. The gutters, fascia, and cornices were copper, which with the passage of years became picturesquely verdigrised.

In the thirty-six-year interval between the construction of these two buildings the American economy passed from steam to electricity. At the turn of the century, *King's Handbook of New York City* identified Western Electric as "one of the foremost electrical supply and manufacturing companies of the world, [which] has been closely identified with the wonderful development of electrical science in the last fifteen years . . . Its dynamos, its arc and incandescent lights, its annunciators and fire-alarm systems, its telephone and telegraph instruments, its aerial, underground and submarine cables are practical testimonials to its enterprise and mechanical skill." The structure on West Street was probably the largest factory of its kind in the world, comprising a foundry, forge shop, and cable department as well as offices and an engineering department on the upper floors, a total of eleven acres of floor space. Some thirty-four hundred people worked there.

The lot also held vestiges of a still earlier economy: lumber and lime yards, a planing mill, and a whiting factory that produced powdered chalk for use in paints and inks. But these were like the small, transient concerns that do business in the shadow of the anchor stores, attracting some small portion of their traffic until they go out of business without anybody really noticing. By the time work began on the Western Electric building, the lumberyard and whiting factory had been succeeded by woodworking firms and manufacturers of fire escapes, children's rocking horses, carriages, and paper boxes and mailing tubes. They too flourished for a while, then closed or moved elsewhere, leaving only their names in a building directory and some surplus stock in a cellar. Decades later a workman clearing the basement to make room for artists' studios might find some decaying crates that when opened turned out to contain old rocking horses packed in excelsior.

The construction of the Western Electric building proceeded in fits and starts, pausing to absorb some of the lot's existing structures and incorporate them into its design. The new building was larger, divided into four sections distributed around a courtyard and separated by firewalls. The sandy ground so near the Hudson River required extensive piling. In the eighteen fifties and sixties this stretch of Manhattan had been extended farther west by landfill until it was dredged in the eighteen nineties to accommodate large-draft steamships; a remnant of that lost Thirteenth Avenue can still be found on the western edge of the Gansevoort Peninsula in Hudson River Park. In nineteen hundred two-thirds of the nation's imports and a third of its exports were funneled through New York Harbor: wheat, corn, soybeans, salt meat, coal, lumber, bauxite, potash, steel. The ships took on and unloaded cargo at narrow wooden finger piers that jutted from the riverbank to point across the Hudson at the bluffs of New Jersey. Their orientation made it possible to cram as many as seventy-five vessels at a time into a limited expanse of shoreline. By the nineteen seventies, when most of New York's shipping had moved across the river, the deserted piers had taken on an eerie *Et in arcadia ego* quality. As if all along they had been pointing at their future obsolescence.

The chief means by which cargo was brought down to the docks or carted from them was the New York Central Railroad, whose freight trains crashed down Tenth Avenue at such speeds that the company sent men ahead on horseback to warn pedestrians out of the way. Nevertheless, the unwary were sometimes run down; Tenth Avenue came to be called "Death Avenue." In the early nineteen thirties the open tracks between the West Thirty-Third Street train yards and the freight terminal at West and Clarkson Streets were replaced by an elevated rail line that ran through thirty buildings along the route; the northern portion would one day be given a new life as a pedestrian path and greenway called the High Line. The railroad and the highway that ran parallel to it, along with the featureless warehouses along Washington and West Streets, made up what the writer Ernest Poole called "an unbroken wall of sheet iron and concrete with NO VISITORS ALLOWED signs and watchmen to exclude the public." Remnants of the elevated were still visible on the second floor of Westbeth in the seventies. Someone who grew up in the building recalls that kids used to rappel down to the disused tracks from the fourth floor roof. "It was filthy but fun."

At the waterfront, the city's grid broke down and gave way to something provisional and chaotic. Its sounds were the roar and clatter of freight trains, the howl of whistles, the shouts of dockhands, the bellow of cattle getting their throats cut in the abattoirs on Washington and Greenwich, the calls of people selling ass in the shadows under the tracks. It smelled bad. In 2021, long after the Meatpacking District had become one of the city's most coveted swaths of real estate, some of its streets were still paved with cobblestones. In the crevices between them, there were still traces of old blood.

A TRANSFORMATIONAL TECHNOLOGY IS ONE that ramifies beyond the original intentions of its creators. Alexander Graham Bell envisioned the telephone chiefly as a means of teaching deaf people to speak so they could abandon the pernicious vice of sign language. In the course of fulfilling its mission of producing telephone-related equipment for industry and the consumer market, the engineering department of Western Electric, which in 1925 became Bell Laboratories, launched a series of innovations that vastly enlarged the definition of telephony, enabling its users to cast the voice greater and greater distances, to amplify and record it, to synthesize it, and eventually to project not only voices but also moving images across the planet. In 1913, the vacuum tube amplifier; in 1916, the condenser microphone, loudspeakers, PA systems, hearing aids. In 1920 and 1922, a pair of experimental radio stations began broadcasting out of the building and became so popular that they were purchased by the Radio Corporation of America. The year 1923 saw the development of a sound-on-disk projector that made it possible to sync sound for motion pictures. Some of the postproduction of *The Jazz Singer* took place beneath the high ceilings, the human voices on the dailies so shocking that nobody cared if they sounded tinny. In 1925, the orthophonic recording system gave rise to high-fidelity long-playing records; the record stylus's soft crackle as it settled onto the disk was the sound of the parting of the curtain of time. In 1927 the image of Secretary of Commerce Herbert Hoover was projected from Washington, D.C., into a room at 463 West Street in the first demonstration of television. Two years later the pictures came in in color. Between 1937 and 1939 the labs produced the first operating electric digital computer. To many of the people who worked there, Bell Labs wasn't a laboratory so much as what one of its senior scientists called an "institute of creative technology." It encouraged the kinds of research more typically conducted at universities. One administrator made a point of tasking research staff "to investigate not 'what is known'" but rather "'what is not known.'"

During World War II, the scientists' energies were focused on radar and radar detection. The radar lab overflowed its quarters on West Street and was moved to the Graybar building on Varick Street, which also housed hundreds of newly hired scientists and technicians. Claude Shannon, widely considered the father of information theory, developed some of the equipment that broke the Germans' supposedly unbreakable Enigma code. Bell Labs also played a role in the Manhattan Project, though the specifics of that role are elusive. The vagueness may not be so remarkable given the secrecy that occulted much of the labs' wartime research; one scientist instrumental in the invention of sonar wouldn't speak about his work until fifty years after the war's end.

On the piers off West Street, barges unloaded uranium shipped down from Canada, which was then trucked to warehouses in Chelsea, a half mile to the north. According to some, the ore may have been used in enrichment experiments. But the painter and short story writer Jack Dowling doubted anything involving radioactivity ever took place on the premises, and he had lived in Westbeth about as long as anyone and knew most of what had gone on there. On the other hand, Murray Bruce, the neighbor who used to watch Gay Milius Spider-Man along the ledge between their apartments, once told me, "There are still rooms in Westbeth that haven't been opened. Rooms where they were doing decay experiments."

This was in 2017, seventy-two years after a prototype atomic bomb had turned the sand at Alamogordo to light green glass. But I knew nothing about Bell Labs' connection to the Manhattan Project, and so I asked Bruce what sort of decay he meant. The decay of sound?

He gave me a significant look. "The life of sound. The life of *things*. It's hard to find a lot out because the Manhattan Project was being done here, and a lot of things have been scrubbed."

It's difficult to imagine what the men and women who worked at Bell Labs—the scientists were mostly men, the women were secretaries, cleaners, and technologists, like the "human computers" who operated mechanical and electrical devices that found numerical solutions to complex math problems—made of the surrounding neighborhood, its Hopperesque isolation, its dirt and squalor. The docks were so thoroughly under mob control that during the war the Office of Naval Intelligence turned to gangsters like Meyer Lansky and Lucky Luciano to provide security. The noise of the trains that thundered through the second floor of the buildings facing Washington Street posed difficulties for electronics work, and as the war effort accelerated, more and more projects were relocated to other sites in Manhattan and then to a new headquarters in Murray Hill, New Jersey. Bell Labs—which was acquired by Nokia in 2016—is still located there today. It closed its operations on West Street in 1966.

By the mid-sixties, New York's shipping industry and most of the businesses associated with it had fallen into decline. More and more of the piers stood idle, with sun pouring through the empty spaces left by rotting planks to cast trembling bars of light on the water below; the warehouses were empty. The future of the neighborhood became an object of contention. Usually such conflict arises in the wake of catastrophes and upheavals that drive out the old inhabitants and leave an attractive vacuum. This was one of the rare moments when the shift took place under auspicious circumstances. In 1961, when the city announced an urban renewal plan for the Far West Village, under which the townhouses and apartment buildings between Eleventh and Christopher Streets would be cleared for housing projects, a group of neighborhood residents led by the writer and urbanist Jane Jacobs mounted a protest, arguing that the proposed site contained "only a negligible amount of blight." The city backed down. When it formed a Landmarks Preservation Commission in 1963, Jacobs insisted that any future Greenwich Village historic district include the blocks along West Street. By then she was no longer just a neighborhood activist, a word that hadn't yet become popular (the city officials' favored term was probably "gadfly" or "crank"), but also the author of what is still considered the definitive text on the spontaneous, unplanned life of American cities, so people listened to her.

Just three years later, Roger Stevens, the chairman of the newly formed National Council on the Arts (later the National Endowment for the Arts), went shopping for real estate. The government had discovered art: art as a source of American prestige; art as a revitalizer of moribund urban economies; art as a building block of liberal small *d* democracy. Art could even be deployed as a soft weapon of the Cold War—because given a contest between abstract expressionism and socialist realism, or, say, between Jackson Pollock, Ernest Hemingway, Alexander Calder, and Duke Ellington and the members of the Leningrad Union of Artists, the Union of Soviet Composers, and the Union of Soviet Writers, who would you put money on, except for side bets on Shostakovich and Vasily Grossman? In 1965 Congress passed the Arts and Humanities Act and New York City enacted the Landmarks Law, which together shifted the goals of urban policy from the wholescale demolition of nineteenth-century factories and tenements to the selective preservation of existing structures for artistic and cultural production. Even cabinet secretaries spoke of building "cities that serve the soul as well as the body." Stevens, who was also a theater producer and real estate developer, wanted to create affordable living and studio spaces for artists throughout the United States. New York, already the nation's arts capital and vying to become the world's, was the logical place for a pilot project. Even back then, the city's rents were forcing artists into cyclical nomadism as they moved from one cramped, ill-lit tenement to another. Very few of them were yet living in the converted factories and warehouses that would become fashionable in the next decade. Under New York's housing code, it was still illegal for landlords to rent out spaces designed for manufacture or industry to residential tenants.

To help finance the pilot project, Stevens approached the J. M. Kaplan Fund, a New York–based philanthropic organization started by a progressive-minded businessman named Jacob M. Kaplan. In 1960 the fund had helped save Carnegie Hall from demolition by private developers. According to Joan Davidson, Kaplan's daughter, "My father was engrossed in business and the foundation was sort of the back of his hand." Davidson passed away in September 2023 at the age of ninety-six. She was a small, upright woman, both regal and elfin and possessed of an exalted sense of purpose and a playful sense of humor. In the course of her very long life she was chair of the New York State Council on the Arts and New York State Commissioner of Parks, Recreation, and Historic Preservation, as well as one of the city's premier philanthropists. She was probably the single person to whom Westbeth owed its existence, and she spoke of it with the proprietary affection of a parent speaking of a child who, despite everyone's misgivings, has grown up to make a decent life for themselves. This after a long period of estrangement during which the child refused to speak to their parent except to loudly blame them for their misfortunes.

"Today the foundation might be regarded as a little vague," she said. "'Do good things for humanity.' Someone might've said it wasn't very clearly thought out." Jack Kaplan's office was on Twelfth Street and Fifth Avenue, and on leaving work in the afternoon, he'd walk back uptown to his home on East Eightieth Street. Davidson mentioned his eccentricity of picking up any trash he spotted on the sidewalk and burning it before he entered the house. "People learned that if you wanted to pitch a cause to my father, you had to take the walk with him and try to persuade him along the way."

This is what Stevens did when he approached Kaplan with his idea for artists' housing. "He knew that my father was entrepreneurial," Davidson said. "And he would move fast, and could make his mind up what he wanted to do. And so the two of them then decided they would do this as a partnership, and they then went chasing all around New York City, these two old geezers, looking for the ideal building." They found eight: the Bell Telephone Laboratory site still comprised that many separate structures. The one that caught their attention was the Western Electric monolith. Dixon Bain, who became the project's construction manager, recalled, "Here was this building essentially a block square in the West Village going up thirteen old-fashioned stories, by which I mean the ceiling heights are thirteen, sometimes eighteen feet. The place was really gigantic. It was roughly three quarters of a million square feet of space." No other property offered so much room in such a promising location—promising both because of the moody splendor of the Hudson and because it was, in Davidson's words, "abandoned territory." With a population density of only six people an acre, there were virtually no neighbors to NIMBY a massive construction project.

In 1967 the National Council for the Arts and the J. M. Kaplan Fund agreed to put up $750,000 apiece in seed money. The amount later increased to $1.5 million each. Some of the money went to establish the nonprofit Westbeth Corporation, which purchased the Bell Labs building. Neither Kaplan nor Stevens had the time or inclination to see the project to completion, so they dropped it in Joan Davidson's lap.

Much of what she did following her appointment as president of the Westbeth Corporation had a similarly impromptu air. Davidson hired Richard Meier as the project's architect. He had recently graduated from the Harvard Graduate School of Design with her older brother; his only previous commission had been a house he'd built for his mother. "We interviewed him and we liked him. And we said, 'What the heck! Let's give him a shot!' It was so informal, the way you did things then. You met somebody, you liked them, you hired them."

Groundbreaking for Westbeth took place on June 28, 1968. A team with more time and money would have torn down the old structures and rebuilt from the ground up. Meier and Bain had to work with the existing envelope. They needed to satisfy both New York City zoning statutes and the funding formulas of the Federal Housing Authority (FHA); the latter was used to insuring mortgages for moderate-income housing, usually in the suburbs, but knew nothing about the needs of moderate-income artists in a major city. And they had to get all of the approvals within the nine months Bell Labs had specified in the sales contract or risk being declared in breach. Meier sought to create maximum living and work space at the lowest cost. He followed the line of the old offices and built duplexes so that corridors would only be necessary on every other floor. You can tell which way the staircases in those apartments run by whether the black arrow on the front door points up or down. In place of fire escapes, he gave adjoining units a shared semicircular balcony—seen from below, each looks like half a Weber grill; in the event of a fire, someone could step out of their apartment onto the balcony and then take shelter with the neighbor on the other side. The old buildings' masonry could be deceptively thick—a wall that seemed to be eighteen inches deep might turn out to be forty-eight and require special drill bits. The FHA almost withdrew support because the units had been designed with moveable interior walls so that tenants could reposition them according to their needs. "Why the hell are we doing this for artists?" Bain described a bureaucrat complaining. "These bedrooms. These are crazy. Who wants a dotted line on a floor plan showing where the bedroom's supposed to be?" The demands of the construction were so overwhelming that he often had to sleep at the site.

Yet somehow, in just two years, Bain and Meier succeeded in building 383 live/work units at an average cost of $12,000 an apartment; in a new construction, the cost would have been $30,000—in today's dollars that would be more than $95,000 and $238,000 respectively. The total cost of construction was $13 million, most of it provided by the FHA. The structural engineer Nat Oppenheimer, who grew up in Westbeth and often cites it as a model for his profession, said, "I've now learned after the fact, but the whole duplexing, the skip floors, all that is very much a piece of foundational architectural design, Corbu[sier] and Mies [van der Rohe]. It's an incredible example of adaptive reuse that should be held up for everybody. In terms of the creativity to turn a big rabbit warren of labs into apartments, it's unparalleled."

The site also included a theater, dedicated artists' studios, a hundred thousand feet of commercial space, and a courtyard that, after the two floors of offices above it had been demolished and peeled off, provided the inner-facing apartments with natural light. As a further brightening touch, Meier painted walls, beams, and columns in the public areas in different primary colors. One of the early tenants recalled, "Those colors were intense, perhaps a bit overwhelming but clearly made a statement." Years later a new building manager had them painted over, and when the tenants approached the architect to see if he could restore the original colors, he demurred: "I didn't make drawings of this. I did [it], you know, by walking through and marking it on the walls . . . So I had no record [of] what was painted what. And I wasn't about to spend three or four weeks of my life redoing it."

"Westbeth really was the pioneering project and it enabled so much else to happen, large and small," Meier later told an interviewer. But when asked where that project led him next, he replied, "Where I went next was never to do another renovation."

WESTBETH OFFICIALLY OPENED IN MAY 1970 with a ceremony attended by Kaplan, Davidson, Stevens, and an assortment of city dignitaries, along with many of the new tenants and their children. There was beer for the parents and hot dogs for the kids. A rock band played. (I like to think that it could have been the Fugs, since one of their members was a resident or would soon become one, but considering their name and X-rated lyrics and the VIP guest list, not to mention the children, it's unlikely.) Artists had begun moving in as soon as the project received its certificate of occupancy in December of 1969, and more than half the apartments already had people living in them. In a roster of those first tenants, a reporter for *The New York Times* found "a hundred and fifty painters, forty-nine sculptors, twenty-seven photographers, twenty-nine writers, twenty-six musicians, thirty-eight actors, eighteen dancers, fourteen filmmakers, eleven playwrights, seven poets, nine composers, seven architects, seven stage directors, seven printmakers, three designers, four graphic artists, five craftsmen, four theater producers, hundreds of children, and a lot of pets." An obvious draw was the rents, which ranged from $110 (some insiders remember it as $99) to $190 a month. The duplex lofts may not have been as large as the ones that were coming onto the market in SoHo now that housing codes had been relaxed and landlords were seeing the virtue of letting artists move in and rehab the unused spaces on their own dime, but the *Times*'s architecture critic Ada Louise Huxtable gave them her imprimatur: "These are Olympian quarters compared to what is on the New York market at geometrically increasing prices, and the ceilings are high and the windows are large and the plumbing works." Another critic went so far as to call Westbeth a "downtown Dakota." Mike Ackerman, the chair of an ad hoc tenants' committee, was more modest: "Most of us are here because there was nowhere else to go," he admitted. Then, maybe feeling the need to boost morale, he added, "It's a big improvement over whatever roach-infested, tiny, crowded fire-trap we came from."

The pioneers were admitted by a committee Davidson had assembled from some of the most prominent figures in the arts: the painter Elaine de Kooning; John Baur, director of the Whitney Museum; Thomas Hoving, director of the Met; the ubiquitous curator and Andy Warhol–film star Henry Geldzahler; Alan Schneider, who'd directed the legendary American premieres of *Waiting for Godot* and *Who's Afraid of Virginia Woolf?*; and the poets Stanley Kunitz and Carolyn Kizer. Kizer became the committee's chair. Even before it began setting criteria for admission, the committee considered what kind of community Westbeth was going to be. As Davidson put it: "Is it going to be a little isolated dormitory, or is it going to be a regular neighborhood of the city? Was it going to be part of the Village in an active way? Or is it going to be isolated like an artists' colony? Very early on we rejected that idea. This is New York, and these are sophisticated people. They want to be part of the city. If you want to be in a colony, you go to MacDowell!"

Originally, the members wanted to give precedence to creative artists over interpretive ones: playwrights rather than actors, composers rather than musicians. Over time this distinction was blurred or abandoned. There were plenty of actors on that early tenants' roster—including Judd Hirsch and Hugh and Merlyn Hurd—along with musicians and singers. There was some dispute as to whether applicants actually ought to be *good*. "How do you define that?" Davidson asked. "Who's going to decide? So should we have juries? No. Should we have site visits? No. These were big discussions, but in the end, I think we mostly agreed, 'No, we're not arrogating to ourselves. You know, we're not an arts institution. We're housing!'" The one unyielding standard was that the community would only accept *professional* artists. This was less a matter of livelihood than of *commitment*. To live in Westbeth one had to not only make art: creating art, appreciating it, thinking about it, had to be the thing one's life revolved around and to which all else paled in comparison. Whatever else residents did to make a living was beside the point. It could never be more than a *B* job.

Everyone agreed that Westbeth would be diverse: multiracial, multiethnic, open to artists across the spectra of sexuality and gender, at least as those spectra were then defined (whether the early tenants included any trans people is not known). Davidson joked that they might even take some Midwesterners. In the early years there were relatively few people of color. Still, the building was almost certainly more integrated than comparable ones elsewhere in the city. While the common stereotype of bohemian artists may have been one of brooding solitaries or horny swingers, the community's biggest demographic was families with children. The swaths of color Meier splashed in the public areas would have suited a Danish grammar school, and the dizzyingly long hallways were perfect for running races or, in the 1980s, skateboarding. "We ran the hallways like they were our own private jungle gym," recalls Jenny Lombard, a playwright, children's book writer, and teacher who was raised in the building. "The hallways were always echoing with the sound of kids screaming. We'd have these games of tag that would span nine floors and last for six hours." The architect Tod Williams, who worked with Meier (today he's considered almost as distinguished) and also lived in the building, said, "There were lots and lots of children. And it was the children that really created the community."

One of the 150 painters on the 1970 tenants' roster was Gay Milius. He's listed in apartment 725-H, on the seventh floor of the H section, formerly 51–55 Bethune Street and 744–754 Washington Street. The 525-square-foot apartment faced Washington Street and didn't get much light, but the quality of light never much mattered to him since he did most of his painting at night, using work lamps that he clamped onto pipes or the racks where he kept his canvases. He was twenty-three, slender, and already a little stooped, and he must have felt lucky to be the age he was and at the start of his painting career with his name on the lease of a small but new apartment (not a scuff mark on the burrowed-oak floors) in a building set aside for artists. His apartment before this had probably been a tenement on Thompson Street where he'd lived with his friend Larry Silverman, whom he'd met when they were undergrads at NYU and who'd brought in a third roommate whose name Gay would later remember as either Alba or Elbow. That, at any rate, was how he wrote it in one of his last letters, but bear in mind that he was a terrible speller (once, during a game of Scrabble, he spelled *boat* as B-O-T-E; he still won). Alba/Elbow turned out to be a junkie. Gay would wake up to see him shooting speedballs in the kitchen, and although he was a stranger to the moralistic horror with which most people view drug addicts, and also to the moralistic pity, he did find the habit unsightly.

He was just out of the School of Visual Arts, where he'd studied painting with the English photorealist Malcolm Morley. Morley's paintings— of ships, airplanes, model toys—had the texture and detail of high-resolution photographs but depicted scenes and objects that didn't, and often couldn't, exist. They were like stills from CGI movies before CGI was invented. It may have been Morley who taught Gay to use the airbrush that quickly became his favored instrument and who encouraged him to paint from reproductions rather than from life. Morley himself often painted from the illustrations on the boxes of models he collected. Gay began with photographs but toward the end of the seventies moved on to the covers of lurid fifties paperbacks that he amassed by the hundreds and displayed on rotating dime-store racks, so many that his collection would later be featured on the evening news. Both Gay and his teacher were collectors of objects that few people back then, before the commodification of just about everything, considered to be of value. They were just drawn to them, the way crows are drawn to shiny objects.

It's unclear how Gay learned about Westbeth. Morley might well have written the reference he needed to include in his tenant application; he seems to have been well disposed toward his student. The apartment must have been a godsend for Gay, for he was only irregularly employed and made considerably less than the building's $11,750 income cap for single applicants (the cap has since been discontinued). He'd grown up in Washington, D.C., the older of two children of parents who'd divorced when he was young. His mother worked for the National Science Foundation and had the pleasant, vague manner of someone who can't quite remember who you are but is keeping up a polite front in the hope that it'll come back to her. His father was a retired naval officer and a ham-radio enthusiast. It's unclear how the men in the family made their money. There seems to have been some on the Milius side. Gay's paternal grandmother Petey lived in a grand apartment near Sutton Place close to the East River. It was crowded with furniture pieces that were both massive and fragile-looking, with bulbous silk-and-velvet-cushioned arms and backs overspreading spindly legs. Petey was imperially rude in the way people with money can afford to be. The one time I met her, she asked me what I did. When I said I was a writer, she snapped, "A writer? Why haven't I heard of you? You can't be much good if I haven't heard of you." Perhaps she said the same kind of thing to her grandson.

Gay wasn't ambitious—that is, he wasn't hustling to build a career—but at that time a career wasn't the fetish object it would become in the eighties. People in the arts weren't yet obsessing over "careers," gloating about them, bitching about them, comparing the ones they had to the ones others had. If a career was what you wanted, you went into business. Gay had come into art through cartooning. He'd started drawing partly to amuse himself and partly as a way of making friends with other boys at the military school where his father had sent him, presumably to inculcate the discipline and team-spiritedness he thought Gay lacked. Just as some boys at schools like that came to be known as the kid who did backflips or the kid who knew dirty jokes, Gay was the kid who drew. Probably every school and summer camp has a kid who draws, but a vanishingly small fraction of them become artists. It would probably take a lifetime to answer the question of why Gay went on to do what tens of thousands of kids like him, some as talented, some maybe more so, didn't. Why he persisted as long as he did, with as little recognition or reward. Why he failed, or whether one can even speak of failure in relation to the arts, whose criteria are always changing, beauty one century, verisimilitude fifty years later, and pure, unreconstructed newness twenty years after that, every hallowed value trashed until some enterprising person retrieves it from the dumpster to introduce once more. In the end, there might still be no answer.

Even after art school, he still drew cartoons sometimes, figures with large knobby features whose movements and gestures revealed an instinctive grasp of anatomy. They were always hunching, strutting, gesticulating, rubbing their hands together in glee or greed. Around the time he settled at Westbeth, he'd started an illustrated children's book called *Baba Ga-nouj and the Astrolarians*. Baba Ganouj was the hero, the name his sole connection to the Middle East; Gay had chosen it only because he liked the way it sounded. The Astrolarians were a two-thousand-year-old secret society plotting to reverse the earth's poles or maybe its magnetic poles. Larry Silverman was involved in the project in some way; he may have written some of the text. What stays with me are pictures of little men with white beards fountaining down their chests and stomachs and hats so big they would make them tip over if they were tilted even a few degrees to the side. They suggested both the Seven Dwarfs and a minyan in an Orthodox synagogue.

Gay drew the cartoons for laughs but sometimes made a little money with them; he had an on-and-off gig illustrating greeting cards. His serious, noncartoon art was influenced by the Pre-Raphaelites, whom he admired for their romanticism and precision, the sodden hair of the swimmer in Waterhouse's *The Siren*, the heavy-lidded appraisal with which Rossetti's Lilith gazes into the mirror. A drawing of his girlfriend Rachel Paine is remarkable for its fine cross-hatching and the delicate expressiveness of her hands, one of which half grasps and half rests on the wrist of the other in a gesture that's at once comforting and possessive. Between the late sixties and the mid-seventies, he also worked at a head shop in Provincetown, taught art at a summer camp for children with intellectual disabilities, and cast latex dildos for a company called the Ram-It Corporation.

During this time Gay's main artistic project was a series of portraits of friends. The figures were always framed by a dark triangular panel or escutcheon set against a brightly colored background. Because of their uniform geometry, they were like gorgeous, meticulously detailed playing cards. The double framing created a sense of depth, as if he had posed his subjects in a hallway, maybe one of the surreally long hallways (a journalist compared them to the ones in the seminal French New Wave film *Last Year at Marienbad*) that were Westbeth's dominant feature, at least from the perspective of the tenants who might spend a significant part of their day walking up and down them. His figures looked frankly out at the viewer. He posed Robin Rathbone, an old girlfriend, dressed in riding habit and holding a crop. The photographer and musician Jonathan Takami was angular, unflappable, and contained, the shadows beneath his high cheekbones almost as dark as his rock-star hair. Gay knew a lot of people and painted many of them; he gathered them to him from the different circles through which he passed, artists and club kids, left-behind hippies, drug dealers and drug dealers' customers. Village characters like Mark Sloan, the proprietor of a head shop on MacDougal Street who was said to have invented the concept button ("War Is Not Healthy for Children and Other Living Things," "Frodo Lives!"). Fallen preppies like Gay's best friend Chris Harms. College friends like Larry, who over the next thirty years would go from designing projectors for rock bands' light shows to developing a prototype of a remotely programmable thermostat that he told people would one day make him very, very rich.

IN RETROSPECT, WESTBETH'S ORIGINAL CONCEPTION had two major flaws.

The first was the assumption that the rents of the resident artists would be subsidized by those of commercial tenants, which were supposed to bring in 50 percent of the complex's revenue. Although Meier had reserved a hundred thousand square feet for commercial spaces, most of it on the lower floors, neither he nor Davidson foresaw that given the general malaise of New York's economy in the early seventies and the remoteness and seediness of the Far West Village, few businesses would want to set up shop there. Christina Maile recalls that "in 1970, it was still a very dangerous neighborhood. It was a neighborhood that no one really knew. So they overestimated the marketability of those commercial spaces. They couldn't get anyone." It may have been desperation that led one of the early building managers to offer certain tenants sweetheart leases, sometimes decades long and with rents Maile remembers being as low as twenty-five cents a square foot. She wasn't being hyperbolic. In June 1977, Gay and his wife Molly Flewharty moved from his dimly lit seventh-floor apartment into a loft on the thirteenth floor of the A building that they rented on a commercial lease. The initial rent was $300 a month, increasing at renewal to $400. The space was eight hundred square feet; Gay built a series of platforms that probably added on another four hundred. So Maile's estimate wasn't far off.

The practical result was that Westbeth would never fulfill Roger Stevens's dream of a self-sustaining model for similar artists' housing projects across the United States. Westbeth would never be entirely self-sustaining. In the following years the consequences of that would become increasingly evident.

The second problem with Westbeth's conception was that no limit was ever placed on how long tenants could stay. The selection committee considered setting a fixed term of four to five years, long enough for artists to get on a sound financial footing before plunging back into the city's pool of unsubsidized housing. Enough people thought that would constitute an undue hardship that the idea was voted down. "But the hope was expressed," Davidson recalls, "very firmly, both by our end—management side—and also by tenants coming in that . . . there'd be a reasonable period of about five years. And then you would move on. PS. Nobody moved. Why would they? The best deal in the city. It still is. But that, I think, is to some extent a failure."

Interlude: A Mirage

WHEN DESCRIBING WESTBETH TO SOMEONE who hasn't heard of it, you can mention it's where Diane Arbus killed herself. Then they get it.

Of all Westbeth's tenants Arbus is the most famous, her fame amplified by the macabre tragedy of her death in 1971, when she was forty-eight. At the time she died she wasn't yet famous outside the art world, and she was piecing together a living from magazine assignments and teaching. She supported herself with editorial shoots the way Lorraine O'Grady supported herself translating the instructions on ATM screens and Jack Dowling did painting *faux marbre* on the walls of rich people's apartments. A difference was that the membrane that separated Arbus's commercial work from her relentless and unflinching art was beginning to tear. In her art photography, she trained her lens on people others labeled freaks: sideshow performers, cross-dressers, a Jewish giant looming and at the same time *stooping* over his tiny parents. She saw these societal outsiders as aristocrats, ennobled by their lifelong intimacy with trauma, the thing the rest of us spend our lives cowering from in the closets of our personality. In her later work, Arbus flung the door of the closet open; then no one could tell who the freaks were any more. Eventually she started doing this in her commercial photos. When she photographed the Warhol superstar Viva for *New York*, she assured her she'd only be taking headshots, but the picture the magazine used showed the actor with bare breasts and her head thrown back in what appeared to be a stoned stupor. Viva threatened to sue, and the fledgling magazine lost a half-million dollars in potential ad revenue. Spooked clients stopped sending Arbus jobs. On some level this may have been what she wanted. Years before she'd walked away from the successful fashion photography studio she'd set up with her husband, quietly announcing, "I can't do it anymore." Maybe she'd come to the same decision about all commercial work. She couldn't do it anymore.

She couldn't be anything but the artist she was. But by today's nosebleed standards, the prices she commanded for her art were pathetic: $100 a photo. The museums that showed them often paid less. MoMA sold her prints for $50 to $75. The Smithsonian beat her down to $25 an image.

It's possible that Arbus made less than Westbeth's income cap, though it's more likely that an exception was made for her. Almost as soon as she arrived in 1970 she was resented for her reputation and because she'd gotten a duplex on the ninth floor that would ordinarily go to a family of four, although neither of her two daughters was still living with her. She also got a separate apartment for teaching; she told her students, "You've got to learn not to be careful." Another tenant who moved in around the same time, the documentary photographer Cosmos, would forage in the trash bin outside Arbus's apartment for her rejected prints and contact sheets. So she too was now an aristocrat.

Because the painter Howardena Pindell lived at Westbeth and worked at MoMA, someone in the photography department once asked her to bring back a package for Arbus, prints or contact sheets, maybe just paperwork. Arbus came upstairs to pick it up, and when Pindell answered the door the photographer gave her a look of frank appraisal, as if she were considering asking her to sit for her. It made Pindell nervous. When asked her impressions of Arbus, she answered without hesitation: "Inward-thinking, deeply serious, and curious. And a solitary. She was like a person with the internal workings of a hermit. And she was deeply, deeply serious about her work. Just the way she looked at me was, you know, kind of sizing me up, like, do I fit into her genre? I was impressed by her."

Not much has been written about Arbus's relations with her Westbeth neighbors: which ones she chatted with by the mailboxes or had over for drinks or, given the spirit of the time, to smoke dope; whom she quarreled with (though she seems to have been more avoidant than confrontational, vague, soft-voiced, indecisive until the moment she locked gazes with you and took your picture); whom, given the spirit of the time and that of the building, she fucked.

It's a cliché to speak of certain kinds of art as "dark," though I'm not sure why the photos of Diane Arbus should be viewed as any darker than the ones in Edward Steichen's wildly popular *The Family of Man*. It's another kind of cliché to think that such work reflects some preexisting darkness of the artist's soul or else casts its darkness on it.

On Monday, July 26, 1971, Arbus slipped a print of Kandinsky's death mask under the door of Andra Samelson, a Westbeth friend, and left without waiting to see if she was at home. Back in her apartment she wrote "The Last Supper" in her diary and placed the diary on the stairs that led up to the bathroom. She took barbiturates. Then, fully clothed, she lay down in the bathtub and cut her wrists with so much force that the tendons were severed. Two days passed before her body was found.

Joan Hall remembered seeing Arbus by the ninth floor elevator from time to time and saying hello, "but I didn't really know her as a friend, as a person. I was surprised by her suicide." The problem with this memory is that Hall didn't move up to the ninth floor until 1974, and by that time the photographer had been dead three years.

Joan Davidson insisted she saw Arbus's body in Westbeth's courtyard, presumably after she'd jumped. She was so convinced of this that I had to look in one of the biographies to be sure she hadn't died that way. Davidson's confusion may reflect two other suicides that took place in 1971, both victims jumping from the roof, or the many suicides that came later, so many that a woman who grew up in Westbeth wrote, "Suicide . . . didn't shock anyone . . . It was a part of life at Westbeth."

Or maybe Diane Arbus, or her work or reputation, exercised some witchy effect on the memories of her neighbors, on the collective memory of the entire building, a shimmer like the shimmer of air above a desert road on a hot day. When you see a mirage in the desert, you're not seeing something that doesn't exist—you're seeing something that exists elsewhere.

Chapter Three

"A very warm welcome to all of you, the first, pioneering tenants of West-beth, the largest living and working facility for artists in the world, and the only one in the United States: may your years here be productive and satisfying in every way . . . . It is our assumption that attractive, high-ceil-inged rooms, abundant daylight, working plumbing, play space for chil-dren, reasonable security from eviction and rent-rise, and other 'amenities' provide a degree of dignity not to be found in discomfort. Only time will tell, I suppose."

—Joan K. Davidson, "Letter from the President," *Westbeth News*, April 1970

———

The Best Present Is the One You Didn't Know You Wanted

BOB GRUEN HEARD ABOUT THE building from his mother-in-law, who was active in the arts. He and his wife Nadya were living on the Upper East Side in an apartment subsidized by her father, since Gruen was just getting started as a photographer and couldn't cover East Side rent on his own. It was embarrassing to be dependent on his father-in-law, and he felt out of place in the staid neighborhood where every morning liveried doormen stood outside their buildings, coolly appraising the passersby. But when he applied to Westbeth, Gruen says, "They told me to forget about it because there was a thousand people on the list ahead of me and it was less than four hundred apartments. And so, basically, I didn't really think about it much. I was late getting on the list. But then, I'll never forget, Christmas Eve, literal-ly like four or five in the afternoon on the 24 of December 1969, the phone rang, I answered it and he said, 'Are you still interested in an apartment in Westbeth?' It was the best Christmas present ever."

✸

On Learning Who to Talk To

WHEN JACK DOWLING MOVED INTO Westbeth in 1971, he was forty-two and homeless, sleeping on friends' couches and in the office of the
mail-order photo catalog house where he'd gotten a seventy-five-dollar-a-
week job as a mail boy. It was a step down from being a rising painter with
a connection to one of SoHo's premier art dealers and an eighteen-hun-
dred-square-foot loft on First Avenue.

Dowling had lost the space after a four-year legal battle with New York
City, which had claimed the land beneath his building under eminent
domain. The protracted stress of the suit had made painting almost impossible. Money stopped coming in. The judge ruled for the city, and
Dowling was given three days to move out. He put his paintings in storage,
called up friends, and told them to come take what they wanted. He got
a job with a mail-order catalog business, filling orders for books of male
nudes. In a nod to the classical pretensions of an earlier era or the post
office's standards of decency, the nudes were notionally draped in skimpy
togas. He sometimes thought, "You were a mail boy at twenty, Jack, what's
going on here?"

He'd built his career slowly, even haphazardly. As a high school student in a small town in New Jersey, he'd applied to Cooper Union only
because his art teacher told him he ought to. Once he was admitted, he
was intimidated by his more sophisticated classmates, most of whom were
from the city, and frustrated because he wanted to paint figuratively, and
in the fifties, American art meant abstract expressionism. If you were a
young male painter, it was an unstated rule that you had to stake out your
canvases with uninterpretable slashes of color in which every brushstroke
was a register of the artist's virility. Beyond that, Jack had no sense of the
extra-artistic skills—social, organizational, and economic—that are now
taught under the rubric of professionalization. "I don't think 'networking'
existed that much in my younger years," he says. "Nobody at the Cooper
Union taught you anything like that. You'd graduate after four years and
be where you were in the beginning. It depended a lot on personality.
There were people who I knew were going to be successful because they
knew what to do and who to talk to." Jack didn't know.

"I really had to get to know the city itself," he says. "That's what was feeding me in terms of whatever creative abilities I was going to eventually have. That was coming not just from going to museums and looking at pictures; it was coming from living in the city and becoming exposed to the whole of the city." He moved from his seven-dollar-a-week rooming house in the East Fifties to another one on Hudson Street. The West Village had yet to be beautified; the cobbled side streets had no trees, just warehouses and once-grand houses that had been subdivided during the Depression and the war. The neighborhood was still industrial. Dowling liked to listen to the freight cars of the West Side elevated coupling on the sidings by Pier 40, "the squeal and grind in the night when all else was quiet, the humping of boxcars banging one another. The sudden silence when it all stopped."

Farther south, where the World Trade Center would one day cast its cyclopean shadows and then collapse into them on a lovely September morning, lay the sharp, footy stink of the cheese market and Radio Row with its bins of dusty capacitors and vacuum tubes. Seventh Avenue hadn't been lengthened yet, so downtown traffic had to turn left on Greenwich Avenue, then turn once more on Fifth, cutting a gigantic Z on its way south. In the Women's House of Detention on Sixth Avenue, prostitutes called out the barred windows to the men passing by below. They might have been setting up future dates or just trying to get a rise out of the squares.

A half mile farther downtown was the circa-nineteen-twenties bar the San Remo, which the writer Ronald Sukenick described as "an actual Village-Bohemian-literary-artistic-underground-mafioso-pinko-revolutionary-subversive-intellectual-existentialist-anti-bourgeois café." With its pressed-tin ceiling and black-and-white tile floors, it was to the Village what the Deux Magots was to Saint-Germain-des-Prés. Dowling liked to sit in a wooden booth and sketch the regulars. There was a woman named Winifred who was famous for unbuttoning her blouse and displaying her breasts to the other customers. "They were quite nice breasts," Jack recalls. The bartender would escort her out the MacDougal Street exit, and she'd come back in through the West Fourth Street door. Once, on a dare, he borrowed a friend's Brooks Brothers suit and went uptown to the Oak Room at the Plaza, but once he got there, he didn't know what kind of drink to order. He was more comfortable at the Astor, a hustler bar on Forty-Second Street where the boys were young and good-looking and nobody judged your choice of liquor.

In 1958 Dowling did what young American artists had been doing since the time of Gilbert Stuart and went to Europe. "It was only after I went to Italy that I started painting seriously," he says. "Partly it was an excuse—'You're in Italy, now what do you do?'" For a while he painted abstractly, inspired by the panoramic landscapes he saw out his window and the excellent quality of Italian paint. But at a certain point he felt he had hit a dead end. He moved back to New York and began to paint figuratively again. Maybe it was that everything in Italy was horizontal and everything in New York was vertical. The city's orientation mirrored that of a standing man.

Dowling kept a cache of family photos dating back to before the war. They were black and white; it'd still be another ten years before color film would be cheap and widely available. But he liked the old black-and-white photographs, their mystery and depth. "You look at snapshots from the twenties and thirties, they have a wonderful light and dark quality to them, a wonderful suggestion of shadow. You wonder what's going on in the background because it's not clear." A painter might choose to fill in the detail that was missing from those backgrounds, or he might simplify them further. The most radical simplification would be to eliminate background altogether. Dowling began a new painting with a snapshot of his parents on their wedding day. He changed the setting to nighttime and placed the newlyweds outside with the lights coming off the porch behind them so that they were like two spotlit actors on a dark stage. The result was more dramatic than anything he'd painted before. It anticipated the ominous suburban family-scapes Eric Fischl would be painting twenty years later, minus the skulking boys and exhibitionist moms—that is, minus the fiction. It was family romance as documentary but with its characters strategically repositioned and its frames darkened. Real documentaries do this all the time.

Dowling continued the experiment with other family photos. The stark contrast between the velvety black backgrounds and the pale figures resulted in a kind of semiabstraction. It was possible to see the latter as pure forms; if you looked at them long enough, you could forget they were human beings. Perhaps out of an unconscious fidelity to the original sources, he kept giving the paintings a white border, more or less announcing that they were paintings of photos. Sometimes, as in a painting of his mother, grandmother, and aunt that he called *Ladies in America*, the subjects' personalities were evident. In other works, the personalities were withdrawn like water into drying soil until only their mineral residue remained. And of course the profound blackness of the background made the figures posed against it seem to glow in a way that somebody might call spiritual.

The art world of the sixties was more open than at any time since, its boundaries more porous. Dowling could call the Leo Castelli Gallery from a phone booth on the corner and then show up with two large paintings and show them to Ivan Karp, the associate director. Karp liked them well enough to pay a visit to his studio and select one of his pieces for an American Federation of Arts tour. While working at a greeting card company, Dowling became friendly with a teenage coworker named Marcia Silverman, who, as Marcia Tucker, would go on to become a curator at the Whitney and a founder of the New Museum of Contemporary Art (as well as a rumored member of the Guerrilla Girls, the feminist artists' collective whose members disguised themselves with gorilla masks). It was Tucker who encouraged him to start making his paintings bigger, even museum-sized. He couldn't have asked for more influential allies. But the support was qualified. Karp placed his work in several shows but never brought him into OK Harris, the career-making gallery he opened on West Broadway after leaving Castelli. Tucker hung one of his paintings at Max's Kansas City—which in 1969 may have been the hippest venue in New York—but never invited him to show at the Whitney.

Dowling still lacked the flair for self-promotion that proved so useful to someone like Andy Warhol. "I didn't handle the business of being an artist very well. I'd go to an opening by myself and Warhol would show up with a party of five or six people. It never occurred to me to ask other people to go with me, I was too self-conscious. That was a mistake. You really should have your protective group around you. People don't come up to a single person at a show, they come up to someone in a group." (The very traits that made Warhol so successful professionally also made him insufferable socially. In 1964 Dowling was throwing a New Year's Eve party, and at the last minute the photographer Billy Name called and asked if Warhol could come. Dowling said no. "I knew how Andy was. He'd show up at a party, stay for a while talking to nobody, and then sweep out with his entourage and the party would be ruined.")

Dowling also made bad choices. In 1969 he was offered a one-person show at the Banfer Gallery. The opportunity looked good, but the venue no longer held the prestige it once had, or else its prestige had emulsified into stodginess. The buyers who came to see work by its more traditional painters had never heard of Dowling or didn't know what to make of him. The show was an underattended embarrassment. So much of becoming a successful artist—or a successful writer or choreographer or composer— depends on learning nuances that are as minute, tacit, and unforgiving as the rules of etiquette of the court of Louis XV. How do you get a gallerist to make a studio visit? What are your headshots supposed to look like? How long should you be prepared to wait after submitting a story to a literary journal, and if they turn one down is it okay to immediately send them another?

Still, Dowling was gifted and productive, and he had some regular buyers who were good for a few paintings a year. "I didn't read it as success. I read it as, 'Oh, somebody likes my painting. That's nice. I got some money for it.'" From the sales and side jobs, he made enough to cover the rent on a large loft at Twenty-Fourth Street and First Avenue. It was eighteen hundred square feet in a city where the average apartment was less than a third that size. The rent was $100 a month, roughly $850 in today's money. The loft was so cheap because the building, along with most of the neighborhood then known as Bellevue South, sat on Title I land, which was designated for public housing. When Dowling moved in, he had no idea that the building would eventually be torn down to make way for a low-income apartment complex: in 1961 that was still a long way off. "To have eighteen hundred feet at the beginning of my career felt like a good move," he recalls. The vast space beckoned him to fill it.

He liked to paint at night; the dark backgrounds freed him from the tether of natural light. He painted incautiously, with grand sweeps of the arm, knowing that if he didn't like something he did he could just paint over it later. He'd put Betty Allen's recording of the "Stabat Mater" on his stereo and play it loud enough to make the windows rattle. He was the only tenant in the building, and at that hour the neighborhood was almost empty. Who was going to complain? When the record stopped, he'd hear the dim rumble of the FDR like an echo of the pop and hiss of the needle in the empty track; it was almost soothing. He'd pause and light a cigarette, walk to the window to see if anything was going on in the street below. There rarely was. New York City has never slept, but back then at certain hours it dozed. He'd paint until the sky over the river began to fill with light, then walk out in a dream to get coffee from a deli. When he got back, he'd look at what he'd painted. Sometimes he'd be happy with it.

"The artists, the writers I knew, it was a small community. Everybody knew each other, it was a really good time." Stonewall was eight years away, but many gay New Yorkers had already emerged from the trance of secrecy and shame that was the general condition of gay life elsewhere in the US. This was especially true in the Village, where you could get dinner at a restaurant owned and staffed by gay people, see a gay-themed play, and have a nightcap at a gay bar. True, the bar owner probably had to pay off the mob or the cops; often enough he *was* mob. (The Stonewall Inn, which began its existence as a tearoom and speakeasy in the thirties, reopened as a gay club in 1966 with $3,500 paid by members of the Genovese crime family.) Still, not even the Village was truly safe. In 1962 Dowling and a friend were coming out of a deli on lower Fifth Avenue when they were attacked by a gang of kids spilling out of Washington Square Park. "I don't read gay and my friend didn't read gay, but we were two guys together. During the beating, we tried to get back into the deli where we'd just been, but they locked the door against us. It was the only time in my life I've ever been assaulted."

Dowling was tall and slender and had the somber good looks of a New York Heathcliff. On nights he wasn't working he roared around downtown on a big, overpowered Moto Guzzi, heading out from his loft to make the rounds of bars in the Far West Village: Keller's, the Ramrod, the Spike, and the Eagle's Nest, where the clientele wore leather and cowboy gear. "At the Eagle, if a guy came in wearing penny loafers, he'd be eighty-sixed. They had an ironclad dress code." (An unstated advantage of a gay bar's dress code was that it screened out clueless tourists who might stumble in looking for a cocktail. A pamphlet issued by the Mineshaft for its fifth anniversary in 1981 cautioned visitors, "those items not approved are those which do not fit into a man's club where visions of leather, cowboys, uniforms, and jocks are a reality, not just sugarplums at Christmas.") He joined a gay motorcycle club. "I was the only one in it who wasn't a leather man, and they only allowed me in on the condition that I'd wear a leather vest. I enjoyed them, a bunch of guys clanking around in leather."

But as the sixties drew to a close, the city began to gnaw at the edges of Dowling's neighborhood, acquiring parcels of land and dispatching bulldozers and cranes to pull down the old tenements. In 1967 it declared its intention to seize the lot where his building stood. He got a lawyer from Legal Aid who took the case to housing court, and for the next four years the struggle to hold onto his home consumed his resources and attention. As the case progressed, it became apparent that instead of putting up public housing in accordance with Title I policy, the city planned to give the property to New York University for its dental school. When Dowling raised the point in court, the judge said he didn't see that art should be allowed to get in the way of progress. In a final indignity, some city workers stole, or at any rate removed, the Moto Guzzi from where he'd kept it chained in his building's entryway. He tracked it down to a garage on Twenty-Seventh Street and found it parked in the back, with some workers standing nearby. He announced, "That's my bike, I'm taking it." Then he rode it out of the building. Nobody tried to stop him.

He never applied to be put on the Westbeth list. One day in 1971 he got a call from Dixon Bain, the project manager, who told him he'd been recommended by somebody at the New York Department of Cultural Affairs and offered him what Dowling called "a starter apartment," because the first thing you did when you moved in was have your name put down on the in-house moves list to get out of it. "It was three hundred fifty-nine square feet. When I had my paintings delivered there, they took up half the apartment. There was my bed, my kitchen and that was it. I couldn't paint in that space, I couldn't even stand back to see what I was doing." Years later he'd have a side gig painting *faux marbre* and *faux bois* effects in Upper East Side co-ops, including one belonging to Charles

Bluhdorn, the flamboyant, hugely wealthy CEO of Gulf & Western. The closet where Bluhdorn's wife kept her shoes and handbags was bigger than Dowling's entire apartment.

One day, shortly after he moved into Westbeth, Dowling came down to the lobby and was greeted by the building manager, who wanted to introduce him to someone. He indicated a woman beside him. It was Joan Davidson, who'd come to check on her project. The manager presented him. "And this is one of our painters, John Dowling." He probably expected Jack to tell his patron how grateful he was. Instead, Jack blurted, "My apartment isn't very conducive to painting. It's very small." Davidson regarded him quizzically and walked away.

On Making an Impression

JOAN HALL ALSO ARRIVED IN 1971. "I was one of the first," she says, so pleased by her longevity in the building that she can't help exaggerating it a little. One of Westbeth's nicer traits is the prestige that accrues to the tenants who've been there longest (as opposed to, say, the ones who are richest or most famous).

Hall has large, soulful eyes and wears her light hair in bangs, and together these give her an appearance of guilelessness. At the time she moved in she was living with another artist who'd applied and was accepted with him. They broke up in 1974, but because her name was on the lease, she was able to stay even after her partner moved out. Which was lucky. "I had no other place to go." That first apartment was a long, narrow corner unit on the second floor, right above the Bethune Street entrance. It was so small that Hall half-blames it for the breakup. That same year she moved up to a larger apartment on the ninth floor, where she still lives today.

She grew up in Brooklyn's Sheepshead Bay, the only child of two artists. Her mother was a painter, her father a photographer. "They were real bohemians. Even though it was in Brooklyn, they were so different from anybody else." For a time, her father worked as a window dresser at department stores, and Hall believes his assemblages may have subconsciously nudged her toward collage, the medium in which she works. Her mother made a living painting portraits, shrewdly and energetically marketing herself to potential clients. She gave her daughter an early model of artistic entrepreneurship. But Hall didn't want to be an artist back then. "I wanted to be a cheerleader. I didn't want to go to an art school. When I went to New Utrecht [a conventional public high school in Brooklyn], my parents were heartbroken."

"I never got onto the cheerleading team either," she adds. She still sounds a little sad about it.

In high school, however, she developed an interest in dance and upon graduating was admitted to Juilliard as a dance major. In another disappointment, she flunked ballet. Fortunately, she did well in sets and costumes and stagecraft. She also got some unintended inspiration from one of her teachers. He'd seen a performance at the American Mime Theatre and spent an entire class talking about how much he'd hated it. Afterward, Hall asked him, "Why would you spend the entire class talking about the American Mime Theatre if it was so terrible? It must have left an impression on you." In an aside, she adds: "Art is about making an impression." The upshot was that upon graduating from Juilliard in 1958, she began taking classes at the American Mime Theatre; a few months later she joined the company and performed and taught in it for the next nine years. This is another instance of a pattern in Hall's life: something meant to be a discouragement becomes an invitation; a disappointment turns into an opportunity.

The next time this happened was when she was admitted to the Actors Studio, the legendary school that defined an American style of acting and whose alumni included Paul Newman, James Dean, Sidney Poitier, Anne Bancroft, and Marilyn Monroe. It took Hall three auditions to get in. Then, as in a nightmare, the admission was retracted. Hall learned that her acting teacher had called Lee Strasberg and told him she wasn't ready. "He hated me for some reason. I don't know," she starts to say, but corrects herself. "No, I do know. I was living with an actor he had a crush on and he was jealous." The words come out in a rush. "But anyway," she resumes, "That's when my life really took a turn. I called my teacher and I thanked him. I said, 'I'll never act again. If this is what it's like, it's too cutthroat for me.'"

Later, while traveling in Europe with her then-husband, the painter Harry McCormick, Hall began to make collages. They didn't take much in the way of supplies, and the compositions recalled her father's window displays. In 1970 a friend photographed some of her pieces, and she took the photos around to see if she could get commissions. She received one to illustrate the cover of *The New York Times Book Review*. "Then I was on a roll." In 1980 she landed the cover of *Time*, the pinnacle of illustration gigs. She was good at dramatizing broad themes and concepts by arraying framed images beside each other or sometimes inside each other like so many matryoshka dolls. The compositions get their ideas across quickly, the way magazine covers are supposed to, but they also have a three-dimensional depth that rewards sustained attention. If they were hung together on a wall, you could stand before them as you would stand before paintings in a gallery, your eye moving among their elements.

It's startling that someone who started out as a dancer and then moved sideways into theater could step through another door and come out as a visual artist. But there are artists who can do many things and ones who can do one thing. They're like Isaiah Berlin's foxes and hedgehogs. Hall is a fox. She's matter-of-fact about it: "I always knew I would be in the arts. It was just in my blood." Defiantly, she adds, "I never wanted a nine-to-five, and I never did take a nine-to-five, ever. I always made a living." It's the freelancer's credo. In it you can hear both the workman's pride in hauling one's own weight and the bohemian's disdain for the straight life.

Naturally, there were side gigs. In the early sixties she waited tables at Caffè Reggio. Evidently Winifred, whose breasts so impressed Jack Dowling, used to come there too because Hall remembers her. She remembers that Bob Dylan used to walk in and sing. "Bobby Zimmerman!" she cries, as if running into him at a reunion many years later. "The Who was performing around the corner at Café Wha?, and Café Figaro was down the block. It was incredible. That was when the Village really was the Village. The Provincetown Playhouse was there, the Open Theatre, Second City, it was all happening." Her expression darkens. "Then it all moved to the East Village, and now I don't know if there's an art scene anymore. There's no . . . the scene is the big bucks."

Where Nobody Looks at You Weirdly

CHRISTINA MAILE AND HER FIRST husband learned about West-beth when they moved to New York and got in touch with Tod Williams, whom they'd been friendly with while they were in college in Michigan. He was now working in Richard Meier's office, and he suggested they apply for an apartment in the old Bell Labs building the firm was restoring. Maile was a playwright who'd already had work staged, but it was her husband who applied, as a painter, and they were admitted on the strength of his application.

"We had one child by then," Maile says. In her seventies, she's still youthful looking, with thick, black hair framing soft, rounded features. Her mouth is striking for its fullness and subtle expressiveness. She often seems wryly amused by her recollections, even those that involve quarrels, embarrassments, and disappointments. "I'm not sure how, what the criteria were, and how they looked at the admissions, but it was an area of the West Village that nobody wanted to be in. We walked up and down Hudson Street when it was really quiet—you can't believe how nonpopulated it was—and we said, 'If we get in, we get in; we don't get in, we don't get in,' because we couldn't," briefly she sounds embarrassed, "*find* the place. We were a little leery because it was the meat market then. There was a lot of, you know, just blood and bowels and cow parts. And there was the Men's House of Detention down the block, so it looked like a kind of suspect area. But we decided that it was great. And a couple of months later, they told us we had been accepted, and we moved in."

The neighborhood had the arctic loneliness of wind-scoured streets and meatpacking plants whose doors clanged down at three in the afternoon, of block after block without a restaurant or laundromat or bodega. In places it was dangerous. People didn't venture beneath the West Side Highway overpass unless they were parking the car or wanted to get their cock sucked or suck somebody else's, and sometimes the trick they'd just sucked would cut them with a knife. All through the night, sirens blared from the Men's House of Detention on Bank and West Streets. Virtually no reference to this facility can be found, even on Google, but Maile and a number of other residents remember it quite clearly, standing on a site that is now co-ops.

There was also crime inside Westbeth. "We had maintenance men who stole from the apartments," Maile recalls. "So that was kind of scary, because you didn't know which maintenance man was doing the stealing. They weren't being violent, but if you let them in and you had to go somewhere, something would be missing. And then there was a whole series of muggings a couple of years later. That's why we had the tenant patrol."

Few of us see the events of our lives in terms of a larger history; really, most of us live as if there were no history or as if the thing we call *history* had nothing to do with us. In the same way, most Westbeth residents relegate the community's history to the background of their stories. Maile, however, presents that history directly, like someone appointed for that purpose. Along with having lived in Westbeth for more than fifty years, she serves on the board of the Westbeth Corporation, the complex's governing body. At the time she moved in, "the building was still half empty, so it was great to be walking down these long hallways and see these really beautiful apartments. You could see the apartments because a lot of people hadn't moved in yet. This was 1970, I don't know exactly what month, maybe April, May. There was still work being done here and there. When we first moved to New York, we'd moved to the Lower East Side, and we were used to pretty dirty apartments. So when we moved into Westbeth it was exciting because the hallways had these nice, bright, neon colors on the ceilings, and the ceilings were curved, and there were all new appliances."

As a couple with one child, Maile and her then-husband got a simplex, a two-bedroom laid out on one floor. After their second child was born, she lobbied the management for a duplex; she later admitted that she'd claimed her sister was moving in with her and she needed a three-bedroom right away. Still, even the simplexes were impressive. The ceilings were high, the construction was solid. "You could do anything you wanted in your apartment. You could build a loft bed, you could take down a wall, you could move the refrigerator, you could add a second bathroom, you could modify the stairs, you could do anything. You didn't have to ask management." A further benefit of their new home was that the neighbors "didn't look at you weirdly because you said you were a musician or a painter. I mean, there were people that understood the need for however you behaved in public." For all this, she remembers paying somewhere between $161 and $200 a month. "It was a little high for us at the time," she says, deadpan. After a pause: "But here it is fifty years later, so the management sent back our security deposits. With interest."

On Becoming What Nobody Wants to Be

EDWARD FIELD BECAME A TENANT in 1976. Along with being one of the building's oldest tenants, Field is the author of twelve books of poetry as well as memoirs and novels, the novels cowritten with Neil Derrick, who was his partner for more than fifty years.

It's a given among poets that they must find some other way of supporting themselves. Many teach. Some give paid readings and tour the country like rock musicians. Field is one of the few poets I know of who once supported himself, albeit briefly, as an actor, a move so improbable that it gives him a sort of Dickensian glamour.

This was in the fifties. Field was ten years out of the air force, for which he'd flown twenty-seven bombing missions over Germany during the war, once crash-landing in the North Sea; the episode figures in one of his best-known poems. He'd moved to New York and gone to college on the GI Bill but dropped out when he realized college had nothing to teach him about writing poetry. There were no poetry programs back then, and poetry was the only thing he wanted to do. It had become that thing as he was riding across the country to report for military training and reading an anthology of poems a Red Cross worker had given him before he boarded the train. "For the next three days I did nothing but read the poems, and when I got off the train I knew I was going to be a poet. A poet was something that nobody wanted to be, and I decided that that was what I was supposed to do."

But ten years later his poetry career was nonexistent. This may have reflected the kind of poetry Field wrote, which was forthright and emotional at a time when the prevailing taste was for murmuring indirection.

Before it won the Academy of American Poets' Lamont Poetry Selection in 1963, his debut collection, *Stand Up, Friend, with Me*, would be rejected twenty-five times. Back then most literary publishers prohibited multiple submissions, which meant a writer might send off a manuscript they'd worked on for five years and wait another six months until it was returned with a rejection slip. Field might easily have had to wait longer if he hadn't followed May Swenson's sensible advice to ignore the prohibition and send the book out to as many publishers at a time as he felt like. (Actually, Grove Press, the house that accepted it, only took *Stand Up, Friend* provisionally, on the condition that it win the Lamont; if it didn't, they wouldn't publish it and Field would suffer the stigma of having been rejected twice.)

"I think I always allowed my heart to rule my poetry. O'Hara and Ashbery don't need hearts, they have wit. I once wrote a poem that had me crying the whole time I wrote it. That doesn't make it a good poem, but that was what I wanted. In the writing process, I think if you're true to yourself, you make people cry. One of the reasons I didn't get a publisher for so long was because I left myself too open. But the poetry of the time came out of the New Criticism, it was cool and cerebral. I don't come out of the New Criticism. I come out of sentimental Jewish people."

Further, there was the matter of his homosexuality. Everybody saw homosexuality as a "problem," the solutions for which were prison or psychotherapy. Field went into therapy. "It was dogma that homosexuality was not good, and that you could change. In my group, there were people who were gay who'd changed. The psychoanalyst said one day, 'Why don't you write prose instead of poetry?' He didn't understand that poetry was my life. The idea was that you have to make a living, and I certainly couldn't make a living from poetry. The idea was you had to make a living to get an apartment, and you had to get an apartment so you could invite a girlfriend over to have sex. And this analyst understood me so little that he thought I could just switch to prose! I walked out of the group.

"After I got out of group analysis, I thought, 'What can I do with my life?' My poetry was getting rejected, I was working terrible jobs in machine shops. I decided to become an actor. I was in an off-Broadway theater group, and I found an acting teacher named Vera Soloviova, who taught the Method, which you *had* to learn. She said, 'If you want to be an actor, learn to be a typist.' So I was working as a temporary typist when I wasn't making the rounds and going to rehearsals. I had just gotten my first sing-ing role in a small theater in Smithtown, Long Island, that was doing Ger-shwin's *Of Thee I Sing*. But before I went away my supervisor at my day job brought over a young man who'd started working there and said, 'I think you two will get along.' At the end of the day, she separated us because we were talking too much, and we lived together for fifty-eight years."

Neil Derrick was a novelist, and like Field, he was still unpublished. Their first apartment was Derrick's cold-water flat in Hell's Kitchen; in winter they used the kitchen stove for heat. Then they moved down to the West Village, where they found a place on Perry Street for a little over $100 a month. Here, Field's fortunes changed: *Stand Up, Friend, with Me* was published. He won the Lamont and then a Guggenheim. Suddenly, he was being paid to give readings. "It was terribly hard on Neil," he says. "We'd walk into a party and everyone would scream my name. And here was this beautiful young man who was in my shadow." Either to salve his envy or because the seventies had arrived with an unspoken mandate that everybody now had to fuck everybody, Derrick began having sex with other men. In 1976 he and Field broke up. Field left New York to travel through Afghanistan; Derrick went to London. At the end of the summer, having nowhere else to go, they both returned to the apartment.

It was an intolerable arrangement. "I came to Westbeth and went to the manager, and I said—there were no apartments available anymore because the West Village was gentrifying so much—I went to the manager and said, 'If I don't get an apartment here, if you can't give me one, I'll have to leave New York.' And he said, 'Oh that's what we're here for, to keep artists in New York.' And so, he gave me an apartment immediately, it wasn't a long waiting list. I moved into Westbeth. Then, ironically, my ex-partner moved in with me. He went blind so I had to take care of him. He couldn't live alone, he kept getting robbed; it was a terribly difficult sit-uation. So he moved back in with me and we lived in Westbeth together. And then we had a very, very good life."

Years after moving into Westbeth, Field learned that the bombsight lens used on the many missions he'd flown had been developed in the building.

A Diorama of His Own

BARTON LIDICÉ BENEŠ GREW UP in Corona, Queens, with a single mother, his parents' marriage having broken up when he and his younger brother Warren were still little. Their mother worked three jobs, and every Sunday, to get the boys out of her hair, she'd give them each a dollar and send them into Manhattan. "We would go to the Museum of Natural History," Warren remembers. "Barton always said that one of these days he wanted to live in a diorama. And he wound up living in one: it was his apartment." Beneš also loved the Egyptian room at the Met, with its stern, gorgeously carapaced mummies. In *Barton Beneš: No Secrets*, a 2004 documentary by the filmmaker Joseph Lovett, he displays a museum-sized glass cabinet filled with Egyptiana whose pièce de résistance is a mummified cat. "I never thought I'd have my own mummies," Beneš muses. Other cabinets nearby overflow with African masks and statuary, antique pottery, bead-and-feather necklaces from the Amazon and South Pacific, and taxidermized animals, including a stuffed mink dressed in a small mink coat.

Beneš is faunlike, not like a baby deer but like a man with the horns and legs of a goat. His features are broad and humorous; his voice is a smoker's rasp. The documentary was made when he was in his sixties, but in his shorts and T-shirt he looks like a school kid showing off his collections. He makes a gesture that takes in the entire apartment, an 850-square-foot studio so completely given over to the storage and display of curiosities that its occupancy by a human being seems almost incidental. "So it's kind of a re-creation of what I did as a kid going to the museum."

Beneš moved into Westbeth in 1970, around the same time he gave up traditional painting. He'd already had indications he wasn't suited for it; Warren has a student canvas on the back of which one of Beneš's instructors at Parsons wrote, "Barton, please don't try to become an artist in your future life." Around the time he landed his Westbeth apartment, he traveled to West Africa, where he was struck so forcefully by the ceremonial masks and statues he saw in every marketplace that whatever he'd done or wanted to do as an artist up until then no longer made sense. "Everything that was around, they made art with," he told Lovett, who was one of his best friends. "Whatever you threw away was picked up and turned into art. I never painted after Africa."

For most of his career, dealers and curators had a hard time describing what it was that Beneš did. "He's not making abstract paintings, he's not making figurative paintings, he's not making minimalist sculpture," says one commentator in Lovett's film. "He really seems to have evolved his own particular, individualistic, odd way of making art."

One might best describe Beneš as a repurposer; it places him in the lineage of the African artists whose work thrilled and humbled him. His materials included cowrie shells—a standard decorative element in West African statues and masks that he started using after returning to the US— money, human ashes, gallstones, pubic hair, scavenged bits of canvas and blobs of paint from the studios of more famous artists, and his own HIV-positive blood, assorted vessels of which were nearly impounded by Swedish authorities from the gallery where they were being shown. It's fitting that a repurposer like Beneš would find a home in an apartment complex that was itself repurposed from offices and laboratories. He told his brother, "When you take insignificant items and you put them together, it then tells a story and becomes art."

The stories he told with his work were fanciful, humorous, filled with visual puns. This was particularly evident in the pieces he made with paper money, which he bought shredded in bulk from the Federal Reserve. He claimed to have bought as much as twenty million dollars' worth. He said money was cheaper than paint. Beneš made up for the drabness of US bills by adding foreign currency. He fashioned the shreds into a pump and hose, attached them to an oversized dollar bill, and titled the piece *Inflation*. He produced an entire series of works entitled *Nest Egg* in which both egg and nest were made of folded, crushed, and chopped-up bills. One of his wealthier collectors used to order one every time he had a grandchild. Beneš's partner Howard Meyer, a weaver, would painstakingly reassemble shredded banknotes on his loom. Once, he went so far as to match the original serial numbers. This might have gotten them in trouble with the Federal Reserve. When the work was shown at a bank, Warren recalls, "some big shot came around and said, 'What is this?' And

Barton said, 'We got the shredded money and we just rewove it.' And they said, 'You got to get that out of here.' Because the whole thing with American money is when you destroy it, you can't put it back together again."

Unlike many of his neighbors, Beneš lived in the same apartment, 956H, his entire time in Westbeth, forty-two years. He moved in while construction was still in progress. His brother says that the old Bell executive suites on the upper floors had fireplaces as big as the ones in mansions. Beneš saw Diane Arbus's body being wheeled out of her apartment. He could remember when the neighborhood was so rough that he made Warren take a taxi from the subway station when he came to visit, but in No Secrets he complains that the Far West Village is now overrun with yuppies. Being childless, and single for most of his years at Westbeth, he was never able to claim a larger unit, but he seemed content with the space he had. It was large enough—though barely—for his collections, which spilled out of the glass cabinets to climb up the walls and populate the apothecary cabinets in which he kept smaller objects, arranged under headings like NAPKINS/TISSUES, CONTRABAND, RELIGION, CELEBRITY, FETISH, and DEATH. There was room for the drafting table where he worked and for the large, refinished dining table where he entertained friends, the cushy recliner that he called "the guest room" and the canopied Chinese opium bed where he slept and in a sense still does more than ten years after his death. His apartment lacked the views and light of those in the A and D buildings, but he did much of his work at night. He was close to Joan Hall, who still owns several pieces of his, and the writer and actor Shami Chaikin, with whom he watched Judge Judy several nights a week.

Beneš never supported himself as anything other than an artist, though in the early days he sometimes depended on the odd five dollars he'd win from his family members when he visited them to play cards, and the five dollars more his mother would slip him before he left. In 1968, he took a job at Bloomingdale's and lasted a day. "He went home," Warren says, "and told our mom, 'If that's what working is about, I can't do it.'" It wasn't laziness. Once he found work that was more congenial to his temperament, he went at it relentlessly.

To date, there is no catalogue raisonné of Barton Lidicé Beneš's art, which ranged in size from gift cards and lapel pins to seven-by-seven foot "reliquaries" holding themed aggregations of found, scavenged, and donated objects. Some of the work, like the *Nest Egg* series, is amusing; some is devastating. His output was prodigious. In this he was a lot like Warhol, another hyperproductive artist of the Czechoslovakian diaspora (though his people were Slovak while Beneš's were Czech). In one of their songs about him, Lou Reed and John Cale have Warhol saying, "The most important thing is work." Beneš would have said so too.

When Everyone Understood Each Other

ON THE LOWER EAST SIDE, crime had been so omnipresent that everyone in Christina Maile's old building kept their doors locked all the time. Even with thieving handymen, Westbeth felt safer. And the management encouraged community by sending out memos urging tenants to seek out other artists in their discipline. Maile became part of the Westbeth Feminist Playwrights Collective. "The men just wanted to write their own plays," she explains, "whereas the women wanted to write about feminist issues. At that time women's lib was a really hot topic. We had two goals in mind: one was to present plays that were sharp and quick and satirical but also loaded with elements of rebellion and meaning, and the second goal was to provide job opportunities for women backstage in those trades that men usually occupied." The set designer, set builder, lighting technician, and sound engineer were all women. The Collective's first evening of short plays was called *Rape-In*. The jaunty title (see Be-In, Sit-In, Love-In) was a provocation. It was scheduled for a Wednesday night at 10:00 p.m., and despite the inauspicious hour, the theater was packed. A subsequent production, *Up!*, featured the actors and then–Westbeth residents Danny DeVito and Rhea Perlman.

"A day-to-day thing with me, because I had kids, was my husband went to work, and then I would go down to the play co-op in the basement because the mothers put together a co-op so we wouldn't have to watch our kids all the time. They would be there for a couple hours. And then I would try to write in that time, and then afterwards my older kid would come home from school, and there would be a lot of kids coming in and out getting snacks. And then at night, we'd go over to our next-door neighbor. Someone in the building was selling grass. So every night we would have these long, intense conversations about art. The next-door neighbors were a painter and an actress. So we talked about theater and then we'd keep getting stoned and then the kids would come in and we'd pretend we were not stoned, and we'd give them cookies and make them go back to bed.

"Everybody was young," Maile says. "So there wasn't that thing that happens as you find your world narrowing. Everything was still open for success, for acclaim, for children growing up happy. There was synergy: everybody understood each other when we talked about things. It was never, 'I don't understand how you can paint all day.' No one would even think that. But at the same time, there were also eccentric people who didn't like anyone. They never joined in. It's not that they were terrible, it's just that everyone understood that they didn't want to be bothered. Sometimes you'd see them carrying paintings inside the elevator, or in summer they would be dressed in really heavy wool clothing because that's what they wore all the time."

The poet Joel Oppenheimer, a downtown celebrity because of his column for *The Village Voice*, was someone who looked like he didn't want to be bothered. Few of his neighbors knew that he'd coined the name for the legendary artists' bar where one of Jack Dowling's paintings was shown: Max's Kansas City. He was paid a dollar for it. Oppenheimer often looked grumpy, with his billy-goat beard and his croaking voice. Kids in the building liked to knock on his door just for the thrill of fear when he opened it and glowered down at them. Often the people who didn't want to be bothered were just used to working alone and wanted to do nothing but that. In time, this became one of the ways in which tenants could be classified: there were the ones who wanted to build a community and the ones who just wanted to make art. You couldn't call them factions. They coexisted without friction except for the rare occasions when one of the community-builders tried to jolly one of the solitaries into driving up to the Bronx at five in the morning to buy produce for the vegetable co-op.

"It was so amazing because I hated vegetables," says Maile, who is a community-builder. "But if someone said, 'This is what we're going to do now,' I'd go, 'Okay.' Every week we would get a box of vegetables; there would be celery and potatoes. There would be enough for maybe one and a half meals, but since I didn't know how to cook anyway, I joined in to get it."

You Have to Be Kind of Tough to Wear a Dress

BOB AND NADYA GRUEN CAME down the day after Christmas and were shown an apartment. There were only four left. "And they were not the best apartments," he recalls. In his late seventies, he has the streetwise matter-of-factness of someone used to negotiating with people who may not be trustworthy. Such people include bands and record companies—since Gruen is one of America's best and most famous rock photographers—and also building managers. Westbeth's management offered the couple a space on the first floor that was being used as a construction office and promised to clean it up by the time they moved in. But when the Gruens arrived at the building with all their possessions piled in the back of a taxi—Bob was holding their cat in his lap—the apartment still wasn't ready.

For the next month, they stayed in a temporary space on the eighth floor. "It was nice. I had a whole view of the neighborhood. I could learn about it. I'd look at all these guys walking up and down the streets because I didn't know that there was a whole gay cruising scene. All night you'd see these guys walking down and going around into the parking lot and going into the back of a truck and coming out pulling up their pants. I'm like, 'What the fuck is going on here?' But I kind of got used to it. In fact, after a little while I realized that the gay guys cruising the neighborhood kept the neighborhood safe. Because even if they were wearing a dress, it was still a pretty tough bunch of guys. You have to be kind of tough to wear a dress, you know, on the streets."

On the Beauty of Being a Seeing-Eye Dog

EDWARD FIELD AND NEIL DERRICK'S first apartment was on the sixth floor. The previous tenant had died of a heart attack after the last of many fights with a noisy neighbor. Seemingly untroubled at having aggravated another person to death, the neighbor continued to make noise. "He was a very difficult man who used to play golf in his apartment," Field says. "He hung a canvas over the windows and would drive golf balls against the windows. But behind the canvas was a radiator that connected to my radiator. So when he hit the golf balls against the canvas and the radiators, it clunked in my apartment. I could see why somebody could have a heart attack."

Derrick had gone blind while still in his thirties, following an operation to remove a brain tumor. In their old apartment building it had made him a mark. When he was seen bringing his expensive audio equipment to the precinct house to be registered in case of theft, neighborhood lowlifes waited for him to go out again, then broke in and helped themselves. In Westbeth there were always neighbors at home during the day. Some of them, like Miriam and Shami Chaikin, whose brother Joe had founded the revolutionary Open Theatre, would look in on Derrick and prepare the meals Field had left for him when he went off to writing residencies or on reading tours.

With the loss of his sight, Derrick had stopped writing. In Westbeth he started once more. Field was staying at Yaddo on a two-month residency but would come home on weekends to care for his partner, and while he was there they began working on a novel together. "I had never written fiction, but Neil was brilliant. He knew about plot and character, which I knew nothing about. So I worked with him, and we plotted a novel for him chapter by chapter. Each week he was expected to write a chapter. He couldn't see what he was doing, but he was a perfect typist, so when I came home, I read him what he wrote and then planned out the next chapter. And I went back to Yaddo and worked on my own stuff. When I came back from my residency, he had a novel." It was called *The Potency Clinic* and, as the title suggests, it was mildly dirty. They published it with a small soft-core-porn house under the pseudonym Bruce Elliott. A German publisher picked it up, and, as *Die Potenzklinik*, it attained some popularity in that country.

With the same work method, the couple wrote *Sticky Fingers*, though this time they used the pseudonym Eleanor Bartlett and made the protagonist a straight woman whose sexual partners included—presciently—the president of the United States; Field maintains that the Rolling Stones cribbed the title for their 1971 album. The new novel was published by Grove Press, which had a racy reputation thanks to its list of titles by Henry Miller and D. H. Lawrence, not to mention some by less illustrious authors that were more or less soft-core porn. Then an editor at the mass-market paperback house Avon invited Field and Derrick to write a mainstream novel about four generations of a family in Greenwich Village. They clinched the deal with a one-page synopsis. *The Villagers* was published under their real names and became a bestseller. The B. Dalton Bookseller on Eighth Street devoted an entire window to it. The catalog copy for the 2000 reprint by a small press begins: "When their effete son Claude succumbs to an opium habit, it is Toom Endicott's lusty bastard son Patrick by Molly, the Irish maid, who carries on his name."

All the while, Field was winning greater acclaim for his poems. He was invited to give readings all over the country, and although the honoraria were low, they added up; ten readings at a hundred dollars each was a thousand dollars, and Westbeth allowed him to live cheaply. A textbook company commissioned him to write a book of poems and stories adapted from traditional Inuit sources. What did a Jew from Long Island know about the Inuit? "I just told them the way my mother used to tell her stories from the shtetl. I gave them to my sister to read. She said, 'Ethnic is ethnic.'"

In 1974 he received the Shelley Memorial Award from the Poetry Society of America. In addition to being one of the most prestigious honors given an American poet, it carries a handsome cash prize.

None of this success seems to have cast a shadow on Field's relationship with Derrick. "Everyone saw us in the neighborhood," he said. "His hand was always on my shoulder. We were an iconic couple. It was a wonderful life being a seeing-eye dog for this blind man."

The Injustice of Living Space

HOW HAPPY TENANTS WERE WITH their new apartments depended in part on how large they were and how well laid out; nobody much liked the little scrap apartments that were tucked into whatever space was left over during the renovation. And of course it also depended on one's art form. Jack Dowling feels that "Richard Meier knew nothing about artists and what they need." Of course he's speaking of painters and sculptors. "They jammed too many people into the building in order to carry the costs of construction. HUD rules specified that a single person could only have a studio and a couple had to have a one-bedroom, and if you had kids you got a duplex, and those are enormous." It didn't matter if the single person was a painter and the family was a writer couple who barely moved from their desks: one got four hundred square feet and the others got eight hundred. At the same time, there were loopholes: if the writers broke up and one of them moved out with the children, the other got to stay on in the duplex at a fraction of the market rate. The actor and visual artist Jan Harding knows of a family that has three duplexes: "The two children are married and have kids. They each have their own big apartment and so does their dad." The unequal allocation of square footage could be the occasion for years, even decades, of resentment, cold stares in the elevators, cold shoulders by the mailboxes. At the same time, not every newcomer wanted it known they were living in Westbeth. According to Dowling, the artists who showed at uptown galleries were especially self-conscious. "Westbeth was a *housing project*, it was a place for poor people. They were afraid it would lower their reputations."

On Counting Dots

THE PAINTER AND CURATOR HOWARDENA Pindell moved into Westbeth in 1970 from the Cézanne building on Jane Street, where she'd been sharing an apartment with a roommate. Westbeth's management gave her a studio but, she recalls, "it wasn't what they had promised. They generally promised that you would have your working and living space together. So what they did was, for people who basically had less than they were supposed to have, they had a building that was right next to them, and they used that as a studio building. You had to share a studio, and it was kind of dilapidated. You know, temporary walls, maybe up to eight feet or so. And then chicken wire—I think the chicken wire was along the top of the wall. In other words, you got some ventilation from whatever poisonous material was coming from one studio to another."

This would have been the I building, the four-story structure on the corner of West and Bank Streets that dates from the eighteen sixties, making it the oldest section of the complex. For a while in the nineteen nineties, it was rented out to a spartan-looking fitness center whose lack of amenities made it paradoxically chic. The building now houses a music school.

"My first reaction to sharing a studio with another artist was I really resented it," Pindell says. "And it worried me that the building was not safe. That was when I was working at MoMA, which meant I was working at night, and I was afraid of being alone. And it turned out that somebody did come and try to vandalize the building. Fortunately, I wasn't there."

She'd been a figurative painter, but the small, poorly lit space and evening hours may have forced her to adopt a new technique: she began using spray paint, which she applied onto unprimed canvas through small circular holes cut in a template. The result was a lush pointillism in which fields of color swirled and vibrated. Almost by accident Pindell was becoming the abstractionist she is known as today, circles or dots—spray-painted or squeegeed or punched out from sheets of paper or oaktag with an office hole punch and then affixed to the canvas—being one of her signatures. The shape evoked a memory from her childhood in Philadelphia when she and her father had gone to a root beer stand, where she'd noticed that the mugs had little red dots applied to their undersides. They identified the glassware as being designated for nonwhites. Pindell is Black.

Another of the artist's signature techniques originated with a studio visit from a dealer who asked her, "'How many spots are on the canvas?' And I thought, 'Oh, well, I'll count.' So I just ended up—I had bags—you know, a bag of punch-outs. And that's what really started that, it started with the spraying, and then that little push, and then I just got a Rapidograph pen, and then [would] use a nail or a tweezer or a needle, or whatever to hold these little spots down to number." The tiny, neatly inscribed numbers suggest a catalog system, the half-effaced instructions for a paint-by-numbers kit, or a kabbalistic diagram.

Pindell says, "The building had a very high suicide rate. I think one of the problems was its architecture. There was a middle courtyard that looked like a prison's, where you have like a balcony and a walkway around it, if I remember it correctly. It was the atmosphere. There was nothing art-related around except in your studios. Now some people who got bigger spaces lied to get their duplex spaces by claiming there were relatives living with them who [were] not. I didn't want to be dishonest about it, but then I got a tiny space. It seemed to be somewhat airless in terms of artistic atmosphere. And the lucky ones, I think, had a river view so it wasn't claustrophobic. My windows faced a parking lot, and the gay community was close by so at night in the parking lot you could hear men having sexual encounters—it kind of woke me up—in the trucks. The area was so quiet that sounds traveled.

"I heard that there was a study authorized to find out why so many people wanted to kill themselves. It was remote, but I was glad that I was in the building. I was glad I was in the West Village. At the time there were no giant corporate buildings. It was really like a *village*, truly, like the name. I did not feel like there was much of a social atmosphere at Westbeth. It was like everyone was closed off in their own little world. I was one of the few people of color there. What I found interesting was that although it was artists' housing, there was no communal space at all. There was a gallery space, if I remember correctly, on the first floor or ground floor, but there was no place where people could gather. You'd just come in and go to your space and leave to go to work or go to your studio. In fact, the only social environment [was] having to share my studio, but we hardly saw each other. But I was so preoccupied by having a day job and doing my work at night that I didn't pay attention to the isolation. It's possible that the people who were there all the time—there was nowhere to run into people except in the elevator. They may have just gone into their own hell or into their own depression. There was nothing to lift them in that building, nothing."

On Waste Remediation

BARTON BENEŠ'S AUNT EVELYN KEPT sending him letters. She wrote voluminously, compulsively, her productivity brought about, or at least given extra *oomph*, by diet pills. (In the late sixties there was a type called Eskatrol. It was brilliant nomenclature, a portmanteau of *escalator* and *control*; the hiss of the first syllable was like one of those shoulder-mounted rocket launchers that can take out a tank.) At the height of the correspondence, she sent Beneš a fifty-page, typewritten, single-spaced, double-sided letter two or three times a week. He tells the story in *No Secrets*. "One day she asked, 'Are you gay?'" He rolls his eyes at the camera. "Oh Jesus! So, I said, 'Yeah,' and that started the whole thing." Evidently under the common misapprehensions of the time, Evelyn took her nephew's queerness as a license to unpack her own sex life from the trunk in which it was usually kept. "She would talk about outrageous things, you name it. If it was typed on pink, it was meant to be very personal . . . to be read only by me. These letters kept coming. I didn't know what to do with them, they were taking over my whole life."

Somebody else would have sent them back stamped MOVED, ADDRESS UNKNOWN. Beneš used them. He copied portions of the letters onto oversized canvases. He wrapped their text around an architectural column; he hand-lettered excerpts on the insides of broken eggshells. He made six hundred books with them. When Aunt Evelyn wrote him about her flirtation with a rep from the company that made her typewriter ribbons ("That man from the typewriter company who I complained to about those dried-up ribbons said, 'I'll bet you can do lots of things.' I don't know what the man had in mind that he felt I could do. He is definitely interested in me personally, especially over the phone."), he reproduced the words on giant spools of typewriter ribbon.

One often reads that certain artists make work to exorcise the unwanted contents of their psyche. Beneš was exorcising the unwanted contents of his aunt's, which she'd forced into his psyche via her barrage of letters. He was practicing a kind of artistic waste removal. Evelyn discharged plumes of grievance and self-praise, coquettishness, advice, scolding, spite—all the particulates produced by anybody's brain on speed; Beneš suctioned them up and sealed them in different media and materials. She sent out more, he scrambled to contain them. He was like poor Mickey Mouse in *The Sorcerer's Apprentice*, frantically bailing out his master's flooded workshop while the brooms he has called to life mindlessly go on flooding it. Except Aunt Evelyn was not a broom, and he hadn't called her to life. Seen in the aggregate, the pieces Beneš called *Selected Parts of Letters from My Aunt Evelyn* are droll, ingenious, whimsical, bitchy, but also exasperated, as if their creator were inwardly groaning, *Will you shut up already!* Eventually, Aunt Evelyn found out what her nephew was doing. For some unknowable reason, the hustler Beneš had hired as a birthday gift for his partner wrote her and told her what use her nephew was making of her letters. "She freaked out and she stopped writing to me," Beneš tells the filmmaker. Then, after a thoughtful pause: "And it was time, anyhow. I always find when I do something a long time and everyone likes it, it's time to move on."

The Company of Famous Recluses

Bob Gruen's apartment was the first one you passed as you entered Westbeth through the door on Bethune Street, next to the mailboxes and around the corner from the elevators. The location was convenient, but it was also noisy. Every time the elevators broke down, as they did several times a week, the sound of the alarm would drill right through you. And being conveniently located wasn't always a good thing. "Since we're in the most public apartment, things would happen," Gruen recalls. "Like two in the morning some guy would ring the bell and say, 'Oh, I heard your music and you're awake, and I just wrote this poem. Can I read you my poem?'" He shrugs. "It got a little weird down there. But I was just happy to be in the neighborhood and have my own apartment at a rent I could afford." He pauses. "Sort of."

He'd been photographing bands, most of them little-known, but the summer after he moved in he met Ike and Tina Turner, who were playing a gig at the Honka Monka club on Queens Boulevard; Gruen took pictures from the floor. "At the end of her act, a strobe light flashed, and Tina dances off and there's a whole bunch of images flashing in front of you and I just opened the camera to a one-second exposure to see what would happen. Three of the pictures are terrible and one of them is the best picture I ever took, because it really just captures the energy and excitement of Tina, like five images in one frame because Tina is way more than any one picture." The photo, which is now famous, depicts Tina as a Hindu goddess, a goddess who doesn't just have multiple hands but also multiple bodies, all in ecstatic motion.

He showed Ike and Tina the pictures. They liked them and invited Gruen on the road with them, and while he was on the road he met Elton John, who was on his first American tour, and began photographing him, and in this way he came to meet most of the musicians who mattered then and others who would matter a few years in the future: Alice Cooper, the New York Dolls, the pre-Blondie Debbie Harry. The money was rarely good: $50, $200, $300 for an album cover. But he didn't care about money: he was still in his twenties, a laid-back kid with frizzed-out hair and heavy-lidded eyes getting paid to hang out in clubs taking pictures of bands he loved and party with them afterward.

Apart from his talent, Gruen owed his career to his coolness and discretion. He wasn't overawed by the increasingly famous people he was photographing, and he didn't view them as gold mines, or coke mines or girl mines or mines of any of the other base and precious metals to which their raffish celebrity—halfway between the celebrity of movie stars and the celebrity of gangsters—granted access. When he brought John Lennon and Yoko Ono some photos he'd taken of them outside the Apollo Theater shortly after they moved to New York, he didn't hang around waiting to make a sale; he just dropped off the pictures and left. Later, Yoko told him that was one of the things that impressed them in his favor. "Nobody just gave them something, everybody wanted something. And I was just biding my time. It turned out to be a good thing to do because when I did meet them, they had more respect, 'cause I respected them and their privacy. Somebody asked me why John Lennon and Joe Strummer and guys like that had my phone number and called me up, and I'd say, 'I don't know, you'd have to ask them.' I don't know why people like me. How do you become friends with John Lennon? The same way you become friends with anybody. You share a sense of humor, you have common ideas, and as you get to know each other, you trust each other."

Lennon came over to Westbeth to visit Gruen in 1975, shortly after he'd moved from the ground floor to a space on the second floor of the A building, facing the river. This was probably the least accessible part of the complex, and Gruen told the former Beatle he should just ask the doorman to ring him rather than try to find his way up on his own. Lennon called when he was leaving his home, only a few blocks away. Gruen waited for him. "And about a half hour later I was just walking across the apartment to ask the doorman if some weird English guy had shown up when John came breezing in and said, 'You have some weird neighbors.' I said, 'What do you mean?' He said, 'I was ringing people's doorbells trying to find your apartment.' And you know, everybody here's an artist and it was a Sunday afternoon in July and John fucking Lennon is standing at your door. So, everybody was, 'Oh, let me read you my poem!' 'Look at my new painting!' 'Hey, I made this sculpture!' 'What do you think of this song I wrote?'" Without actually imitating his fellow tenants, Gruen somehow magically conveys the neediness and self-absorption that are the standard character defects of many creative people and that must have been greatly amplified by the presence of arguably the most famous creative person in New York City at that time. Gruen sighs. "Everybody has something."

A friendship with Lennon could be taxing. One weekend, he invited Gruen to go out drinking with him and the singer-songwriter Harry Nilsson, who was coming to town from L.A. As someone who knew the city's club scene, Gruen was indispensable. They made plans to meet at Ashley's on Thirteenth and Fifth. But Gruen was in the middle of finishing some prints, and by the time he got to Ashley's, Lennon had left and gone up to Trax on Seventy-Second Street. He followed him uptown, only to learn he had left for JP's. "He would go to a club, he'd get so mobbed that after twenty minutes or so he'd have to leave and go to the next place. And he had just left JP's, so I said fuck this and went home."

Still, the friendship made possible some transfixing photos of Lennon as an immigrant in New York, poised, restless, guarded, open, defiant—the defiance understandable if you know that in the first years of his residence he was under constant surveillance by the FBI, and the Immigration and Naturalization Service was trying to kick him out of the country. Perhaps the most famous of Gruen's photos shows Lennon standing on a rooftop silhouetted against a backdrop of high-rises, his arms folded across his chest, his eyes hidden behind round-lensed sunglasses. He's wearing a sleeveless NEW YORK CITY T-shirt, a ubiquitous piece of tourist kitsch that the photo instantly made hipper than shit. The rooftop was on Fifty-Second Street by the East River, above the apartment where Lennon was staying while he recovered from the infamous "lost weekend" (it was actually eighteen months) he'd spent with his and Yoko's former personal assistant May Pang. Gruen initially told me that Lennon's apartment was next door to one belonging to Gloria Swanson, then decided it was another star of the same vintage, and we went back and forth over possible candidates until he and his wife blurted in unison, "Famous recluse: *Greta Garbo!*"

"Yeah, his building was one floor lower," Gruen says. "He could see her apartment. And he said, 'I'm hidin' out here, just like her.'"

On the Difficulty of Living Without Rules

WESTBETH WAS A COMMUNITY OF bohemians, and it had a corresponding attitude toward sex. Many newcomers quickly became involved in an illicit, jerry-rigged phone system of noisy, polyamorous affairs that entangled several floors. "We were all running around from unit to unit," Jack Dowling recalls, "and returning home in the middle of the night or the next morning."

Often, Christina Maile says, it was more casual. "Every now and then there'd be kind of a group of guys, some of them married, some of them not. I mean, they were friendly. But they would just go around knocking on doors of single women. And many times the door would be answered, and a guy would be invited to stay. And then the other guys would just go on. One woman used to answer her door stark naked. It was fun. And then there was this one time when these guys are wandering around and one of these women said, 'Just come in.' At the time there was a lot of mugging going around, so the Westbeth tenants organized a security patrol. Whoever volunteered would be on call, and if anything happened a tenant could call and one or two guys would show up. On this occasion, when this woman invited this guy in, she decided that she didn't want to have anything to do with him, but he wouldn't leave. So she called up the guy on the tenant patrol, and he came. And it turned out that the two guys knew each other, so they both stayed and just hung out."

Tod Williams described Westbeth as a community "where there was always some drama, whether the story of the horse coming into the building, or the cat that fell out and was imprinted on the pavement in the center of the courtyard from the window." He himself lived next door to a couple in which the husband "was an artist, but he wasn't really an artist." For a while, Williams thought he might be in the military because he wore some kind of uniform; he turned out to be a guard at the Playboy Club. The wife was a curator at the Met. "And they had children, and the apartment . . . was unbelievably filthy, with the children allowed to run in the hall naked and shitty and peeing in the hall. And it was tough because there were no rules. Absolutely no rules."

Among the gigs the poet Joel Oppenheimer cobbled together to support his family was writing for "gentlemen's" magazines such as *Oui* and *Cheri*. This was back when those magazines included nonporn content— maybe to support some readers' claims that they only bought them for the literature. Oppenheimer wrote about baseball. Still, no one would make a serious argument that those magazines were about sports, and when Oppenheimer's son Nat arrived at school one day wearing a *Cheri* T-shirt, the principal promptly sent him home. And when a stack of porn magazines that might have been his father's was left out by the garbage chute, kids swarmed to it like rats swarming to an open restaurant dumpster. "It was like the grapevine at Westbeth," Nat's younger brother Lem recalls. "People would go run and strip that stuff as quick as it went out."

Westbeth may have been a place where horny guys could casually knock on their neighbors' doors until they got a friendly answer, but Jack Dowling feels this only applied to the straight people. The few times his gay motorcycle club met up at his place, it didn't go over well, and at some point, somebody put up a sign by the mailboxes that chided, this is a family building.

What Psyche Saw by Lamplight

LIKE MANY NEIGHBORHOODS WORKINGMEN PASS through on their way somewhere else, the Far West Village had prostitutes, particularly trans prostitutes. Some of them were made up and padded so artfully that the only giveaway was the size of their hands. Others weren't trying to fool anybody; a trucker who just wanted a ten-dollar blow job wasn't checking a girl's hands. Still, a lot of the early Westbeth tenants were disturbed by the sex workers, and it was hard for a parent to explain them to their children if they passed one on their way to school, a very tall lady unfolding herself out of the cab of a parked truck to clop down the street on heels that made her even taller. Sometimes she'd blow the kids a kiss as she clopped past.

In the seventies, the neighborhood had two economies: the daytime economy of meat and trucking and the nighttime economy of sex. Their respective workers filed past each other at five in the morning, when the cutters put on their white jackets and tested the edge on their knives and regulars at the Anvil toweled off and settled their bar tabs, though some hardcore partyers would stay on until the club closed a few hours later. By the end of the decade, street prostitutes occupied a smaller niche in the sex economy, at least in the heterosexual one. As if in anticipation of the changes that would radically transform other industries forty years later, the pros had been driven out by amateurs. What emerged for a little while was a utopian economy in which the haves were happy to give to the have-nots; or else everybody was a have-not, rendered equal by the longing that begins with the apprehension of lack. The men who came to the Mineshaft and the Toilet paid for drinks and coke and poppers; the Mineshaft had a "membership" fee. But they didn't pay to fuck. Fucking was free. It was free in the trucks that parked under the West Side Highway until a stretch of it collapsed in 1973, and it was free in the rotting warehouses on the piers along the Hudson.

The piers appealed greatly to the artist David Wojnarowicz, who described prowling them with a friend as if through an eroticized Piranesi labyrinth, drawn by aesthetic appreciation and sexual suspense:

We . . . sat on the waterfront board walk and watched the characters easing
in and outta the shadows of the pier warehouses, along the brick walls like
rats and emerging into the phosphorescent shine of bathing streetlamps
along the lapping posted walls through various darkness and passing no
one—once inside it was difficult to see, a few dim shapes of white T-shirts
or the pale gleam of white skin in the darkness, and standin' still for a while
our eyes adjusted and we walked toward the back of the pier warehouse
where there was one middle doorway shining with a contained section of
river and lights . . . we turned and walked back in the deep darkness of the
pier warehouse and stood against a side wall talking quietly and watching
the movements of anonymous characters driftin' back and forth and up
and down staircases against the back wall, occasional voices from upstairs
and then we strolled back out and onto the bank street pier and towards
the end of the pier, avoiding the large gaping holes that open onto the
river, my foot almost disappeared down a large pipe aperture, over to the
side materializing in the darkness were two men, one giving the other a
desperate blow job . . . and further on were two men one bent over getting
rammed by the other guy, the fucking was brutal and fast and almost violent but both were into it and then at one point the guy getting rammed
was rammed so hard he flew over and his palms landed on the surface of
the pier boards and he continued in that position.

A lot of the bars tried to re-create these found spaces' mood of disrepair
and clammy menace: Man's Country went so far as to mount a dummy
truck on its roof. Inside or outside, the great, horny coalition of the willing
enacted what some sexologists described as the pure male strategy, the
one all men would adopt in a world without women or one where women
were "more like" men, taking and giving sex without pretense or restric-
tion, with no distinction between consumers and providers, every man in
the room both trick and hustler.

In another Joseph Lovett documentary, *Gay Sex in the Seventies*, Barton Beneš reminisces, "I'd be working in the studio, and it was like the
call of the wild. 'Oh, I gotta go out! There's the trucks!' And even though
you're in the middle of a really creative, interesting thing, I'd put it away

and go out to the trucks." Before he left his apartment, he'd take his wallet from his pocket and replace it with a piece of paper with his name and phone number written on it in case someone had to identify his body. "You'd enter the trucks from behind. It was absolutely dark inside, you couldn't tell who was doing what to whom. There was always somebody who'd take a match"—Beneš mimes striking one—"and hold it like this, and look around to see the faces."

This may or may not have been a good idea.

When Cupid took Psyche as his lover, he granted her every luxury and indulgence. He just wouldn't let her see him. They made love in the dark. But goaded by her jealous sisters, Psyche broke the prohibition and stole a glimpse of Cupid by the light of a lamp she had smuggled into the bedchamber and was so stricken by his beauty that she wounded herself with one of his arrows and was made lovesick. And in her trembling she spilled some lamp oil on him, and he woke and fled. More or less the same thing happens to the heroine of "Beauty and the Beast," except the Beast, being only a monster, is more forgiving. You can read the stories as lessons in the danger of knowing, knowing both in the sexual sense—*Where are the men which came in to thee this night? bring them out unto us, that we may know them*—and in the other. Adam and Eve weren't damned for fucking but for eating knowledge. There's a school of thought that sex *is* knowledge, that it's only in fucking that the other is wholly revealed, not a social construction but the bare self, red-faced and bawling. The photo on the cover of Hanya Yanagihara's novel *A Little Life* shows a handsome young man whose face appears to be knotted in pain or grief. But the photo's (it was taken by Peter Hujar, who was Wojnarowicz's lover and mentor) title is *Orgasmic Man*. He isn't crying but cumming.

"Barton would try anything," Lovett says. His tone becomes measured, the tone of someone delivering a serious warning. "I had to tell myself very early in our relationship that Barton might be able to do things and survive, but I would never survive the things he did if I tried to keep up with him."

✳

"IT WAS THE VILLAGE," EDWARD Field sums up. "There were rent parties, there were drugs, there was rustling in the halls at night. It was different, it was very *Village-y*. It was much more anarchic."

On Czech Hedgehogs and Voguing

IF YOU SPOKE OF SOMEONE as "gay" within his earshot, Gay Milius would snap, "You mean homosexual." It was the only indication he was bothered by the popular connotations of his name—but the snapping was meant to be ironic, a joke. He was no more homophobic than other heterosexual men of his generation and artistic disposition. (Someone recently reminded me that his childhood nickname was 'Butch'; it may have made him a little more secure in his heterosexuality.) Still, he was oddly prudish. He spoke of *Lolita* with horror, as a work of pedophiliac erotica. "You can't tell me that guy wasn't a pedophile," he'd say, meaning not Humbert Humbert but Vladimir Nabokov. He hated the bridge-and-tunnelers who invaded the neighborhood looking for prostitutes. He made miniature tank traps—the whimsical term for them is *Czech hedgehogs*—out of twopenny nails that he soldered together and then scattered in the street to puncture the tires of their cars. The two of us once spent a day planting the hedgehogs the way two other guys might have spent the afternoon bowling. My recollection is that they didn't work, and we just watched as horny shitheads from New Jersey ran over them and drove away unscathed.

Not long before Gay killed himself, I introduced him to Christopher, a little boy from a poor neighborhood in Brooklyn who spent a few weeks with my wife and me in the country every summer and later a few days at Christmas and Easter as well. He'd been coming up since he was six and had met most of the grownups we knew and been mostly unimpressed. At first he was suspicious of Gay, this cranky, seamed, stooped, disheveled, very white and borderline old man with a junk-filled van and an enormous, regal, silent husky dog that indifferently bore his attempts at petting. But within a few days, the boy was clearly in awe of him. It may have been because Gay teased him—roughly, sometimes even insultingly—and at the same time paid him attention, probably more attention than he'd ever gotten from any grownup except his mother and my wife and me. I remember Gay giving Christopher a drawing lesson, molding the boy's blunt hand around the crayon, then guiding it across the paper as he showed him how to shade and crosshatch. "He's cool!" Christopher told me afterward. His voice was full of wonder. *Cool* was the last thing he'd expected any friend of ours would be.

This was pretty much the way I felt the first time I met Gay in 1976. He had curly brown hair and the cunning, pointed face of a Beardsley satyr. He was twenty-eight. I was twenty-two. And I suspect I subconsciously thought of him in the terms I would have used ten years earlier, when I was the same age Christopher was when he met him: as "a big kid." It was always the big kids I wanted to hang out with.

Gay showed up at a New Year's Eve party my girlfriend and I were giving wearing a seersucker jacket and a T-shirt appliquéd with two rows of latex dog teats. The jacket was a breach—an ironic one—of his Waspy dress code; he said seersuckers should be worn only between Memorial Day and Labor Day. He'd cast the dog teats himself, having learned to work with latex at a job as a sex-toy fabricator at the aforementioned Ram-It Corporation. It's one of the few jobs I remember him holding. A job would have gotten in the way of his painting, though he usually did that at night, keeping himself going with speed and coffee and Wanda Jackson records while Molly slept upstairs. I don't know how she slept through the music, which had the speed and torque of a muscle car taking a curve on two wheels; even turned down, Jackson's voice was like an engine being gunned.

Like other big kids—the thirteen-year-olds who'd started shaving, the fourteen-year-olds who were screwing—Gay had acquired some of the skills and experiences of adulthood. He was married, he'd been to art school. He could make cocktails, in a brushed-aluminum cocktail shaker, no less, and cook a roast; he rode a motorcycle—no, a motor scooter, which was not yet a hip mode of urban transport, so it seemed like another badge of his rakish eccentricity, especially when he broke a leg wiping out on it in Jersey City. There was an unauthorized aura about his acquisitions, as if he'd borrowed them without permission, the way another big kid, somewhere else in America, might borrow his old man's guns to bring to school. Many of Gay's acquisitions, like the art deco cocktail shaker and the green and pink Depression glass on the kitchen shelves, were things he'd picked up secondhand in the shops that lined Hudson Street, staffed by fussy, old-maidish men who may or may not have wanted to actually sell their merchandise—they seemed to only want to arrange it on the shelves and talk about it knowledgeably with anybody who wandered into their store: *This is one of your third-generation Kewpie dolls, the originals were made of bisque and then they started making them out of composition in the twenties, but this one is celluloid, which is how you can tell.*

Gay enjoyed this too. He could chew the fat with those shopkeepers for hours, oblivious to your boredom and indifferent to everything else he was supposed to be doing, including painting. To the end of his life, he was a collector, and he'd never collect something without wanting to know about it. He knew odd facts about the Pre-Raphaelites and the Masons. His father had been a Mason and had expected Gay to become one and was disappointed he didn't. Maybe that was just a story Gay had made up to cover up other ways he'd disappointed him.

At twenty-two I had very little idea of what constituted adulthood. For this reason I didn't see that Gay's performance of it was a boy's performance. This, after all, was somebody who came to a party in a dog's-teat T-shirt. If Molly tried to kiss him in front of company, he'd push her away like a twelve-year-old fending off his mom. He was a great cartoonist, and I often felt he preferred cartooning to painting, both because it was quicker and because it had a point, a punchline, like the card he sent out one Christmas that showed a group of little Christmas trees with arms and legs surveying a beautifully rendered figure of Saint Sebastian that they'd draped with lights and mounted on a stand. He insulted people's origins and appearance to their face, as when he met a woman I was seeing who was a great-great-grandniece of the Apache war chief Geronimo and mused, "You're what my grandmother would've called a *savage*." Years later, when I introduced him to the girlfriend who is now my wife, he immediately began to warn her of my defects. "He's very clumsy," he told her, "and he knows it. You notice how slowly he moves? It's because he knows he's clumsy." Abruptly he became magnanimous. "Still, somehow he survives. And very well."

As time went on, Gay refused to earn a living, though maybe the truth is he simply couldn't earn one because of incompetence or some debility for which there is no name.

When I met them, he and Molly had only recently moved from his old apartment on the seventh floor into the loft that was one of three commercial spaces on the thirteenth floor of the A building. They paid more rent than their subsidized downstairs neighbors, but it was only $475 a month, $75 of that being utilities, and although Molly had been a film student when they got together, she now worked in finance and probably made twice that much every week. The space was raw, and Gay had to build it from the subfloor up and run his own plumbing and electric from the basement. It couldn't have been a picnic. When I moved into the loft almost twenty years later, I had to haul four-by-eight-foot sheets of drywall up four flights of stairs, my legs trembling, my hands cramping from the weight of those slabs, which left my clothing powdered with gypsum dust.

I lived in the loft on and off for eleven years, from the time Gay left New York with his second wife to shortly after his death. I remember it as a single immense room with a ceiling as high as the ceilings of churches and a window that stretched its entire length, opening onto the Hudson and the jagged apartment blocks of the town in New Jersey where Aaron Burr shot Alexander Hamilton in a duel: Weehawken. The ceiling was rippled, a feature designed to increase its load-bearing capacity, and this made the room look like a deep, inverted swimming pool. When I dream of it, as I often do, I feel I am barely inside at all but suspended hundreds of feet above the edge of the city and the broad river, which is sometimes a lightless gray-green, sometimes the silver of fish scales, and at dusk a chromatic swoon of violet only a little darker than the sky. The breadth of the room and the height of the ceiling and the grandeur of the view outside could make you feel like an elated tyrant surveying his realm from a parapet. But there were times, especially at night, when all that space brought on an icy, agoraphobic dread. I suspect this is part of what Gay was feeling when he took his life thirty years later, how small he was and how great the dark.

Of course, dreams, like memory, cheat. The loft had more than one room, and it wasn't really that big. Gay had taken advantage of its height by building a series of stepped platforms that turned it into a triplex, with a painting studio, dining room, kitchen, and guest room on the ground level, a sitting room on the level above that, and on the highest tier, which was really an *L*-shaped balcony, a bedroom and a bathroom from which you could look down at the tugs and barges humbly plying the Hudson. Sometimes you'd see an ocean liner being towed downriver, looking like a great black utility knife cutting the horizon. I remember this happening once during a party and the whole room falling silent. I went to many parties in that loft and stayed over many nights when I was too fucked-up to make my way home.

Gay and Molly always had dogs, whom they named for baked goods; the pair they had in the seventies were named Cracker and Crumbs. (My friend Ray made them characters in a long poem that began with a stranger pronouncing a curse on them: "Your names are Cracker and Crumbs, you're a pair of bums, and one of you is dead.") Later they got some ferrets; one of them once slithered into my briefcase as I watched and then slithered back out with my checkbook in its mouth. There were always friends sprawled about the loft, louche, good-looking men and women who might've been figures from the crowd photos on the sleeve of Lou Reed's *Berlin* album. They gave off a smeary, postcoital haze. Still, the overall vibe owed less to fucking than to getting fucked-up. I remember Gay sprinkling carrot greens on Jonny Takami's head after he'd nodded out at the kitchen table. Gay's ex-girlfriend Robin had a screaming fight with her new boyfriend at a Kentucky Derby party where she'd gotten smashed on mint juleps and had to be dragged off the roof before she could pitch herself over the edge as she was threatening to. Nobody thought she was serious; there was just a tacit consensus that she ought to be discouraged.

Nobody I knew in the city had an apartment that big or one with such jaw-dropping views. In his dance studio two floors below, Merce Cunningham would tell audiences before a performance, "If you get bored with the dancing, you can look out the window." If you ignored the worn furniture and junk-shop clutter, the shelves of Depression glass and Rookwood pottery, the brass diving helmets, novelty wall plaques, the racks of shrieking fifties paperbacks, the art supplies, the half-finished canvases, you might've been in one of the dream flats of movies from the thirties, though those are usually implicitly somewhere in midtown, with windows that look down onto the glittering web of streets and out onto rows of mirroring windows in mirroring skyscrapers, and convey a sense of being situated simultaneously at the center of everything and far above it, so that the bloodthirsty clamor of midtown traffic—the ten thousand horns blasting *I'll kill ya!, I'll kill ya!, I'll kill ya!*—comes through the high windows as a demure *beep-beep-beep.* Gay's loft might've been at the edge of the world. There were no apartment blocks across the river back then, just the husks of abandoned factories. It was only when you stepped out onto the roof and peered over the cornice that you saw the nocturnal life of the city swarming below.

It was a nightlife of men, hundreds of them, many stripped to the waist in the warm air, some just in blue-jean shorts that were almost loincloths, some in motorcycle jackets and chaps, parading along West Street and up and down the piers. They were indolent, receptive, desirous, yet there was also something martial about them. They were the fuck soldiers, the sex army, the ones who'd chosen to make love not war. And for a little while, you could believe they'd won the war. Sometimes they scared the shit out of me, the way groups of men always have: street gangs, football teams, soldiers, cops. Sometimes I envied them. Gay liked to run a long industrial extension cord out onto the roof so he could train his theatrical spotlight onto the crowds below. Some men, on seeing the halo of light that suddenly bloomed around them, would start to vogue, though the word didn't exist yet. They framed their faces with jazz hands. They spun on a heel and glared over a raised shoulder, as if at invisible catcallers. They were fantastic.

What made them fantastic was their courage, the courage to be what they wanted, to take what they wanted, even the ordinary prize of sexual pleasure, so necessary and so disesteemed, though scarcely a pop song would ever have been written without it, and not much opera either. Taking pleasure ought not to require courage, and for most heterosexuals—that is, heterosexual men—it didn't. In time, that would be true for queer people too. And their pursuit of happiness would be as heedless, as ruthless, as foolish, as base as the pursuits of their straight neighbors, and no more worthy of commendation. In grade school we learned that those walking ax-heads the Puritans came to the New World in search of religious freedom, but our teachers neglected to mention that having ob-

tained that freedom, they set about strenuously denying it to their hereti-
cal neighbors, a practice they passed down to their doctrinal descendants.
Taking pleasure requires courage mostly when law and custom deny it
to you. In 1978 they still denied it to homosexuals. It would be another
twenty-five years before the Supreme Court ruled that a man couldn't be
thrown in prison for sucking another man's prick. And God have mercy
on you if you were to walk around Bensonhurst in cutoffs and an un-
zipped motorcycle jacket. They'd cut your balls off.

It was probably homophobic to train a theatrical spotlight on a group
of queer men as they performed an essential ritual of their queerness and
maleness, as those things were constructed in that place and time. (If
they'd been in Naples and had more clothes on, you could have said they
were taking their evening *passeggiata*.) Would we have done the same
thing with a group of women? With Boy Scouts gathering for a jamboree?
I can't remember much of what was going on in my head back then: I
was almost always high. And I can cite few times that I was deterred from
doing something because I thought it was wrong. What Gay had in mind
is beyond retrieval. He would have said he was having fun.

The Meaning of NOTHING IS FOREVER

"TODAY, THE BUILDING'S IN QUITE good shape," Jack Dowling points
out. "The floors are polished and gleaming, the walls are freshly painted,
and even the pipes are covered with clean sleeves. But back in the seventies it was pretty grubby, with graffiti in the stairwells and dirt everywhere."
(Joel Oppenheimer's son Lem confirms: "Nothing in Westbeth seemed
clean. I had been in the deepest parts of it and it was a nasty, nasty place.")
In winter the heat would go out for an entire stack of apartments. The
doorbells in the Bank Street entryway often stuck, and if someone rang
an apartment whose occupant was out, the unceasing rasp of the buzzer
would have neighbors pounding on the walls for hours, pausing only to
make pissed-off calls to the management.

Some of this was a consequence of the miscalculation of rental income from the commercial spaces. Whether the rent charged was too low

or Westbeth was too ill-situated to justify charging more, the money wasn't enough to cover operating expenses, let alone payments on the $11.2 million mortgage. Management should have corrected this, but Westbeth's board of directors never pushed it to do so. Christina Maile points to "the realities of running a building that had no endowment, very little money, owed a big mortgage. The board didn't exactly want to be involved with all of this." Then Bankers Trust, which held the mortgage, threatened to foreclose. On July 1, 1972, the management sent out new leases that raised rents 17 percent, with indications that a further increase would be forthcoming.

Maile recalls, "And so there was a huge firestorm of tenant opposition and complaints. There were petitions, there were accusations of fraud, corruption, mismanagement, inefficiency." About a hundred and fifty tenants refused to sign the new leases and were sent eviction notices. Fairly or not, some people looked to the Kaplan Fund to issue another grant so that the increases could be revoked. When it didn't, they blamed Joan Davidson. Davidson announced that the fund would be withdrawing its support and leaving Westbeth as a "legacy" to its artist residents. Writing for the striking tenants, Joel Oppenheimer (apparently more willing to be bothered than anyone had guessed) responded, "A legacy that requires you to go broke paying for the funeral is not such a great legacy." Davidson had second thoughts and insisted that the fund would be "sticking with Westbeth and will continue to stick as long as is necessary."

"The real issue raised by Westbeth is a *housing* issue," wrote the art critic Barbara Rose. "Artists are chronically among the lowest-income groups in the country. Although a handful of artists earn as much as middle-management executives, the vast majority are simply poor people with the added problem that their work requires more space than ordinary living quarters. Somebody has to subsidize art. There is a certain reality in the fact that the Kaplan Fund, a tax-exempt foundation, has money, and artists do not have money."

To anyone who hoped New York City would come to the rescue, Rose pointed out that the city's total budget for visual arts programming that year was $10,000—"roughly the cost of materials for one reasonably successful artist."

Looking back at these events fifty years later, Maile believes they "demonstrated how profoundly important the housing and the mission were to these artists. In everything, whether you were opposing the rent increase or supporting it, what came through in all the flyers placed under everybody's door was: *We have to save this building.* Either we have to save it from management or we have to save it from the banks that are wringing the last bloody dollar from us. So that's how the community was forged in those early years, because we were constantly meeting about how to fight the rent increase, how to fight FHA, how to fight HUD, who took over the mortgage.

"I signed every petition. My first husband and I, we gave money for the lawyer. We put out these huge banners outside a window. And mine were very cryptic, as it turned out. I thought I was being clever. I had one hanging outside my balcony. And it said, NOTHING IS FOREVER. So everyone thought that meant I was either for the management or for the rent strike. They couldn't figure out what 'Nothing is forever' meant. Everyone kept asking me, 'What does that mean? Who are you with?'

"Hal Miller was against everything, but he was an actor. And so he would get up and he would talk for a half hour, about whatever it was. And he would blame Joan Davidson and blame the board of directors and blame everybody and get everyone all excited. A lot of these people have passed. What's sad is that there's a whole history of this building that tends to be overlooked. We have an installation downstairs called *Fifty Mile-stones in Westbeth*. It's creative events in Westbeth. And, yeah, that's great, but you would not have those events without these people who came to every meeting, wrote out the petitions, went door-to-door to get people to sign something or to, you know, march down to Washington, raise money to hire lawyers. It was an amazing thing. They were saving a community. They had suddenly had this realization that this was their—their *home*! And they didn't want the financial incompetency of the management or the corporation to take it away from them. So that's actually what created the community: In many ways it was the rent strike.

"And so then the rent increase kind of got settled. We did a much lower increase. And so that kind of went away, but the distrust of the mortgage companies, of the government, of management, of the board of directors, that stayed with the tenants. That really marked a beginning of a kind of adversarial relationship that the tenants would have with anyone telling them what to do. And at the same time, there was all this other energy with people putting on festivals, doing shows, having exhibits. Plus it was also the youth of the people living here. And because there were two-bedroom and three-bedroom apartments, there were a lot of kids, and so the kids, either through playing or babysitting or visiting—that's how people got to know each other. The fight about the rent increase was the inciting moment."

Oppenheimer put it more elliptically in a poem that begins, "I am his majesty's poet at westbeth"

    all we
    are asking is a little cave somewhere,
    where we can do the work. even
    cro magnon allowed that, and,
    possibly, even gained by it.
    at least we think they found where
    the animals were, by the paintings.
    if only we could find our consciences
    as easily, this is the fight we
    are fighting. and asking for
    space to build our own perimeters
    in defense of such. believe us,
    or drop the history of man.

Looking back at Barbara Rose's statement, the one point that might be argued with was her assertion that "somebody has to subsidize art." But it would be at least another decade before such an argument was made with any seriousness. For the time being, the artists in Westbeth had caves where they could do their work. As long as Gay had his, at a rent so low that someone looking back from 2024 can only laugh in incredulity and envy, you would've thought he'd be happy.

Interlude: The Chimney Girl

IN WESTBETH SHE'S KNOWN MOSTLY as the Chimney Girl, so that's what I'll call her. She was a child of the building, as was the tenant who first told me her story. Her parents were musicians. By the time she was twelve she was already showing signs of trouble, though those signs may not have been apparent—may not even have existed—until later. The past looks different when viewed in the glare of the future, which magnifies irregularities and small disfigurements while at the same time blinding you to everything else. Afterward you remember only the disfigurements, the issues At the time, however, she was just a girl. In pictures she's quite pretty.

It was summer; a cousin came to visit. The cousin was older, already a young woman, but making up for the difference in their ages was the fact that the Chimney Girl was a New Yorker, which adds five years to any child's age, and lived in a labyrinthine fortress of artists, some cool and some just weird. Still, she wanted to impress her cousin, and so one night she took her up thirteen stories to the roof. She showed her the city the way another child would show a visitor her room: the grid of glowing streets that to the south became a web of diagonal and zigzag strands; the ghostly high-rises thrusting toward the moon; the softly lapping river where late ferries glided between the banks. Perhaps feeling that wasn't enough, she pointed to the chimney that rose another two dozen feet overhead. There was a ladder attached to it. The tenant who told me this story remembered that the kids she'd grown up with used to mess around on it. The young girl climbed the ladder. I don't know if the cousin climbed behind her or watched from below. At the top, the girl struck a pose, maybe heroic, maybe clownish. Then she pitched backward and disappeared soundlessly into the chimney's gaping mouth.

The cousin froze.

An instant later she was brought back into her body. Maybe she took the elevator, maybe she leapt down the stairs three at a time. She pounded on the door to the apartment and told the girl's father what had happened. He called 911. Some firemen arrived; Westbeth's super led them down into the basement and then to a steel door that opened into the base of one of several chimneys. A lieutenant poked his fingers through a crack, and a small hand appeared on the other side. He jumped back. He hadn't expected to find someone alive: people are killed by falling three stories, and this girl had fallen more than thirteen. When the door was broken open, he saw eyes and a mouth floating in the sooty darkness. It might've been an image from a cartoon. You hear of people laughing in relief, even people who are used to opening doors and finding the dead behind them—maybe especially such people.

The blackened face spoke. "Am I dead?"

She had fallen 180 feet and landed in a mound of soot and ash, years, maybe decades of it, soot so deep she'd had to claw her way up to the surface. The soot had saved her. The lieutenant thought she'd fallen headfirst and landed on her back. At the hospital she was found to have a dislocated hip and multiple fractures. In the storyteller's memory, the injuries were worse than that; she thought the girl had also suffered lung damage from inhaling ash. "I think she ended up having a pretty serious drug problem. Whether that was a factor before or after I don't know. She must've been on lots of painkillers. Her parents live in Westbeth. I don't know where she lives. I don't know what her deal is. After that the building got wise to some of these things. They clipped the ladders, they put up fences so that kids couldn't crawl into places. There've been many generations of kids who've grown up in Westbeth."

The story has become part of the folklore of the building, a cautionary tale for parents, a legend passed down to the next generation of Westbeth children, who hearing it may feel not just frightened but also secretly thrilled. Because, after all, the Chimney Girl lived.

Chapter Four

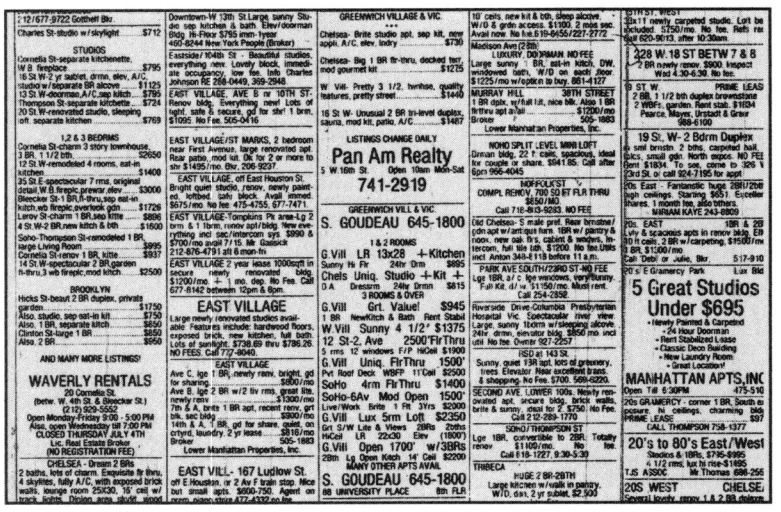

ART SALES 1987-1989

1987
$39,784,600 | Vincent van Gogh *Tournesols*
$53,900,000 | Vincent van Gogh *Les Iris*

1988
$24,566,225 | Claude Monet *Dans la prairie*
$24,750,000 | Pablo Picasso *La Maternité*
$38,390,889 | Pablo Picasso *Acrobate et jeune arlequin*

1989
$24,200,000 | Paul Gauguin *Mata Mua*
$26,400,000 | Pablo Picasso *Le miroir*
$47,850,000 | Pablo Picasso *Self-Portrait: Picasso*

On Becoming a Mockery

IT'S NOT EVERYBODY WHO GETS to be a muse, especially a muse who doesn't just inspire a work of art but helps bring it into being, not just once but twenty-five times.

Black-Eyed Susan met Charles Ludlam as a theater student at Hofstra University in the sixties, when she was still going by her birth name, Susan Carlson. One day she was watching a production from the wings when a voice beside her murmured, "You love the theater, don't you?" She whipped around and cried "Yes!" Somebody else would have jumped. Ludlam, the owner of the voice, was unfazed: "Well then, stick with me, baby, and you'll see the East."

Even as a college student, he had a pro's assurance and a love of the showbiz tropes of the past. In time he would incorporate those tropes into original plays like someone rummaging through a trunk for old props and costumes to find new uses for them, but in the beginning he just tried to loosen the seams of existing works enough to accommodate his sensibility. In one of the first plays in which he cast Susan, he gave her the part of a young girl who'd been struck and killed by a car while taking a walk with her boyfriend. Now, as a ghost, she was conducting him through the underworld to meet her departed relatives. Because the actor playing the boyfriend was more than a foot taller than the leading lady, Ludlam had him play the underworld scenes on his knees. The play mystified classmates and professors. "It was too modern for them," Susan says. "And Charles wouldn't let us take a curtain call because we were playing dead people. And they were just furious that he would do that. But he made them furious all the time. I got used to that."

Ludlam moved to New York, and when Susan graduated a few years later, she moved there herself and reconnected with him. He was working with John Vaccaro's Playhouse of the Ridiculous at Café La Mama on East Fourth Street. Although they were performing Ludlam's play *Con-*

quest of the Universe, his position was contested, thanks to Vaccaro's towering egotism and histrionic rages. "I was told to be very careful of him," Susan recalls. "He was very violent, and he was weird. Charles, when we walked into rehearsals, knew I was shy and he would hold my hand so the guy didn't come near me and didn't start yelling at me." Eventually Ludlam and Vaccaro had a falling out, and he left the company, taking Susan with him, along with the actors Lola Pashalinski, John Brockmeyer, and Bill Vehr, who would work with him for the next twenty years. But Vaccaro kept the rights to *Conquest of the Universe* and continued to perform it. The only way Ludlam could stage his own play was under a different title, *When Queens Collide.* He may have had payback on his mind when he called his new enterprise the Ridiculous Theatrical Company. Vaccaro outlived him by almost two decades, but Ludlam was the winner of their rivalry. When people speak of the Ridiculous Theater or the Theater of the Ridiculous, they are usually speaking of Ludlam's company.

His plays were Frankensteins with the torsos of gothics, the limbs of four different films noir, and heads stitched on from 1920s vaudeville productions; some of the plays had two heads, which quarreled with each other. Ludlam often did this himself, playing two—often female—roles at a time and snapping back and forth between them with microsecond speed and precision. Travesty, in the sense of both cross-dressing and mockery, was an essential part of his aesthetic. Rights to perform *The Mystery of Irma Vep,* Ludlam's most popular work (in 1991 it was the most-produced play in the United States) stipulate that both actors, who between them play eight roles, be of the same sex to ensure that the production contains some drag. Where Vaccaro was bent on shocking audiences, Ludlam liked to leave them dazedly entertained, as if they were staggering off an amusement park ride that had them laughing uncontrollably even as it scared the shit out of them.

Today, many of Ludlam's trademarks—the drag, the mash-ups of tone and genre, the cavalier attitude toward realism—have found their way into mainstream theater as well as movies and TV, but in the seventies and eighties, what he was doing was revolutionary. Like any proper revolutionary, he wrote a manifesto, among whose tenets one finds: "You are a living mockery of your own ideals. If not, you have set your ideals too low." And: "The theater is a humble materialist enterprise which seeks to produce riches of the imagination, not the other way around. The theater is an event not an object. Theater workers need not blush and conceal their desperate struggle to pay the landlords their rents. Theater without the stink of art."

"Charles and I became very good friends," Susan says. "And he introduced me to other wonderful friends. And they became close friends, like the ones I didn't have in high school. We'd go to the theater together, and he would be talking to me all the time and educating me. He talked a lot; he would talk and talk and everybody listened. He was interesting. But it was him that ruled. He ruled everything."

This seems like a fair thing to say about someone who changed your name, as happened one night when Ludlam came upon her putting on makeup before a show. Susan was trying to conceal a black eye she'd accidentally given herself. He told her to darken it instead, make it blacker. "I think I'm going to call you Black-Eyed Susan from now on," he declared. When she protested, he told her, "Your last name's not so hot."

"He would stretch out the way people behaved," says Susan. "He understood when people did things, how they meant them. Sometimes they were hiding things"—she demonstrates with a stealthy sidelong glance—"and sometimes they were just"—angrily blurting—"letting you know how they *felt*. But they were very funny."

A common misconception about the Theater of the Ridiculous is that the acting was campy and over the top. The truth is, the acting was disciplined and contained. "It's larger than life what we're doing," Ludlam once told Susan, "but you cannot seem like you're not real." His characters may not have behaved the way people behave in day-to-day life, but they behaved the way people would behave in the circumstances of the plays. A woman trying to persuade her lover to kill her husband isn't behaving naturally, no matter what Zola said. Susan's genius was to make her actions seem logical. The logic might not be evident at first, and indeed part of the pleasure of her performances was the moment in which you saw the logic of what she was doing. She treated each part as an opportunity for discovery, the sudden understanding of an action or a character, as if those characters hadn't been written so much as briefly captured by the playwright and were now breaking free to be captured by her.

As a young woman she was slight, with a shield-shaped face that could be impassively regal or mobile and cunning. She was unsure of her looks, but Ludlam taught her to "sit next to the drag queen" (who was often Ludlam himself) and copy the way they put on makeup. Even in roles that required stripping down to pasties, she gave an impression of modesty. Her femmes fatales knew how to drive men out of their minds without losing their own. One night the troupe played a gig at a derelict theater on the western edge of Hell's Kitchen that hosted strip shows during the day. The manager invited Susan to join the talent, and Ludlam told her she ought to think about it. The minimally clad dancers got $125 a performance, which was about $100 more than she was getting acting for him. The Ridiculous was so broke that it had trouble paying venues. Still, she stayed. She supported herself with typing jobs. She performed in twenty-five of Ludlam's plays, more than anyone in the company but Ludlam himself. She played the Infanta Eulalie Irene. She played the Polish actress Maia Panzaroff. She played the Empress of China. She played the Queen of Saturn. She played an ex-stripper named Zena Grossfinger who was trying to reunite with the child she'd given birth to when she was six, having been "well-developed for my age." She played the jealous wife of a ventriloquist who spends too much time with his dummy, whose name is Walter Ego.

"We don't call them *dummies*," Susan corrects herself. "We call them *ventriloquial figures*." Ludlam taught her how to throw her voice, and she picked up the skill almost at once. "I have the kind of mouth where my lips don't move when I'm speaking for the ventriloquial figure, and it's interesting to just go and play around."

In 1978 the Ridiculous found a permanent home at 1 Sheridan Square in the West Village; the street outside the theater is now named Charles Ludlam Lane. It's not a bad monument for an artist who set out to be a living mockery. During these years, Susan lived in the sort of housing that every off-off-Broadway actor lived in. Her first apartment was on Avenue A, a railroad flat that rented for fifty-seven dollars a month. It had a separate bathroom with a shower stall, which meant it was "nice." A not-nice apartment would have had a bathroom in the hall that was shared with two other flats. As the theater company bounced from one venue to the next,

Susan moved from apartment to apartment. She moved into Westbeth in 1980. She'd only been on the waiting list a few years when a woman she knew who lived in the building invited her to stay in her flat while she chased her errant boyfriend around the country, and although Susan's benefactor married the boyfriend and almost immediately divorced him, she never came back to reclaim her space. At some point the management became aware of the interloper's presence and summoned her to the office. The manager was, if not exactly crooked, something of an operator: eventually she'd be fired for giving an apartment to her boyfriend. "She had certain ways of dealing with people," Susan recalls. "She never looked anyone in the face. She had me in her office and gave me a seat behind the desk, and she sat with her back towards me. But that's how she dealt with everybody. I understood why people would meet with her and come out of the office looking confused. She asked me a few questions. And then she said, 'Okay, I'm going to put you down for the apartment. You've been there long enough, that's fine.'"

In her years performing, Black-Eyed Susan had never made much money. She'd been priced out of one flat after another as the city's engine of gentrification ceaselessly ate up whole neighborhoods. Her parents had never come to see her onstage. She had the satisfactions of her art and the vital, nurturing friendships of the independent theater, a camaraderie based on common self-sacrifice and the sweetness of doing something illicit together, for what's more illicit than pretending to be somebody else? It's what con artists do. And now she had a home.

"It saved me because I could have my own apartment, and it was affordable. And I could have a part-time job to help me pay for it. And I could be rehearsing and performing at the same time. And it was just amazing that I was able to do this. And I think that there were other artists who felt the same way. We were lucky, really lucky."

She's thinner than she was back when she was acting for Ludlam, but even in her eighties she has a youthful, even childlike, air. She still makes up stories the way she did as a child. She wears her hair in pigtails and roller-skates around her apartment for exercise. Although Walter Ego was donated to an archive, she has another large puppet that Ludlam gave her, and she amuses herself by practicing throwing her voice with it. One imagines what her neighbors make of the sounds that come from behind her door, the swish of skate wheels and a pair of voices performing an old burlesque routine:

> Voice 1 [a licentious croak]: What's big and hairy and sticks out of a boy's pajamas?
> Voice 2 [exasperated]: Oh, Walter!
> Voice 1 [triumphantly]: His *head*!

The Children's Hour

JENNY LOMBARD COMES FROM A family of actors, so even as a kid she knew the miseries of New York housing. The Lombards' old apartment on Perry Street was five hundred square feet; not ideal for a family with two children. The one they moved into on Westbeth's third floor looked out on the inner courtyard and the blank brick wall of the I building. It had almost no light. But it was more than twice the size of their old place and had separate bedrooms for Jenny and her brother. So everybody was happy.

"My father had been this sort of Middle-American farm boy with a big talent who came to New York, and he'd met my mother, who was sort of a gypsy. And my grandparents were notable vaudevillians," Lombard says. Still, her father lacked the ruthless hunger for the limelight that distinguishes (or afflicts) most actors, and it kept him from getting very far. "He was not the kind of guy who would do anything for a chance. A lot of actors now are so single-minded about themselves that I myself find it . . . kind of off-putting. Even when I was at my theater company, I was working as the literary manager, I was writing, but most of my close friends were writers or directors because actors always seem to"—and here she reaches upward desperately—"*want* something from you." She reconsiders. "That's sort of a facile thing to say about an entire profession.

"We were kind of *square*. My parents were very middle class in their values, unlike the other families that were around us." She laughs. Maybe she's thinking of the people Tod Williams spoke of, the father in his grandiose Playboy Club uniform, the mother with her Masterpiece Theatre accent, and the kids pissing in the hall. "So there was always this tension because when we moved into the building, it was simply a free-for-all. The children were . . . we were just . . . there was just a massive amount of kids because they were all . . . I mean, now the building skews so *old*, right? Everybody's quite elderly. But *then* everybody who moved into the building was at the beginning of a career, and they all had young families, and it was just *heaven* for children. There are pictures I've seen of courtyard events where there must be fifty kids sitting around listening to a storyteller. There were so many of us."

In the apartment next door to the Lombards lived Ed Sanders, who may have been the first poet to start a rock band—that band, the Fugs, being the first to record songs with titles like "Kill for Peace," "Coca-Cola Douche," and "Boobs a Lot." In 1962, he'd founded the avant-garde journal *Fuck You: A Magazine of the Arts*, whose credo was "I'll print anything." A few doors down lived a man who beat his wife; Lombard became used to her screams and the sheepish remonstrations of the cops who were called in when the noise got too bad. Across the hall were the sculptor Ralph Martel, the actor Jess Osuna, the poet Joel Oppenheimer, and the Guatemalan painter Rodolfo Abularach. The Oppenheimer and Abularach boys became part of a group of Lombard's friends that sprawled over floors and across buildings.

Some of those friends went to grade school with her, and a few went on together to middle school and high school. She's still close to many of them. The "good" kids went to Stuyvesant, long known as the best of the city's public high schools, the wild ones went to Music and Art. A last resort was Charles Evans Hughes in Chelsea, which before it shut down in 1983, had such a bad reputation that not a single child who graduated from the middle school across the street was willing to go there. "A lot of the kids of my generation, they were either successful and moved on or . . ." she flutters her hands helplessly, "they were just disasters in their lives." She grimaces, worrying whether she should have said that. Along with being a playwright, Lombard teaches drama in a New York City public school, and she has the outsized gestures and facial expressions of someone who's used to grabbing the attention of young children.

"There was an immediate community. We ran the hallways like they were our own private jungle gym. The hallways were always echoing with the sound of kids screaming. Skateboards, because you know those long, smooth hallways. I think somebody cracked down so skateboarding became illegal. We'd have these games of tag that would span nine floors and last six hours. A whole-day thing was playing tag in Westbeth."

"Back then the building was sort of unfinished, so a lot of dangerous stuff was available to us and we . . ." she shakes her head, "we did some *insane* stuff. I wasn't really that reckless. I was the only girl that was part of that scene, but I wasn't fully part of it because I was too chicken. But there was a group of boys that did . . ." shaking her head again, "*crazy* things. You must be familiar with the layout of what was the Merce Cunningham Studio and is now the Martha Graham?" The dance studio, which was directly downstairs from Gay Milius's apartment, took up the eleventh floor of the A building. As in Milius's loft, there were tall windows that looked out on the Hudson, the view even more impressive because there was no sitting platform obstructing it; Cunningham wasn't just being puckish when he suggested that audience members who got bored with the dance could look out the windows instead. Up on the roof Lombard and her friends found a ladder that led to a mysterious stairwell that in turn opened onto a little balcony that ran around the walls of the Cunningham studio. From it, they could look down on rehearsals or, more rewardingly, peer into the dressing rooms. But the balcony was outside the building, not much more than a broad ledge with a wall too low to keep a child from falling. Lombard shudders. "To this day I cannot believe that I would do that! It was not a place where a person who valued their life would ever go. But we would climb onto the Spanish tile on top of Merce Cunningham — there was a gabled roof up there — and we did that. But somebody saw us and we got in big, big trouble. They shut us down over that. A person who lived in the building saw us and called the other mothers."

Lombard is referencing a version of what Jane Jacobs called "eyes on the street," the informal network of mostly mothers (but also grandmothers, aunties, shopkeepers, off-duty schoolteachers, and local busybodies) that surveilled, regulated, and protected the children of a given neighborhood, calling out those children's misbehavior and blowing the whistle on any threats to their well-being. What Jacobs described was mostly what she saw from the windows of her house on Hudson Street, just a few blocks away. Yet, architecturally, Westbeth was one of the overplanned, utopian super-buildings that she was generally suspicious of. Those dizzying, oneiric hallways had no windows from which parents could watch their kids potentially breaking their necks on skateboards, and, unless one lived in the C section and had windows that faced onto the Bank Street courtyard, the only places where one could surveil them comfortably were the semicircular balconies that floated over the interior light court like so many hovering flying saucers.

The children were also drawn to the basement, which was huge and dark, crisscrossed by pipes of various gauges, some of them hot to the touch, and divided into many rooms—artists' studios, storage spaces, and others seemingly without purpose. There were vermin. Someone had painted the boilers with murals of Mickey Mouse characters. Lombard knows of two kids who once entered a ventilation tunnel and got stuck there for an entire day.

Some of the older boys were tough, and there were tougher ones in the neighborhood outside the building, like the ones in the dreaded Go Club, who reportedly stabbed someone to death in Westbeth's courtyard. The actor Vin Diesel, who grew up in the building, often speaks of those kids as the crew he ran with as a teenager. But Lombard scoffs, feeling that Diesel exaggerates his hard-knock origins, maybe to bolster his cred as an action star. "His father directed *soap operas*."

"But not everybody had an easy life. There was a whole contingent of guys who were very much on the punk scene, they were at CBGBs and the Mudd Club. Some of us went on and had lives and some of us didn't do very well, you know, had problems with drugs and whatever."

And, of course, there were the suicides. A boy Lombard's age was almost struck by a body that plummeted into the courtyard in front of him; the dead woman turned out to be the mother of one of his friends.

Still, Lombard's memories of her childhood are mostly happy. "In the summertime they had these huge tables that they would put out [in the courtyard]. It was sort of like a puzzle thing. The tables all fit together and they made a performance stage that went over the fountain. Now there's just a garden, but that was the fountain back then. Merce Cunningham would bring his dancers and they would perform on that stage. There was a children's theater company that used to come and set up in the courtyard. And, of course, Ralph Lee."

Ralph Lee was Westbeth's puppeteer. In 1974 he commandeered the courtyard for a Halloween parade for the entertainment of the community's children. "There were swirling puppets . . . witches flying in the sky, skeletons dancing, and snakes swimming," one of those children remembered as a grownup. "People in costumes danced and whirled around us, and yet they seemed elevated. Maybe they were on a dais. Maybe they were dressed as skeletons. Maybe actual magic was happening." Lee and his assistants began assembling the giant puppets in the courtyard a month out from Halloween; it was how you could tell the holiday was coming. The parade proved so popular that within a few years it had grown too large for its original location and too spooky and anarchic to be just for kids. It's since been rerouted up Sixth Avenue and become the world's largest Halloween parade, as well as the only major parade in the United States to take place at night. Its transformation parallels that of Halloween from a children's festival to an occasion for general license, America's sexiest holiday. "To have been there really at the start . . . that to me is Westbeth," says Lem Oppenheimer, the poet's youngest son. "It's like, 'Yeah, let's create a community thing. We happen to have a giant puppeteer here.'"

"There've been many generations of kids who've grown up in Westbeth," says Lombard. "I think my generation and the one right after were the ones that were most engaged with the building. My son grew up in Westbeth, but he doesn't have that same view. When my son was born, I think he was maybe the only baby I knew, there were no young children in the building at that time. I mean, there's been some movement, the last few years. Some of the larger apartments have been vacated and there are more families coming into the building." She's trying to sound optimistic, but doubt overtakes her. "I mean it didn't, you know, it didn't exactly . . . I think that originally they thought people would be moving out of the building, that it would be this temporary thing. But there are many, many people like me that grew up in the building and continue to live there. Now, some of them were admitted as adults. There's a woman on the tenants' council who grew up in Westbeth and then took over her parents' apartment. That's what I did. I know you could say we're taking advantage, but on the other hand I think about the effect that having affordable rent has had on my life. I was able to go to graduate school. I'm the most middle-class person in my family because I hung on to the apartment and figured I could get a graduate degree and afford to do it. Having affordable rent is such an essential thing.

"I can't think of my life in New York without Westbeth. I don't know where I would be or even who I would be. My husband is a painter and graphic artist, and he's lived in a million different places, did a million different jobs. He doesn't understand how when I walk down Bethune Street and in the block between D'Agostino's market and Westbeth I say hello to ten people. That freaks him out. They're people, some of them, that I've known since I was a child. Westbeth is sort of taking the place of the small town where you *do* know everybody.

"Living in Westbeth has made me a more tolerant person. It's also hard not to have a sense of humor, because there's so much nuttiness around. I think it's very significant to see people working at their art when they're adults and older adults. Not that I actually admire everybody in Westbeth. Sometimes there are people that you look at it and just go"—squeezing her head as if to keep it from exploding—"'Oh my god! I've seen this person's painting in the gallery show. How could this be the focus of someone's entire life?' But it's meaningful for anybody who's doing something artistic to see older people who make art a central part of their lives. I'm fifty-eight years old and I'm starting to write a play for the first time in who knows how long. But if I didn't have the background of knowing I could do that or knowing people who do that . . . I think it makes you less afraid of failure."

Thank You, Colt Studio

IN TIME JACK DOWLING SUCCEEDED in moving to a larger apartment, but it was on the second floor, quite dark and pervaded by the exhaust of the trucks that idled on the street while men had sex in the back. There was always "the *clomp, clomp, clomp* of boots going up West Street to the bars." There was a man he kept seeing around the scene, who always seemed to be watching him. One night Dowling went up to him at the Eagle. "I said, 'Everywhere I go, you're always staring at me. Why?' 'I like you,' he said. 'You don't even know me and you like me?' 'I like what I see,' he said.'" His name was Stanley; he was an antique dealer in his early twenties, twelve years younger than Dowling, and very beautiful and wild. They were together for seventeen years. Dowling once had the unenviable experience of recognizing Stanley sucking cock in a Jack Wrangler film that was being projected on the wall of the bar where he was drinking.

The catalog house where Dowling worked as a mail boy was called Colt Studio Group. It specialized in photos of male nudes barely concealed by swags of cloth that might pass for something an ancient Greek might wear. The business was in trouble. In the seventies there was a diminishing market for gay art photos with classical pretensions. Although he didn't yet realize it, Dowling had a strong entrepreneurial streak, a sense of how a business should be run, and he saw how this particular business was falling short. He persuaded his bosses to try a different look, men with mustaches as big as Civil War generals' posed in leather and ripped denim. They were like the guys you saw every night on Christopher Street; they *were* the guys you saw on Christopher Street. The look caught fire. The new photos were so popular that at one point Dowling, who'd been promoted to junior partner, had to fly to London to stop an English outfit from selling bootleg copies. The first album by the Village People—the prefab disco band that was to gay men of the late seventies and early eighties what the prefab boy band NSYNC would be to preteen girls twenty years later—had a prominent thank-you to Colt on its cover. Dowling went from being homeless to owning half the company. Though he never became famous as a painter, he was instrumental in promoting what would be the archetype of gay masculinity for the next two decades.

Just six years after he'd started working there, Dowling's partner at Colt bought him out for $100,000. The business relocated to California. Dowling sent out the remaining inventory, though he kept some small portrait books, *Man, Another Man,* and *Olympus,* that he later sold to collectors willing to pay top dollar on eBay. "There is not one piece of Colt in this apartment," he tells me. "If, when I started at Colt as the mail boy, I had kept a copy of everything we produced, it would be worth millions today."

With his earnings, he built a house on Fire Island that he rented out for income and bought a second house in Beacon in the Hudson Valley. He turned that one over to Stanley, who renovated it for his antique business. It came back into his possession ten years later, when Stanley, like many of the men Dowling knew back then, died of AIDS.

You Can't Put Your Arms Around a Memory

JOE LOVETT'S DOCUMENTARY GAY SEX *in the Seventies* opens with Barton Beneš sorting through a collection of what appear to be fragments of pottery. He calls them "my shards." Each is inlaid with a small photograph—no bigger than the photo on a driver's license—of a man. The photos on driver's licenses notoriously make their subjects look stiff and dazed, but the men in these photos are strikingly handsome, their expressions candid, inviting, even poetic. Beneš explains that they're friends and lovers who died of AIDS during the worst years of the pandemic. When asked for the concept behind them, he says, "Memory. Like you find pottery shards, memories of civilization." By itself, each piece preserves the memory of an individual; in the aggregate, those individual memories coalesce into the memory of an era, the memory of a scene. You could say that a scene is a civilization writ small. It rises and falls at a particular place at a particular time—*this* neighborhood but not the one three blocks to the north; *this* club, which was cool for six months in 1982 and then got turned over to the bridge-and-tunnel crowd who read about it in *The Village Voice*. And although you can certainly memorialize someone who is still alive, Beneš's snapshots of the scene are enhaloed by death.

Beneš was interested in death—he was, after all, named for the site of a massacre: his middle name, Lidicé, commemorated the Czech village where in 1942 the Nazis executed 340 of the 503 residents. Even in childhood his taste ran toward the funereal, the museum dioramas of preserved animal corpses posed in a fiction of aliveness, the gilded sarcophagi of mummified human ones whose black eyes gaze impassively at the viewer as if declaring death's indifference to mere life. At some point he started to indulge those tastes by buying mummies from Robert Brier, a senior researcher in paleopathology at Long Island University (when a *National Geographic* documentary brings in an expert on ancient Egypt, it's likely to be him). More accurately, Beneš traded for mummies. "Out of the blue," Brier says, "I got this phone call from Barton Beneš, not knowing who he was. He was sort of an interesting guy, so I said to him, 'I have mummies because when I was in Egypt I'd bring them back—animal mummies—to use when I was teaching my classes.' And I asked him, 'What do you do?' and he said he was an artist. And it was kind of a risky thing to do but without seeing anything of his, just over the phone, I felt he was a good artist. And I said, 'I'll tell you what: I'll trade you a mummy for your art.'" The mummy he traded was a fish; it was sort of a grade C mummy, and Brier didn't especially want it. Evidently the Egyptians mummified all sorts of animals as offerings to the dead. There were fish cemeteries, cat cemeteries, there were farms that raised cats for sacrifice. When Brier X-rays those mummies, he always finds that their necks were broken or their skulls smashed. "These weren't beloved pets, noooo!" Brier and his wife Pat went down to Beneš's studio and fell in love with his work. "I saw Barton's place, we struck up a friendship right then and there that lasted for decades. We bartered for many, many years."

By the eighties, Beneš was a successful artist, even if, to the bafflement and indignation of people who knew his work, he had never had a major museum show in the United States. His pieces didn't command the highest prices (they went for four or five figures, not six), but, as Brier explains, "He was the most prolific artist I ever met. He was cranking out good stuff. That's all he did, that was his life. He didn't leave Westbeth very often. He did a lot of cocaine. He had so many pieces he could sell or barter or whatever. But he was never really mercenary. I was in the house several times when Barton was given orders for commissions that he simply didn't do because he just didn't want to. *Nest Egg* was a nest made of shredded money with a few eggs, also made out of money. He must've made thirty or forty of them. He used to say, 'Don't tell anybody,' because everybody got it, and he sold a lot of them. He was selling them for $1,500 each. Years later I was in his house and he gets a phone call, and it's Malcolm Forbes. Malcolm Forbes collected eggs. [It should be noted that the kind of eggs Forbes—who in the eighties was one of the world's richest men—usually collected were made by Fabergé.] I'm only hearing one side of the conversation, but it's Malcolm Forbes on the other end, and Barton's saying, 'No, I don't make them anymore. No, it's not a matter of money. *Nest Egg* is in the past now. No, sorry. Bye.' That was it, he wouldn't make one for Malcolm Forbes. He moved on."

Beneš was generous. Much of his earnings went to support his mother, whom he adored. He became friends with Joe Lovett when they were both in their twenties, and for the next forty years would bring him pieces of art the way someone else might bring over wine for dinner. Lovett was shocked the one time Beneš told him he'd have to pay for a shell piece that was left over from a show at the Kathryn Markel gallery. "It didn't sell so I said, 'I want that.' And he said, 'You'll have to buy it from Kathy.' I said, 'What do you mean, buy it?' He said, 'You'll have to buy it from Kathy. It's on consignment.' And I said, 'I've never paid for a piece of yours.' And he said, 'I know, but this is through a gallery. You have to buy it.'" Lovett's physician husband is a serious art collector, so he understood: "If we don't buy their work, how are they going to eat?"

When she was barely out of her teens, collage and assemblage artist Joan Hall came across one of Beneš's early watercolors at an outdoor art fair and was so enchanted by it that her boyfriend of the time bought it for her. By the time she and Beneš became Westbeth neighbors years later, the painting had been lost, and although he wouldn't paint her another one, he gave her one of his money pieces, a far better gift—or at any rate a more desirable one, at least going by Malcolm Forbes. One wall of Hall's apartment is devoted to Beneš's work, notably a photo of the toilet stall where Republican Senator Larry Craig from Idaho was busted for soliciting, with a piece of what Beneš claimed was the original toilet paper attached to the frame. A later artwork, which he gave Hall on one of their nightly visits, is a photo of a perfume atomizer filled with pearls, with the inscription, "I couldn't find anything valuable in time for my kissy-poo. This was the best I could come up with. Love, Barton."

Women in the building doted on him. He was so close to Shami Chaikin that the other members of his coterie called her "the first wife," though he assured Hall that *she* was the real first wife: she didn't believe it for a second. Yet for all his popularity and social ease, Beneš rarely went out. If Brier wanted to have him up to his home in Riverdale for dinner, he'd have to drive him both ways while Beneš cracked jokes about going to Mongolia. Toward the end of his life, when he could no longer leave his apartment without an oxygen tank, Hall recalls that if he got bored at a dinner, he'd nudge her under the table and announce, "I'd really love to stay, but my oxygen is running out." She laughs. "And nobody could say anything."

Even as a younger man, he preferred staying at home among his spectacularly weird collections, sleeping in the day and working through the night. The chief breaks in that routine were cruising and coke. "You walk along and you look, you walk and you look," he tells Lovett in *Gay Sex in the Seventies*. "You make believe you're looking at something in the window when you're really looking at the reflection in the window, of the other person. It's like watching two birds mate. As time went on, there was no ritual, you just did it. Someone would stand there and they'd touch themselves. That was the invitation. 'Here it is, take it.'

"You could have sex several times a day. You go to the supermarket, you meet someone you go off, it was no problem."

Well, there were problems, a lot of them arising from the pyrogenic chemistry of sex—anonymous, multipartnered, often rough—and cocaine. He cautioned his younger brother Warren: "Don't ever do cocaine. Once you try it, you're probably going to like it, and you're done."

"It became manic," he says in *Gay Sex in the Seventies*. "It became like, 'How much can I get?' and 'This isn't enough.'" From off-screen, Lovett asks what it was that he couldn't get enough of, and Beneš impatiently says, "Sex! You had a lot of sex and you go from one to the other to the other. And it also takes down inhibitions. You'd let anybody fuck you, you didn't care. You'd get gang-fucked." This was part of the reason he carried around that slip of paper with his name and phone number. Once he picked up, or was picked up by, a piece of rough trade in a public bathroom, who without warning shoved his head into a toilet bowl. Beneš was so shocked he began to cry. Suddenly contrite, his trick offered to let him shove *his* head in the bowl instead.

Obsessive collector that he was, in 2006 Beneš still had one of the numbered cards that used to be given to drop-ins at the city's clinics for sexually transmitted diseases, back when an STD was an annoyance and not yet a death sentence. He used it, mounted above a sentimental illustration of a pioneer oxcart train, in a piece called *Chelsea VD Clinic*.

In 1981 Beneš's partner Howard Meyer was diagnosed with an odd and previously unseen illness that a year later would be given the name AIDS. "I remember Howard got sick," Brier recalls. "What happened was [they] went to the doctor, and what happened was the doctor was a very handsome gay doctor . . . They come back, and they call me. I went to medical school, so they often asked me for medical advice—like I knew. So anyway, they call me and tell me that this gay doctor told them that Howard has this kind of cancer that only gays can get. 'What do you think about that?' 'I never heard about this,' I said. And they decided that the doctor was jealous of their relationship and had told them this about this kind of cancer only gays can get [out of envy], and they didn't believe it. So they didn't do anything about it. It was like another six months before it came out that there really was this thing called AIDS, and they said, 'Well, I guess that's what we got.' It sounds unlikely when you hear about it the first time. You can't figure out the mechanism. *Gay cancer? Yeah, right.* So they sort of blew it off."

By the end of that year, 213 cases of AIDS had been diagnosed in New York City; seventy-four people had died of it.

Meyer developed Kaposi sarcoma. Brier used to drive him to his weekly treatments at Sloan Kettering hospital. It took some agility and spatial intelligence to fit the patient, his wheelchair, and Beneš, who insisted on coming along, into his red MGB, but Brier performed the errand every Tuesday for two or three years until Meyer got too weak to leave the apartment. "It was never a downer," he says. "The three of us would go and we'd be joking. Everybody who met Barton became a friend."

Howard Meyer died in 1989. None of Beneš's work specifically references his death, and all the pieces that might be called AIDS art (a term Beneš hated) date from the nineties onward. The one possible exception is *Death Museum*, which, alongside embalming eye cups and a skull fragment of a victim of the Black Death, contains an object labeled "cotton used to wipe the face of Howard Meyer after he died, July 10, 1989." "Everything I do is because of something that's happening in my life," Beneš says in *No Secrets*. "My Aunt Evelyn was happening in my life, I did Aunt

Evelyn. Africa, I was doing the shells. It gets rid of my fears . . . When Howard was so sick, I was with him when he died. I went through the whole thing with him. It took my fear of dying away. So when you're working with stuff and experiencing it, you get over the taboo, the taboo goes away." Maybe that was why, in the gleefully mercenary eighties, Beneš's favored medium was money. "You give someone a dollar and say, 'Tear it up,' they can't tear it up. They're terrified to tear it up. But once you can tear up money, you're free."

This Is What It Is

THE LAST TIME JACK DOWLING saw his lover was at the house he'd bought him in Beacon. When he came up from the city, he found Stanley emaciated and too feeble to walk; he could only push himself around the house in a wheeled office chair. He'd wanted to end his life at home, but his nurse said he needed to go to a hospital. Dowling took him to one in Poughkeepsie, where he died four or five days later. It took years to straighten out his affairs. He'd had three checking accounts, and when one was overdrawn he'd just move on to another. Like many men with the illness back then, Stanley had maxed out his credit cards and cashed out his other assets: he knew he wouldn't live long enough to have to settle.

In the beginning, Dowling remembers, before it was AIDS—before it was even GRID (for Gay-Related Immune Deficiency)—it was sometimes referred to as "a gay brain disease." But the idea of a gay brain disease was as baffling as the idea of a gay cancer. On first reading about it in the July 3, 1981, *New York Times*, one gay man dismissed it as "insane. There's no heterosexual illness," he muttered, and turned the page. The void had yet to be filled by science because the science didn't exist yet, and so people filled the void with myths and rumors. Some were scary, some were comforting. Dowling says, "We'd tell ourselves, 'It's them, the people who use poppers, the people who use drugs. They get it, we won't get it.'" One can read this as primitive, crowdsourced epidemiology or as an attempt to moralize the disease. Moralizing the disease lessens the anxiety that you yourself might contract it. To place its victims in the category of the sinful is to place yourself by default in the category of the safe, because of course you are not a sinner. A year later, when the disease had a name, heterosexuals were telling themselves it only affected the people who got fucked in the ass. The problem with an emerging disease is that its etiology is uncertain, its causative factors liable to shift. What did people who congratulated themselves on their heterosexuality tell themselves when AIDS began to show up in heterosexuals? To speak of fundamentalist Christians as modern-day Puritans is unfair to the Puritans, for the Puritans at least understood that sin is slippery and amorphous and almost anyone may, one morning, without having done anything truly wrong, find that they have become one of the fallen. One of the things that made the COVID-19 pandemic so contentious was that anybody could get it. One couldn't stigmatize the victims, so the stigma of the illness attached to the measures people took to protect themselves or to the ones they refused to take. Depending on where in the country you lived, you could be fined for going in public without a mask or mocked and threatened for wearing one.

"I probably lost a hundred guys, friends, lovers," Dowling remembers. "A lot of people on my block in Cherry Grove, everybody on my walk died. Couples, roommates. The house across from me had five guys, and they all died." Some houses on Fire Island saw so many deaths that people began to speak of them as if they were haunted.

By the early nineties, AIDS was the leading cause of death for male New Yorkers between the ages of twenty-five and forty-four. The Village and Chelsea had more infections than entire towns elsewhere in the United States. On any given day, approximately two thousand people with AIDS were occupying beds in the city's hospitals. Even getting admitted for an AIDS-related condition took ingenuity and persistence. At one well-known hospital, an executive of one of the largest corporations in the city who had Kaposi sarcoma and was running a 104-degree fever was denied a bed until his doctor told him to simply show up in the emergency room, where by law the staff couldn't turn him away.

Dowling spent more and more time caring for friends who fell ill. This became a common occupation. The genius of queer New York had always been a genius for community, but now a community that had been organized around pleasure gave way to one organized around sickness.

Just as you used to see everybody you knew at Stonewall or the Roxy or the Cubbyhole or the Saint or on the line at the Met, you now saw them in certain doctors' offices and pharmacies and hospital waiting rooms or at meetings of Gay Men's Health Crisis. "NYU had something called Co-op Care," Dowling says. "It was more like a hotel where you could stay with your partner or friend while you took them to their medical appointments. The first time I entered the dining room, I was shocked to see so many people I knew." Many of those people were dying. Some died meekly, quietly, withdrawing into the rooms where their struggles finally came to an end. Some went out publicly, even triumphantly. Dowling recalled being at an outdoor party in Cherry Grove early in the epidemic. "A young man from the Pines arrived. He was incredibly good-looking, and it was almost a point of pride for him that he had Kaposi's spots all over. He was almost a warning. I had enormous admiration for him that he had the courage to go out like that. His manner was charming. *This is what it is.*"

Several Westbeth residents are said to have died of AIDS between the eighties and early nineties. Dowling only knows of one: the actor and playwright Seth Allen. Few people remember him now. In 1967 he won an Obie for his performance in *Futz*, Rochelle Owens's play about a man who chooses to love a pig—in the playwright's words, "domestically, affectionately, and sexually." The plot is worth mentioning because before the Supreme Court's *Obergefell v. Hodges* ruling in 2015, many attacks on same-sex marriage hinged on comparisons between homosexuality and bestiality, as in Senator Rick Santorum's infamous remark that "in every society, the definition of marriage has not ever to my knowledge included homosexuality. That's not to pick on homosexuality. It's not, you know, man on child, man on dog, or whatever the case may be." Some thirty-five years before that, *Futz* had imagined an entire town of Santorums who were so outraged by their neighbor's flouting of sexual norms (not to mention domestic and affectionate ones) that they killed him.

✳

Last Guests at the Party

IF THE SIXTIES CAME TO an end, as Joan Didion suggested they did, on the day news of the Manson murders broke, maybe the seventies ended the night John Lennon was shot outside the door of his apartment building, the Dakota. When he heard the news, Bob Gruen was developing pictures of John and Yoko he'd taken for *The Village Voice* a few days before. He slid to the floor. "My mind was reeling with the shocking permanence of the news and with how unbelievably wrong John's death was." A moment later, the calls started coming in, and he began to think of what to do with the photos he'd just made. He called the papers. Then he made his way up to the Dakota to see if there was anything he could do for Yoko. "It was a scene, people crying and crowding around John's home. People were in shock and wanted to gather together for solace. There was a lot of hugging and handholding and tape recorders playing John's music." As Gruen approached the vestibule, he saw a bullet hole in the window. By the time he got back to Westbeth, he had calls from every major media outlet in the world, all wanting photographs.

A few days later, Gruen got a request from the producer who was putting together a public memorial for Lennon in the bandshell in Central Park. He wanted him to select an emblematic photo to be enlarged and displayed during the ceremony. Gruen had taken a lot of iconic photos: the one of Lennon playing guitar in an army jacket; the meditative portrait that had run on the front of *The New York Times* in which the musician faces the camera but glances off to the side as if at something more interesting to him than the gluttonous attention of the world. His final choice was inspired by a full-page ad in which Yoko implored fans, "Please don't blame New York for John's death—it could have happened anywhere." The ad reminded Gruen that Lennon was a New Yorker, and so the photo he chose to hang above the bandshell that day was the one of the musician in a sleeveless NEW YORK CITY T-shirt.

By 1980 Gruen was working relentlessly, touring with bands from KISS—who were hugely popular in Japan, maybe because their makeup and stage costumes suggested both kabuki and anime—to the Clash. When he was in New York, he spent the night pinballing among music venues and after-hours clubs, double-parking outside one to dash in and take a few shots of whoever was playing, dashing back out before he got ticketed. His marriage had broken up. His lifestyle was a low-budget version of those of the musicians he photographed. Sometimes he couldn't get a hotel room and crashed in the back of a tour bus. He once snapped a monumentally fucked-up Sid Vicious shoving a hot dog into his mouth and smearing ketchup and mustard over half his face. The photo was later exhibited at the National Portrait Gallery in London as part of a show called *Faces of the Century*. At a party in Japan, Gruen ran into a woman he went to high school with. She exclaimed, "Oh my god, you were the AV guy!" In the first story, we see where art can come from — that is, from squalor as well as the sublime — and in the second, we see where Gruen came from. All these stories can be found in Gruen's buoyant memoir, *Right Place, Right Time*. Often, he had trouble getting paid. A French magazine that owed him money for shots of the Rolling Stones couldn't pay him unless he came to Paris to pick up his fee in person. He got so hip to his clients' obfuscated and exploitive contracts that his office manager took to erasing their suspect clauses with Wite-Out.

Gruen saw Westbeth and the surrounding neighborhood change a lot in the years he lived there. "When we moved in, there was a highway out here. And under the highway, the city rented space, and they'd park all the trucks underneath the highway, and they'd leave the back of the truck open so somebody wouldn't break in to steal something. They'd leave it open to show there was nothing in there. Well, all those open trucks became little motel rooms for all the gay cruising people. There's all kinds of stories and even songs about going down to the trucks.

"But then, in the eighties they took the highway down, and the trucks were gone and for a while it was just bare asphalt. And you'd see like ghouls, like zombies, kind of staggering around. And then a car would show up and the zombies would kind of shuffle over to the car and either put down some money and get something or someone would just suck their face down, get a hit of crack, and then walk away, and then they're all happy and bouncing around and stuff. Crack was everywhere, and people were fucking crazy."

One night, coming home late and drunk, Gruen went out on the pier across from Westbeth and got jumped. A man who was out cruising came to his rescue. By that year, 1984, the great sexual night market of the West Village waterfront was emptying out as people became more conscious of its risks. Of course, fucking strangers in public had always been risky, but evidently the risk of being robbed or beaten or stabbed paled beside that of contracting a fatal disease that shifted shape, appearing here as a cancer once seen only in elderly men of Mediterranean ancestry, there as a kind of bird pneumonia, elsewhere as an illness commonly transmitted by house cats. You could die from petting Fluffy. Depending on how you were wired sexually, one risk could be a turn-on, the other not so much. A year later the city would close the Mineshaft. Inspectors from the Department of Consumer Affairs cited men having unprotected sex with multiple partners in full view. *The New York Times* reported, "Two of the inspectors said they heard sounds of whipping and moaning but did not investigate 'for reasons of personal safety.'"

I like to imagine that Gruen's cruising rescuer was a holdover from the long free period of the previous decade, the last guest at the party standing amid a wreckage of broken glass, crushed poppers, and discarded pieces of clothing, wondering where everybody had gone. The fun was just getting started.

On Counting the Dead

NOT EVERYONE BLACK-EYED SUSAN MET in Westbeth was friendly. Some of her older neighbors gave her dirty looks, and at least one called her a *slut* apropos of nothing—a peculiar accusation in a community where not ten years before guys on the make had wandered the halls knocking on the doors of female neighbors like Halloween trick-or-treaters. Susan adds, "And they hated the shows I was in with Charles [Ludlam]. There was a man who lived around the corner from me, whenever I happened to be outside my apartment at the same time he was, when he passed me, he would go *eucchh!*"

For a long time, she made no friends in the building. It's only in recent years that she's been recognized as a Westbeth Icon, an honor given "senior Westbeth artists who continue to work passionately in their field." If you watch the video of her 2019 induction ceremony, with its reverential career summary and clips from past performances, you'd never guess that anyone in the building ever said *eucchh!* as they passed her in the hall. It's possible she mistook an exclamation of general disgust—with the garbage the neighbor may have been hauling to the trash chute, with the hour, with life—for one directed at her. Maybe the neighbor believed that the Ridiculous Theater Company was an enemy of theatrical tradition, when in fact its creators loved the tradition and just wanted to enjoy it without the stink of art. But a number of otherwise sophisticated people made similar misassumptions. When Susan was hired to play a small part in the 1987 movie *Ironweed*, one of her rare roles in a Hollywood feature, Jack Nicholson, the male lead, figured that because she worked with Ludlam, she had to be a lesbian and evidently took that as a challenge. "Jack Nicholson, you can take him, I don't want him!" she exclaims, mocking and indignant. "He was making sexual advances to me during the whole thing."

Still, she was deeply impressed by Meryl Streep, who played a ladylike down-and-outer. "From Meryl Streep I learned how to direct myself. That's what she did. Film directors don't direct the actors. They tell them where to stand and when they're overdoing it. But Meryl Streep, while they were setting up the cameras, she would be at the sink in the room, playing the character herself. I saw her doing her own speech, talking to herself. She was directing herself, and I thought, 'That's what I have to do.'" Susan's performance as a hard-mouthed slattern who baits Nicholson's character about a shoelace (she keeps telling him to "Put it *in!*") is terrific. For the two or three minutes she's on screen, you can't take your eyes off her.

On the whole, movie work didn't interest her. She wanted to be directed. Around the time she got the *Ironweed* job, she played a female Hamlet in the drag performer Ethyl Eichelberger's exhilarating, breakneck *Hamlette*. Eichelberger played Gertrude, Claudius, *and* the ghost of Hamlet's father. The Player King was a hand puppet.

In the spring of 1987, Susan was costarring with Ludlam again in *The Artificial Jungle*, which transplanted the plot and characters of Zola's *Thérèse Raquin* to a Lower East Side pet shop. Mid-performance, Ludlam collapsed onstage and had to be rushed to St. Vincent's Hospital. He'd been diagnosed with AIDS only a few months before. Talking about it many years later, Susan recalls that Ludlam, who had always been health conscious, had for a long time followed a macrobiotic diet but stopped the night they went to a talk by Michio Kushi, macrobiotics' great popularizer, and Kushi began to hold forth on the unluckiness of blue eyes. He cited instance after instance of blue-eyed people who had died gruesomely, starting with John F. Kennedy. Ludlam had very large blue eyes. Afterward, he was visibly upset. "He just was silent. He was just looking down, and his mind was going a mile a minute, I could see. He never followed macrobiotics again. And I think that if he had, he might have lasted longer." In his last weeks, she'd bring her friend chicken soup in the hospital; it went uneaten. When he died on May 28, it made the front page of *The New York Times*, the first AIDS death to be reported so prominently.

Susan lists the friends she'd lost to the disease: "John Brockmeyer, Bill Vehr . . . it just went on and on. Ethyl Eichelberger. People that we worked with. They were *young*!" She remembers visiting Vehr in the hospital when he was dying. "He was just lying still, he was almost dead. And the nurse came in, and she couldn't stand it that we were all huddled around him. Well, what did she think?" For a moment, her face is lit with wonder; it's the face of someone seeing a thing for the first time. "I never thought I—who could predict that? That one would live through that."

EARLY IN 1981 THE NEW York Police Department reported that the year just past had been the worst year of crime in the city's history: 710,153 reported incidents, with 1,814 homicides. Ten years later, total crimes had climbed past one million, and there had been more than 2,200 murders.

In January of 1980 a tenant was raped in an unlit area of Westbeth's Bethune Street entrance. This is probably why the guards' station was subsequently moved from the Bank Street entrance to the one on Bethune. The old arrangement did little to promote safety. Entering the building from Bank Street meant crossing the courtyard between the I and L buildings, then climbing a flight of broad, shallow steps to the set of glass doors before the guards' station, and during that time one was both concealed from the street, which never had much foot traffic at night, and exposed to whoever might be lurking in the shadows of the low buildings. The man on night duty might not even see someone being mugged twenty or thirty feet below. With the new arrangement, one could come in through the door directly off Bethune Street, under the benign gaze of the guards who staffed the desk day and night: among them were a humorous Haitian gentleman named Jacaman who knew the name of every child in the building; baby-faced Anthony Crooms; and the scholarly Bayan Abdelbaree, who could discourse with ease on the history of Kool and the Gang and the differences between the Old Testament and Quranic stories of Job (in Arabic, Ayub). None of the night men was especially big or threatening, and none was armed, and it's a small miracle that nothing much worse than stickups took place in the building during those years. However, in the early nineties someone broke into the building, dragged a tenant into a stairwell, soaked her with lighter fluid, then tried to set her on fire.

The Misfortunes of the Artist's Family

By 1980 THE WESTBETH PLAYWRIGHTS Feminist Theater Collective had dissolved. Part of the problem was that it had been too successful at securing grants. Each grant placed conditions on the recipient, usually concerning the kinds of plays it could put on. As Christina Maile puts it, "We were spending a lot of time making up programs that would fulfill the obligations of the grant rather than being just allowed to be creative and get money and just do whatever we wanted. So there was a certain amount of bureaucracy that we just couldn't deal with, and it kind of dampened our enthusiasm." She's philosophical about it. "Everyone had the best intentions. The grantmakers also had the best intentions, but they also had to manifest what the money was going to, so they had their own kind of requirements that probably they wouldn't be that happy with ei-ther, because they—both of us, the grantor and the grantee—were just locked in this endless paperwork."

Maile had been supporting her family as a carpenter, building the plat-forms and dividing walls that were in high demand among tenants in the undefined spaces of the new Westbeth apartments, but when the theater collective broke up she enrolled in the landscape architecture program at City College. Designing stage sets had gotten her interested in volume and space. The problem was that City College's school of architecture had a long list of requirements, including calculus. City's urban landscape program, which was housed in the same building, had no calculus requirement. Maile is amused that her entire career going forward was determined by her distaste for higher mathematics. She got into the program on the strength of some set designs she brought in to show the dean.

On graduating, she went to work for New York City's Parks Department. "I love the Parks Department because it has a real impact on people's lives. I mean, the Parks Department, interestingly enough, doesn't only do the playgrounds and parks, they also are in charge of all of the historic landmarks, like the Diamond House, for example, or the Jumel Mansion, or Washington Square. They're in charge of restoring and maintaining historic landmarks. And they're in charge of all the recreational stuff. They're the pools and the pool buildings. I mean, they have such an impact on the city. And when I was there, it was one of the smallest departments. My work was mostly in Manhattan, but once I had to do some restoration in an area in Prospect Park, and Prospect Park is really beautiful. I like it actually better than Central Park because Prospect Park is a much more sinuous, organic kind of shape. There are little paths that people have forgotten, and so the area that I was assigned to renovate was like a room in a big house that everyone has forgotten. The asphalt had unraveled, the benches had fallen apart, all of the planting had burst through all of the hardscape. And it was like nature had come back and had softened all of the hard surfaces that years ago people had put in and had reclaimed it as it had once been. And so my recommendation was that we just leave it alone."

On the whole it was a happy time for Maile, except that she and her husband divorced. This was hardly uncommon in the building. There's a lot of reasons that an artistic marriage is sometimes very hard to maintain. Because of jealousy, because of finances. You have maybe one artist who's so totally obsessed with his or her work that she doesn't pay attention to the marriage or the family. So there was some amount of stress on the kids when either the mother or the father left. But whoever remained, the amount of community around was so great because if there were kids involved, the kids had really, incredibly close ties. They could always go to someone else's apartment for a meal. It was kind of like a village in that sense.

"I did a whole bunch of video interviews with some of the kids here, and one of them said that her father had left and her mother raised her, and she said the reason she didn't become an artist was because she didn't want to be poor. She didn't want to worry about where their next meal was coming from."

On the Origin of the World

ON A LIST OF THE top ten art sales of the eighties, the dominance of Picasso is evident at a glance. Five of the ten paintings that blotted up freakish sums at auction were his, which makes the inclusion of two Van Goghs, including one at the very top of the list, seem almost like a consolation prize awarded to a sentimental favorite. Given the vibrant strangeness of his vision, the brushstrokes that render the furious aliveness of stalk and leaf and blossom, those colors that at first viewing seem all wrong and then suddenly become the only possible right ones, Van Gogh is an incongruous sentimental favorite, but by 1987 he had become one. That Picasso had also become a sentimental favorite, or maybe a *logical* favorite, an artist it made sense to love, and to collect even at the cost of tens of millions of dollars, may be even more incongruous: How *does* an artist go from being an affront to popular taste to being its beneficiary? Time surely has something to do with it. Three of the top-selling Picassos in the eighties were painted in 1905, that is, eighty years before they sucked all the oxygen out of the auction chamber, and much of the money. *Irises* was almost a hundred years old when somebody bid nearly $54 million for it. Great art doesn't die, but it does age, and sometimes age mutes the brilliance that once made people shield their eyes when they first looked at it and makes it easier to think of as an investment.

"At its most basic level," Louis Menand writes, "the art world exists to answer the question, 'Is it art?' . . . You don't know it's art by looking at it. You know it's art because galleries want to show it, dealers want to sell it, collectors want to buy it, museums want to exhibit it, and critics can explain it. When the parts are in synch, you have a market."

Joe Lovett puts it another way: "When I was growing up, I don't think that anyone ever expected to make money in their art unless they worked in graphics on the side or fashion illustrations. You made art because you were obsessed with it. You made art to make art. You made art because you couldn't not . . . It used to be art, and then it became the art world, and then it became the art market, and then it became the art industry."

By the eighties the art world had become a walled city, its fortifications so high and thick that it took extraordinary measures to breach them. The days when Jack Dowling could bring a canvas up to Ivan Karp in his office at Castelli on the strength of a phone call were long past. The conceptual artists and curators Stephen Eins and Joe Lewis had to go all the way up to the South Bronx to establish a space that would feature work by younger and more experimental artists, especially artists of color. In time the walled city got wind of what was happening elsewhere and sent emissaries to seek out selected talents and escort them in. Jean-Michel Basquiat began the decade tagging buildings in lower Manhattan with his friend Al Diaz under the name SAMO or SAMO©, the tag often accompanied by an epigraph: SAMO© 4 MASS MEDIA MINDWASH, SAMO© AS AN ALTERNATIVE 2 GOD. He is supposed to have sold his first painting to Debbie Harry for $200. By mid-decade he was earning $1.4 million a year, and his feverishly animated, category-shattering paintings were being shown at *documenta* in Germany and the Whitney Biennial. Lorraine O'Grady called him "a black Picasso." In less than ten years, Basquiat went from making art for nothing to making it for hundreds of thousands of dollars, much of it in cash. Some art dealers paid him in drugs. This may have struck both parties as practical and efficient, but it eventually proved fatal. He died of a heroin overdose in 1988. He was twenty-seven.

In 2017, Jean-Michel Basquiat's *Untitled* from 1982 (its central image is a black skull with a gaping square of mouth like the open door of an empty warehouse) sold at auction for $110.5 million. This made it the sixth-most-expensive painting ever sold and placed the artist, according to his dealer (who may not have known he was echoing Lorraine O'Grady thirty-four years before), "in the same league as Francis Bacon and Pablo Picasso." The buyer was Yusaku Maezawa, the billionaire founder of the Japanese clothing line Zozo; a year later he would sign up to be the first customer for a circumlunar voyage on the SpaceX rocket.

On Who Gets to Tell What Kind of Jokes

GAY MILIUS HAD A HABIT at parties of going up to strangers and asking them to name five artists. Picasso came up most often. Everybody knew Picasso. Many people could also name Warhol. But after that, most drew a blank or rummaged their memory to produce Van Gogh, Monet, or Leonardo da Vinci. While Gay might give somebody a break on the recently deceased Picasso, he drew the line at the deceased of the previous century. "Come on, he's *dead!*" he'd scold. "He's been dead a hundred years!" It was a kind of performance art, an art of discomfort that if staged more artfully might have been compared to the provocations of Karen Finley (if it had been funnier, it might have been compared to the routines of Andy Kaufman). But Gay's indignation was real. So was his glee at having exposed some stranger's ignorance, for the stranger was a representative of a public that couldn't name five living artists, that could barely conceive that there were people living in the world who made art the way other people made cars or air conditioners or sandwiches; that art wasn't just something hanging on the walls of museums or reproduced in textbooks or on postcards sent from distant countries with the faces of defunct royalty on their postage stamps. It was *here*, it was being made at this minute, unrewarded and unseen.

By the eighties, Gay's painting had changed. The formal portraits of friends and lovers had given way to tableaux based on the covers of the fifties paperbacks and photos from the old copies of *True Detective* magazine he'd been amassing. Maybe he started collecting the paperbacks because he was consciously researching new subject matter and wanted to know, for example, what a man might look like as he tried to choke a woman with one hand while keeping her from clawing his eyes out with the other. Maybe he started collecting the paperbacks the way he

had Depression glass and Rookwood pottery, and then found the accu-
mulated books, with their repeated images of men with guns facing off
against women with tits, influencing his painting, haunting it. At one
point he had so many volumes that he had to display them on swiveling
wire bookstore racks spaced so closely that you had to step between them
sideways, as if you really were in a bookstore, a disheveled, slightly seedy
one. The paintings, which were almost always oversize—five by six feet,
six by nine—were scenes of men inflicting violence on women. They
shot them, slapped them, twisted their heads back in the prelude to what
might be a kiss or a vampire's bite. They were both brutal and campy, and
it was easy to read them as gorgeous jokes. That may be why they never got
picked up by galleries, though other artists of that period, such as Ronnie
Cutrone and Kenny Scharf, were also painting jokes, just not gorgeous
ones. Their work, populated by iterations of Woody Woodpecker, Felix
the Cat, and Fred Flintstone, either skimped on technique or slathered
it on like Marshmallow Fluff on Wonder Bread. According to his friend
Edie Vonnegut, Gay's technique was "rigorous and time-consuming . . . so
time-consuming that it took years to complete anything." Maybe that was
the problem: If a joke goes on too long, by the time you get to the punchline people have forgotten that they're supposed to laugh.

Of course, nowadays no one would laugh at the joke at all.

AT THE START OF THE eighties, Gay was working intently and, for him,
productively. The first things you heard when you came in off the elevator
were the buzz of the compressor and the caressing hiss of the airbrush.
Finished canvases leaned against one wall and lay stacked on the overhead racks. Apart from the tools and detritus of work laid out around him,
it wasn't actually clear that he was working. A writer might need monastic
silence to create, but a painter could do it amid noise and chaos. The
stereo would be on, he'd be talking to Molly or some friends who were
sitting around the dining table across the room. Someone would be mix-
ing cocktails.

Maybe a poker game was going on, which Gay would ignore unless his
best friend Chris Harms was playing. The two men, both Waspy and slen-

der and similarly dressed in button-down shirts and pullovers like wastrel brothers from a good family, were bound in a mutual trance of competitiveness. If one played, the other had to play against him; it didn't matter what else was happening. Gay would try to stay focused, but as the bets passed around the table, he'd keep glancing over at Harms, waiting for him to discard and pick up or pass. Then he'd step away from his painting; he couldn't stop himself. He'd sit down hurriedly, pick up his cards, discard one, pick another from the pile, make a bet, then stride back to the canvas and give it his attention until it was time to bet again. One or the other of them might get testy; Harms because he resented having to wait while Gay dithered at his cards, Gay because he felt guilty for betraying his work. And also because Harms needled him. "If you just sat down and played poker instead of getting up all the time, maybe you could remember what you had in your hand."

And it's true that Harms usually won, though Gay insisted that he won because winning was all he cared about. "He's a genius," he'd say. "You've never seen anyone so intelligent, but the only thing he's intelligent about is games. Poker, bridge, fucking Monopoly. You don't stand a chance against him, he's one of those idiot savants." Personally, I never thought Harms was an idiot, but calling him a genius seemed a stretch. He was good at games, and at lighting movie and TV sets, which was what he did for a living, and dealing coke, which he did on a small scale to underwrite his own use. He was laconic where Gay was talkative, incurious where Gay could take an interest in virtually anything and soon after taking it would tell you why everything you knew about the subject was wrong. Like many good-looking people, Harms had a face that was almost immobile, fixed in an expression of slightly amused appraisal. The expression might be a product of nature or genetics, or he might have figured it out by trial and error and dedicated himself to maintaining it; his blankness was probably behind some of his success at cards.

It would be another few years before artists became celebrities, but there were already celebrities who collected art. Gay had another friend named Hunter who painted gorgeous hyperdetailed portraits in the style of the Renaissance masters on Shrinky Dinks. When baked in the oven, the portraits dwindled or de-blossomed into glowing miniatures that would fit inside a lady's locket. But the thing Hunter was proudest of was that he'd once painted a mural in the bathroom of his fellow Tennessean Dolly Parton. He bragged about it all the time; Gay took to introducing him as "Muralist to the Stars." But there was no ignoring the power of celebrity. When Norris Church, who had recently become Norman Mailer's sixth wife, asked to see some of Gay's paintings, it was all anybody could talk about. She was going to come over to the loft; maybe Mailer would come with her. (At the time Norman Mailer was the literary equivalent of Picasso: the writer that even people who didn't read had heard of.) Gay made a show of indifference. Still, you could tell he was excited and nervous by the way he cleaned in the days before the visit and groused at Molly if she moved one of the objects he'd arranged with curatorial exactness on the shelves. I know nothing about Mailer's taste in visual art, but I think he would have dug the paintings' theme and overall gestalt; the misogyny blown up like a balloon in the Thanksgiving Day parade until it was buoyant and harmless, the creamy magnificence of the technique. Some of Gay's paintings would have made perfect covers for Mailer's novels; one can imagine the art director of a prestige paperback house buying rights to the entire series so they could put out a line of uniform editions. But the Mailers never bought anything. According to Edie Vonnegut, who was connected to the literary world through her novelist father, the Mailers weren't collectors.

In 1981, Gay had a show at Central Falls, a bar and gallery in SoHo. It was mostly a bar, but the SoHo location had an incantatory power. Gay's friends were always talking about "the SoHo show" the way other people would talk about "a Broadway show" or "a Hollywood movie." The opening was glamorous and well attended. Lots of people crowded into the bar and stood before the big paintings, whose pastel pinks and blues were reflected onto their faces and made them appear younger and more vital. Edie Vonnegut came with her father, another writer famous enough to be name-checked in a party game, who looked both mischievous because of the upward surge of his hair and saturnine because of the droop of his mustache and the bags under his eyes. Some of Gay's friends think the show sold out. Afterward, though, he was dissatisfied. Maybe it bothered him that there hadn't been any reviews. Maybe the event, which he must've been looking forward to since he entered art school, couldn't live up to his expectations.

He took out some of the dissatisfaction on Molly. Their relationship had always been low on sentimental display, but also when Molly kissed him in front of company now, Gay wasn't just embarrassed but also angry and would tell her to cut it out, not caring that he was embarrassing her or anyone who'd witnessed the rejection. She worked late—people in finance did, even back then when the eight-hour workday wasn't yet an elegiac memory for everyone—and came home tired in the way of people who spend their workday in absurd and uncomfortable business clothes, heels and jackets with padded shoulders and blouses with pussy bows, a uniform designed to project masculine power while making the necessary gestures at femininity (there was also the item that Molly showed friends at a bar one night: a funnel-like device that allowed a woman to piss standing up like a man, shaving minutes off wasteful bathroom breaks), and the last thing she wanted was to go out clubbing at eleven on a weekday night and wake the next morning hungover with the sting of cocaine in her throat. Gay complained she wasn't fun.

Sometimes he'd bully her into going out anyway. More often he'd leave her at home and go out with friends, the bars or clubs differing according to which friends he was out with that night; there were some who went to Area and Studio 54 and others to the Mudd Club or the World or the East Village galleries, Fun or PPOW or Gracie Mansion. The distinctions between the different kinds of space were notional: galleries were turned into pop-up clubs by the addition of a DJ or a live band; clubs turned into galleries when some artists painted on their walls. All the spaces could be called "bars" since they served liquor or had it lying around in ice-filled trash cans or, in one venue, a urinal. It was in these spaces that you first started to see the work that thirty years later would sell for as much as work by Picasso. It's hard to imagine what Gay thought of Ronnie Cutrone or Kenny Scharf or Basquiat, whose visionary wildness was apparent even then. Maybe he recognized Keith Haring's radioactive babies and milk-carton-headed dogs from the Westbeth gallery, where Haring had his first show, or just from the subway. When Gay went to an opening, he was more interested in the scene than what was hanging on the walls. He may not have been interested in any art that had been created since Edward Burne-Jones's in the late nineteenth century. He spent most of his time watching the room's ripples and eddies of human motion: a woman in a beautifully cut lipstick-colored dress and matching elbow-length gloves casually stroking the face of a cranky boy who looked like he'd just woken up on a bench across the street in Tompkins Square Park, maintaining the contact even as she turned to walk away; a scrum of gallerists and art writers swarming around some kids from the Bronx who pretended not to notice they were about to be eaten; a poised and very handsome man in a three-piece suit standing stock-still in the center of the room as if posing for a portraitist. Gay always wore his "good clothes"—Oxford shirt, jeans, and loafers, the shirt ironed; they were the clothes of a college kid of the mid-sixties, a little drab. When someone suggested he ought to take the T-shirt with the latex dog teats out of storage and wear it to gallery openings, he said, "People would think I was some asshole trying to get attention."

But what does any artist want but attention?

The triumph of the artists of the eighties was that they found new ways of breaching the walls of the city of art and making themselves visible to the inhabitants. Some of them bypassed the city altogether. Mao showed that a people's army could conquer a nation that way. Lee Quiñones, Futura, and Fab 5 Freddy wouldn't deign to set foot inside a gallery until the gallery owners were begging them in. Why bother when they had an entire subway system as a canvas and millions of people a day marveling at what they'd painted there? Even the haters marveled. David Wojnarowicz appropriated the abandoned piers and warehouses along the Hudson as private galleries where visitors would look up from fucking to see his dreams exploding from the walls.

While this was happening, Gay continued to paint on canvases he stretched himself, to draw his subjects from the trash culture of thirty years before, and to limn its figures with a care and specificity not much inferior to those Raphael devoted to the saints. But maybe he grew tired of the lack of return. His painting changed again. It became cruder, with a more restricted palette. There were almost no people on his canvases, or just faceless crowds. One painting showed an empty frame with a bunch of price tags hanging from it, each price discounted from the one above. You could say Gay's problem was that he delivered his jokes with too much artistry, and it confused people. You could say he gave up too soon. If you look back at the earlier paintings—you could call them "the *True Detective* paintings" or "the noir paintings"—and consider the figures' blurred outlines and the soft colors in which they're rendered, the instability of the expressions that shimmer on their faces, you realize they're suffused with yearning. Maybe this was why they wouldn't fit in at galleries like Holly Solomon or Gracie Mansion: In the eighties, who gave a shit about yearning? If you wanted something, you got it. Sometimes you bought it; sometimes you just took it.

It's not clear why Gay didn't try to mount another show. It would have given him something to work toward. Lacking that thing, he became aimless. He spent more time in secondhand stores; he spent more time in bars. He traveled with Molly on a business trip to Hong Kong, which was still a British colony. Rather than board the dogs at a vet, they asked me to house-sit. This is how I discovered that Cracker, a mostly even-tempered shepherd mix, would start growling when you danced in front of him, or at least danced by yourself.

Before he left, Gay warned me not to introduce myself to anybody in the building. Under no circumstance was I to tell anyone where I was staying. The information, he feared, might be used against him. "They all hate us," he said of the artists down below. "They think we're rich and have this big luxury apartment that we pay practically nothing for. I keep telling them, 'I'm *not* rich! *Murray* and *Gail* are rich!'" He was speaking about the people whose window he shinnied out of from time to time. "Let them hate Murray and Gail if they want to hate somebody. I'm sure they've got an eye on my apartment. Why don't you tell them that? No, don't tell them anything."

True to his instructions, I kept a low profile, coming home late and skipping the crowded elevators so I could ride up a few minutes later in an empty one. If the elevator was empty, I could lean my forehead against its cool metal wall to keep from getting sick. At least once during that time I took too big a shot and came to on the bathroom floor, looking up through the window at the pale sky of early spring, that blue so tentative it's almost white. I hadn't been out that long; the blood I'd squirted onto the mirror when the gimmick clogged was still wet; it wiped off pretty easily.

Eventually, Gay found a new purpose in scuba diving. He'd been at it for a few years and gotten good enough to do more than dangle in the clear turquoise waters of a vacation resort looking at tropical fish. Off the coast of Honduras there was an island called Roatán that was popular among divers for its proximity to the Mesoamerican Barrier Reef in the Caribbean, the largest reef of its kind in the western hemisphere. What excited Gay were the wrecks of Spanish galleons that were rumored to be lying at relatively shallow depths, tons of silver ingots from the mines of Potosí gone black with tarnish in their holds. He'd grown up watching *Adventures in Paradise*, though I guess he'd forgotten that the series was set in the South Pacific and not the Caribbean. Toward the end of the decade, he drove down to Honduras in a van he'd furnished with a fold-out bed and a propane cooktop. He went by himself; the trip would take at least a month, and Molly couldn't get off work that long. But he brought along Wheatie, the Airedale terrier he'd adopted after his older dogs died. The new dog sat in the passenger seat as they drove through Mexico, Guatemala, and Honduras, occasionally jostled off when they hit a pothole but hopping back up in an instant. In profile Wheatie looked like an American president of the previous century, the facial hair and the calm. Gay had to get a passport for him, a pet passport complete with a small black-and-white photo above the designations: NOMBRE: WIDI. ESPECIES: PERRO. CRIAR: TERRIER AIREDALE.

The trip was difficult in many ways. For one thing, Gay had little facility for languages. When he left he was still learning to pronounce the Spanish *r*. He'd pace around the apartment, trilling "r-r-r-r" like a broken lawn mower that somebody was trying to start. But a problem with language is not the same thing as a problem with communicating, and Gay was a genius communicator. I witnessed this myself years later in Indonesia, where he persuaded flea marketers who spoke barely any English (and he spoke no bahasa Indonesia whatsoever) that he was a member of their fraternity so they should give him a break on their prices, which, incredibly, they did. One can imagine him joshing a stone-faced border guard into letting him and Wheatie enter Honduras at a prohibited crossing or arguing with customs officials who might shoot him dead on the spot and somehow making them dissolve in laughter or ordering a round for the patrons of a roadside bar festooned with fly strips and nobody minding how he mangles *aguardiente* when he calls out to the barkeep. All these years later, it's unclear which of these things actually happened to Gay and which were imagined, whether by Gay or myself. Although he often exaggerated his stories, his exaggerations dwelt on his cluelessness and incompetence. If he triumphed in a story, it was against the odds, even against his inclination. More often, he did the opposite of triumph: the guards barred the border crossing until he paid a crippling bribe; the customs officials impounded his scuba gear; the drinkers thought he was telling them to fuck their mothers. He was his own butt.

In truth, this isn't such a terrible thing to be. Life will make a butt of you anyway.

However, I remember Gay telling me that sometime in the course of his travels, he got ahold of a horse and not only rode it through a flood but also somehow rescued Wheatie, who'd fallen into the water and was in danger of drowning, pulled him up, and deposited him in the saddle, where he sat obediently until they reached dry ground. Can this be true? Where did Gay get ahold of a horse? Who even knew he could ride? And how did he manage to lean forward far enough to scoop Wheatie out of the water—an adult Airedale can weigh fifty pounds—without falling off the horse? Is this another Mark-Twainlike invention? Probably the water was no more than two or three feet deep, and Gay dismounted from the horse and coaxed Wheatie to jump up onto its back. Afterward, a stranger watching would have seen a man and a dog awkwardly perched on a horse as it sloshed through a river of murk that rose to its hocks or its croup or some point in between, all three animals drenched and smelly. If it had happened to me, I'd be telling that story for the rest of my life.

Who Should You Hate If Not Your Neighbor?

AFTER THE RENT STRIKE, WESTBETH'S finances quickly slid back into disarray. Half the commercial spaces remained vacant; the other half, rented at well below market rate on twenty- and twenty-five-year leases, brought in only a fraction of the needed revenue. Management was so haphazard that some tenants had no idea who was running the building; this was the era of the manager Black-Eyed Susan spoke of, who gifted an apartment to her boyfriend and conducted interviews with her back turned toward you. In 1975, the mortgage passed from Bankers Trust to the federal Department of Housing and Urban Development. Those tenants who expected a federal agency to be more forbearing than a privately owned bank were disappointed.

"Oh, HUD!" Christina Maile exclaims. "Yes, the mortgage got transferred to HUD, and HUD at the time couldn't deal with our mortgage because the building [which only accepted tenants who had artistic references] couldn't fit into any of their [HUD's] slots. So they were not interested in it at all. And so once again we fell behind in our payments to them." In 1979 Westbeth could pay only $383,000 of the $530,300 it owed the organization each year.

"HUD refused to recast the mortgage," she remembers. "We wanted them to recast, we begged them to recast it, they refused. They said, 'You're supposed to pay your bills.' Once again, as with the rent strike, people began blaming the management, blaming the board of directors. So the tenants came up with the idea, over a long period of memos and meetings, of doing a limited-equity co-op [under which people who didn't want to buy their apartments could continue to rent them]. And that engendered the worst civil war the building has ever seen. The tenants once again banded together. But they banded together in two separate conflicting parties. One was for the co-op and one was against the co-op. And the fight was rancorous and became personal. It became really ugly."

This was in 1983 or 1984. By now Westbeth was roughly $3 million behind in its payments and looking at foreclosure once more. The impetus for the co-op came from members of the Westbeth Artists Residents Council, who argued, in Maile's words, "that we would buy the building from HUD and run it ourselves, and we would get rid of the corrupt management and the aloof board of directors. That we would become our own landlord and thereby be a much more efficient building." And also one that remained true to the project's original character and purpose. For anyone familiar with the New York real estate market of the 2020s, in which a one-bedroom walk-up on the third floor of a circa- 1900 building a few blocks from Westbeth lists for more than $1 million, the prices are almost pornographic. "For my apartment," Maile says, speaking of the triplex to which she was upgraded in the seventies, "I think it was supposed to be like $7,000 or $10,000, something like that, very low." The highest price listed in the conversion plan was $18,402, with an estimated monthly maintenance of $763 and a 19 percent tax deduction. The sponsors estimated initial sales of at least 240 of the building's 384 apartments, which would bring in $2.7 million. Of that, $1.1 million would be paid immediately to HUD to meet its minimum terms for settling the arrears. Another $1.3 million would be allocated for much-needed repairs.

Still, tenants who opposed the conversion pointed out that the 19 percent tax deduction was much less than what was usually available to shareholders in co-ops. In fact, co-oping the development might have threatened all the various deductions and exemptions it had been given by federal, state, and city agencies, including a city property-tax abatement of 76 percent. Another objection was that three of the principal sponsors sat on Westbeth's board of directors. To some people that looked like a conflict of interest. More fundamentally, there was the question of whether a building that had been conceived and explicitly described as a trust could be legally transferred to a cooperative business corporation.

"The people who opposed the co-op opposed it for purely philosophical reasons," says Maile. She'd supported the plan, but she viewed her old adversaries in a generous light. Her chief criticism was that they'd been too rigidly idealistic. They were Red Guards. They were yippies at a time when Jerry Rubin, one of the original yippies, had rebranded as a yuppie and was promoting salons for business networking. "They said that this housing was not for rich people, even though the cost was low, that it was meant for artists who could only afford a couple hundred dollars a month, that it wasn't a way to get real estate. That wasn't the mission of the building. The mission of the building was to provide affordable housing. And that as part of our articles of incorporation we were termed a charitable trust. So *they* hired a lawyer, and their lawyer's argument was that a charitable trust cannot turn itself into a limited equity co-op even if it poses as nonprofit, because the articles of the trust prevented that."

A spokesperson for the anti-co-op faction promised that if Robert Abrams, New York State's attorney general, "allows a co-op plan to take over a public trust and convert Westbeth into a business, I'm quite prepared to sue Robert Abrams."

Maile continues: "But we wrote letters, there were articles in *New York* magazine, there were articles in *The Times*, we got [Senator Daniel Patrick] Moynihan involved. We went to HUD, we begged HUD to have that [the co-op plan] as an option. And so, the building, which at one time had been, if not close, a reasonably friendly place to be, became opposing camps. If you were for the co-op, everyone knew you were for the co-op. If you were against the co-op, everyone knew you were against the co-op. There were really mean-spirited letters under your door, accusing the people for the co-op of being capitalists and taking the housing away from artists. And then there would be letters from the co-op people saying, 'No, we're not doing that! We're trying to save the building!'

"Whatever community that had been built up with the rent strike fell apart with the co-op controversy. Neighbors stopped talking to each other. HUD relented and reinstated our mortgage again, but the passion that had been ignited by the fighting, both philosophically and financially, really damaged the psyche of people living here. So the building became a darker kind of place. There were people that you just didn't have anything in common with anymore. And everyone looked at each other as a traitor. That first initial blush of being an artist began to face the reality of earning a living. So the whole enthusiasm of putting on shows and performances also became dampened. Sometimes there'd be months where there'd be nothing in the gallery, not a show, nothing. There'd be nothing happening.

"And because we were constantly fighting each other or fighting *something*, and therefore not presenting a lot of art, Westbeth in a way disappeared for years. I met someone about two, three years ago, who lived on Bank Street just in the middle of the block, before you even got to Greenwich, and he had never even heard of Westbeth! And he's lived there for thirty years."

In the end, the co-op proposal never even went to a vote. Seeing the rift it had torn in the community's social fabric, the organizers withdrew the offer. Years later, George Cominskie, a longtime president of WARC and a former chair of the Westbeth Corporation's board, explained. "I know I understand the downside to it: that we would have been responsible for our own future and our own fate. But, you know, the tenants are constantly saying, 'We should have this and we should do that. And we don't have the power to make those decisions. It's up to the Board.' So, with power comes responsibility, and a lot of people wanted the power, but they didn't realize what a responsibility it was. And others realized, 'That's a lot of responsibility, and I don't want [it]. I want somebody else to take care of me.'"

The news of the co-op offer struck Gay with terror. He was sure he'd be driven out of the building if it went through. In retrospect, his fear seems paranoid. The most he and Molly would have had to pay for their apartment was $18,000 or so, and Molly could certainly have afforded that. Maybe on some level Gay already understood that their marriage was coming to an end, and without his wife he would never be able to come up with $18,000. Not even $1,800.

Interlude: The Chimney Girl Part Two

Grace Bergere's musician parents moved into Westbeth when she was eight. They divorced when she was eleven. After that, she shuttled back and forth between her mother's apartment on the first floor and her father's on the sixth.

Bergere is vague about dates. "I attribute my brain to a few things, one of which is the accident. I hit the ground at seventy-something miles per hour."

As a young child, she used to visit a boy on the eighth floor who'd rigged an intricate network of plastic tubes in his room: you'd drop a marble in one end and hear it rattle through the system until it popped out someplace else. Sometimes they'd go out into one of the narrow hallways and brace their feet against one wall and their hands against the opposite one and inch their way up almost to the ceiling, then drop down onto a mattress they'd dragged there for that purpose.

Elsewhere she was unhappy, especially after she transferred to a new school: "I never did well in school, I was always a weird outcast And I didn't have many friends. And then when I got to IS 89 because PS 3 was a hippy school where we were fingerpainting and singing all day long, and now we're at a math school . . . where I didn't learn any math. I felt stupid and chubby and stinky. And I had acne, and nobody wanted to talk to me."

She was twelve. Her cousin Lily visited from California. "It felt nice to have someone sort of my age to hang out with. I mean, she wasn't really my age, but she feels like my peer, and I didn't have any siblings. I don't remember what led to us being on the roof except that I thought it would be interesting for Lily. And it was nighttime. It was dark.

"I did not have a cell phone, I did not have video games. The way that I knew how to play was using my body and climbing things. I'd been climbing things my whole life, you know. Like in Central Park we would climb the rocks, and trees, and buildings, and whatever. I've talked to a lot of people from New York, and that's how they are. So anyway, I saw the ladder. And I didn't know it was a chimney, either. I don't think I would have done what I did if I'd known there was a hole at the top of it. And, by the way, I didn't slip and fall. I was just mistaken about the nature of what I was doing. I hate to sound like an asshole, but I mean, I'm a juggler. Climbing a ladder and sitting on something is not challenging to me. And it wasn't challenging to me when I was twelve."

It's here that Bergere's story departs from the official version you can read in *The New York Times*, though you can see how it might drive a fact-checker crazy. It still sounds more truthful. No one was with her when she fell, and if she can't entirely say what happened she can come closer to it than anybody else. "Okay, what happened was, I climbed the ladder, and I put my hand out to sit on it. I thought it was asphalt, the blackness. And I put my whole weight onto nothing. It didn't occur to me that there wouldn't be anything there. It never occurred to me, you know, that there would be an industrial-size chimney in New York City in my building, which is an apartment building, because I'm twelve. In my mind, I thought it was a tower. I don't know why there would be a tower, but I thought it was a tower."

The hole was as wide as her outstretched arms. "I remember I put my hands out. I was falling, but I didn't *know* that I was falling because it was so . . . I didn't know what the fuck was going on. See, if I had known it was a chimney and I'd slipped and fell, I think I'd be dead. Because I was . . . I was so relaxed. It felt like I was falling through water. It felt like water because the pressure of the air hitting me felt like . . . like a . . . *substance*. I just remember it felt like I was touching something and something was cradling me. It was just the air pressure. And then I remember hitting the ground. And they calculate that I fell for a few seconds. You know, I mean, it's like pretty high."

It was 180 feet.

"And I think what happened was I made a full rotation. I don't remember what part of my body hit first, but I think I went in headfirst, and then my hips kind of balanced me out. My feet and then my ass, and then my shoulders and then my head. If I was tense or flailing, I could have landed on my head. I remember when I hit the ground, I heard my neck break.

Everything was white. And it was like, in my head there was just this crazy, loud, static sound. It felt pretty psychedelic — just the whiteness and the crazy fucking sound, and my whole body was kind of vibrating.

"And I wasn't scared because I didn't know what the hell was going on. I knew something really bad had happened, but I didn't know what it was. And I wasn't scared because it had already happened. There was a part of me that was like, *steadfastly calm* about it. Like I knew that whatever was happening was normal. I know that sounds like a lot of crazy, weird lies, but it really felt wholly okay with me because I wasn't in pain. Like my brain had shut off my pain sensors . . . like I'd lost all sense of my body. It didn't feel like I was in a body at all. I was like, 'Damn, what the fuck is happening to me? This isn't so bad, I guess.'

"It was completely black. And what I was saying before, which is kind of important, is that . . . and I know this sounds too much like a movie . . . but I really did think of my mother. That really was the main thing driving me, the desire to not pass out and die. If I had done nothing, I would have died because I had ashes shoved down into my mouth and chest, and I couldn't breathe at all. And it turns out that one-and-a-half lungs had collapsed. So I had half of one lung working. And I remember I had to remove all the soot out of my throat. I couldn't cough or anything, so I was using my hand to pull the shit out of my throat. And at this point my skin was burning. My whole skin was on fire, I think because of shock. But I didn't feel any pain in my back yet; it turns out I broke my back in, I think, eight places. And my hip, I dislocated my hip. And my shoulder, too. And I had all kinds of fractures all over the place. And I ruptured my spleen. I don't know what that does.

"So then I sat up, and that helped with breathing, and I leaned against the wall, because it was like a big chamber and then a little echo chamber, from what I remember. And there was a hole, and I could see the basement light through the hole. The wall had been cemented shut. If no one had been with me [on the roof], I would be dead. No one would have known where I was. So, I started putting my mouth up to the hole because the air down there was so fucking disgusting. I used my arm and I broke the hole bigger with my arm. And I put my hand out, and I was waving my hand around and trying to breathe.

"I think while I was still kind of on my back, my cousin went down to get my dad. She didn't really know what happened because she just saw that I was climbing that thing, and then she turned away, and then I wasn't there anymore. She didn't know it was a chimney either. And as soon as she told my dad what happened, he knew what it meant. And he was really freaking out, obviously. And he got up on the ladder and waved his phone down at me. Because, you know, he thought I was dead. Everyone thought I was dead. He was the first person to know I wasn't dead. He's like, 'Are you alive? Are you okay?' I was like, 'I'm okay. I broke my leg or something.' The only thing I knew is that I couldn't move my leg.

"He told me he called the fire department, so I wasn't really that scared. I knew that I was okay. But apparently the firemen didn't believe him at all . . . that I was okay. They thought he was hallucinating or something. And I remember when the firemen came, they told me to back up from the entrance, and they broke the door with a sledgehammer. The EMTs dragged me out, and I just wanted water immediately. And they won't let you have water because if they have to do surgery, they don't want you to vomit. They laid me out on the stretcher. Man, I don't know how this happened, I think they were probably nervous. They didn't know what to expect. But they started forcing my leg down, and my leg was broken. It was dislocated, it wasn't in the socket, and they were pushing it down. I remember telling them, 'I can't put my leg down!' They were like, 'You have to!' and I was like, 'I can't!' A piece of my hip was broken.

"I remember they took me up, and I remember looking up at the ceiling in the lobby and looking around, and everyone was standing around and looking at me. Like people in the building. And then I was in the ambulance, and I remember the ambulance guy had to cut my clothes off me. And I didn't want him to cut my clothes off me because I liked my pants. And he's talking to me about Barney, Barney the dinosaur. And I was like, 'How old do you think I am?' I was immediately giving them shit. They took me to the hospital, and they had to put me through an MRI, and I had three or four piercings in my ear cartilage, and they had to take them out. I remember yelling at them about that.

"They took me to Bellevue, and then NYU. Up until this point, I was not in any pain. And then I remember, I must have finally passed out. I think they must have given me something. And then I remember I woke up and I was all alone in this room. And all of a sudden, I was in fucking agony. My whole body was just screaming. I was screaming. And I didn't know why I was alone, either. I was just alone in this room. I think my parents were at the door, but I couldn't see them. And I was just screaming.

"And then I was in the ICU for a while, at least a month. They never did any surgery on me, they just relocated my hip and put it in traction where they put the bar through your knee. It was like being held up in the air. And then they had me in a brace in bed, so it was just time. And they had me do these exercises, where I would like blow into a tube."

This was probably an incentive spirometer, meant to help her reflate and strengthen her lungs.

"And they had me on morphine. And that's a whole other story. I remember, I *loved* the hospital. To this day I love the hospital. I love going to the hospital. I feel like I'm being taken care of when I go to the hospital. I have really positive body associations with the hospital and the doctors because they just had me on morphine. I would go to sleep with that [pump] just rigid in my grip. And I needed it, I really needed it. I was so fucked. The first time I went through withdrawal was in the hospital. They said that I was having a psychotic episode, because they transferred me [to a rehab facility] and they didn't tell them that I was on morphine. So not only was my back shattered, and I was still in a brace, I had to wear a brace for a year after that. But I was in excruciating pain. And I was going through withdrawal. And I was twelve."

GRACE BERGERE IS THIRTY NOW. She's a working musician whose first album was released by Casa Gogol Records in 2024. Her songs are suspended between the grim wisdom of their lyrics and the shimmering lushness of their harmonies and lent authority by the directness of her voice, which is devoid of melismata or any of the other techniques singers use to court the sympathy and admiration of their audience. It just states its case. As one of her songs puts it: "I did nothing wrong."

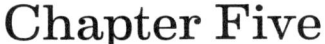

Chapter Five

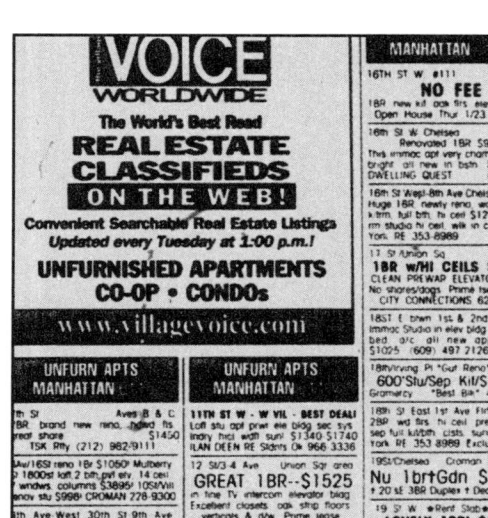

ART SALES 1990-1999

1990
$78,100,000 | Pierre-Auguste Renoir *Bal du Moulin de la Galette*
$82,500,000 | Vincent van Gogh *Portrait du Dr. Gachet*

1997
$31,902,500 | Pablo Picasso *Les femmes d'Alger (Version O)*
$48,402,500 | Pablo Picasso *Le rêve*

1998
$33,057,596 | Claude Monet *Bassin aux nymphaeas et
sentier au bord de l'eau*
$71,502,496 | Vincent van Gogh *Portrait de l'artiste sans barbe*

1999
$45,102,500 | Pablo Picasso *Nu au fauteuil noir*
$60,502,500 | Paul Cezanne *Rideau, cruchon et compôtier*

On Living

FOR GAY MEN LIVING IN the West Village in the eighties and nineties, Edward Field and Neil Derrick were singularly untouched by AIDS. No one close to them got sick; no one died. It was as if they floated through the pandemic sealed inside an invisible bubble, protected not just from the protean bio-horror of the sickness but also from the horror of seeing one friend after another succumb to it: the friend who called you every morning to dish about the night before; the friend you met for breakfast at Manatus or La Bonbonniere; the friend with whom you shared your opera subscription; the friends who had once been lovers but so long ago that you barely thought of them as sexual beings anymore; the friends you still wouldn't mind fucking once in a while and once in a while did. A whole generation gone—the deaths of its members first ignored, then treated as macabre moral pedagogy, most notoriously by the right-wing columnist (and future presidential candidate) Pat Buchanan. It was Buchanan who gloated, "The poor homosexuals. They have declared war on nature, and now nature is exacting an awful retribution."

Some forty years later Field seems almost shamefaced about their good fortune. Of course, after they got back together early in the seventies, he and Derrick lived a fairly sedate life, and by the eighties they were like an old married couple. They didn't go to the clubs or the trucks. What they did was travel, often for months at a time. "When [Neil] lost his sight, he said, 'I can't travel anymore,' and I said, 'Let's go to London for the Christmas holiday.' His sister was living in London. We came to London, he knows London far better than I do, and I'd say, 'I don't know where we are.' And he'd say, 'Is there a tower to the left?' He knew exactly, he'd had vision all those years, and he really knew everything and still remembered. So the trip to London was a great success, and from then on we traveled everywhere. We lived in Amsterdam, Berlin, Tangier, and we went to other countries. We went to Istanbul, Cairo, we went everywhere."

Derrick's sexual adventuring had ended when he lost his sight. But sometimes they'd go to the bathhouses, and in one such bathhouse in Europe Field saw a young man and was so struck by his beauty that he went up to him and brought him over to Derrick and then wordlessly guided his lover's hand over the stranger's beautiful face and then watched as the hand began to move on its own, remembering.

One of Field's best-known poems is "A Minor Accident of War." He reads it in voiceover in the 2019 documentary of the same title. With reportorial straightforwardness it tells the story of his bomber's crash-landing in the North Sea in the closing months of World War II. Afterward the survivors huddled in a life raft while waves reared and smashed against it, the water so cold that someone who fell in had only twenty-five minutes before he froze to death. Field, who'd been one of the last men out of the plane, could only hang on to the side and tread water. Just as his strength gave out, one of the gunners, "a skinny kid from Arkansas," offered him his place in the raft, and Field took it. The boy died.

> That boy who took my place in the water
> who died instead of me
> I don't remember his name even.
> It was like those who survived the death camps
> by letting others go into the ovens in their place.
> It was him or me, and I made up my mind to live.

On Imagining a Stranger

AIDS NEVER CAME TO AN end. It just slipped out of the crisis category. This happened when it went from killing almost everybody who got it to killing only some of them while sparing the ones who could afford the right doctors and the right drugs. In this way it was like other American crises of the late twentieth and early twenty-first centuries. That AIDS had stopped being a crisis was of no consolation to the thousands of New Yorkers who died of it, their passing marked by memorial services and vacant apartments, piles of fashionable men's clothing donated to Housing Works or put out in lobbies for the neighbors to pick over, medicine bottles in the trash. It was of little consolation to their loved ones. Who wants to be told that they're mourning a statistic, that the numbers have gotten much better?

Jack Dowling stopped attending memorials. This was common among the survivors of the time; at a certain point you bottomed out on mourning. He went into therapy. It gave him some relief. So, for a while, did alcohol—until he saw it was becoming a problem of its own. Once at an event on Fire Island, he "charged at the bar like a bull in a stockyard, and came back to my friends and burst into tears: 'I have to stop drinking and can't do anything about it!'" People took notice. "It was costing me status. My lover at the time was a heavy drinker, and when you live with a heavy drinker, you either don't drink at all or you drink with them." Dowling drank, then stopped. His lover eventually died of emphysema, and he cared for him in his last months. It was a painful echo of what he'd gone through with Stanley. He says, "It told me to lay off the liquor and boyfriends."

His response to the sickness around him was complicated by his upbringing. His mother was a disciple of Christian Science. As a teenager, he'd contracted spinal meningitis and come close to death in the hospital, but she refused to believe he was sick and his father wouldn't stand up to her. "So I was in the house in pretty bad shape before anyone called the doctor. They told my parents. My mother wasn't there, she was sitting in the park reading her Bible and her *Science and Health* and her *Sentinels* and all her other things that she always read all the time, no matter what was happening. If the coffee pot overflowed, she'd go to *Science and Health* to make sure it wasn't some terrible thing that she did. It's not uncommon for people to talk about having near-death experiences and just going off into space somewhere. And I did that. I went into the sky and saw airplanes that had my friends on them, sitting on the wings, and my father was there trying to get my attention. He intimidated me a lot, but I remember paying him absolutely no attention at all. On reflection, I thought, 'Wow, how'd I get away with *that*?'

"Anyway, I survived that, but it sort of put in place a sense of acceptance and . . . be careful. Be careful what you allow people to do to you."

Dowling had been sociable by temperament, but AIDS made him a recluse. When at last he reentered society, it was by way of Westbeth. The early nineties wasn't a good time for the community. The neighborhood was even more dangerous than it had been twenty years before. Muggings were so common that many of the female tenants carried whistles, and the Westbeth Artists Residents Council engaged the services of an organization similar to the subway vigilantes the Guardian Angels, which sent uniformed guards to patrol the floors and courtyards at night. It was an unaccustomed role for WARC, which had come into being chiefly as a liaison between the tenants and the management. In the early years every meeting included a half-hour open forum, during which anyone who had a complaint could bring it up for consideration by the president, who would then decide whether it was worth bringing to management. "It gave people a place to speak," Dowling says, "and made WARC a buffer for management so that it didn't have to be bothered by foolishness."

By the nineties, though, the organization had shifted its primary focus to the tenants' interactions with each other. It offered many opportunities for service, depending on how close you wanted to be with your neighbors and how deeply you wanted to dive into Westbeth's politics. You could join the In-House Moves Committee that was formed to regulate internal migrations rather than have tenants snapping up more desirable apartments the moment they fell vacant. (Back in the seventies, when Dowling left his grotto on the second floor for a space on a higher floor, he'd simply moved his stuff and then gone downstairs to tell the management.) You could join Beautification and plant flowers in the boxes outside the Bethune Street entrance or work for the flea market that originated as a recycling system for residents' castoffs but in time became one of WARC's principal moneymakers, paying for repairs in the building's public spaces. You could join Admissions to help select new residents from the ten-year waiting list; it's not the worst thing to have some say in who your neighbors will be.

For more than two decades, Dowling resisted being drawn in. But in 1996 Barbara Prete, the chair of the Visual Arts Committee, asked him to fill in as secretary because the old one had stepped down and they needed somebody to take notes. He proved to be so good at it that instead of posting the vacancy, the committee simply appointed him secretary. There was no dissent. One of his first orders of business was to do something about the Westbeth Gallery. Like other parts of the complex back then, it was dirty and in disrepair, and the previous gallery director—who had coasted by with an air of entitlement and an entourage of artists whom she regularly placed in shows—had apparently been helping herself to the operating funds for years. No one on the council dared say anything. Dowling pushed the other members to pass a motion of cause: the gallery was shut down. It was, he remembers, "in disgusting shape."

That Christmas, though, it felt important to keep up the tradition of the annual Westbeth holiday show. This is the most important of the gallery's in-house events, the one where Westbeth artists show who they are *as artists* to neighbors who may know them only as faces in the elevator. Dowling agreed to put something together. But given the decline in the gallery's status, he wondered how he'd get any art worth showing. He says, "Barbara Prete knew all the best artists in Westbeth and persuaded people who would never have shown in Westbeth to donate work. It was really a great show, and I got a lot of slaps on the back. And at the next election in 1997, I ran for Visual Arts chair and ran every two years until 2012. I wasn't working, so I had the time to take care of a lot of stuff. I learned how to hang the work and learned how work should look on a wall. It's a creative field because you're making something. You're not just slapping work on the wall haphazardly. You're thinking it out and thinking about the relationships between the pieces. Sometimes we had ninety paintings in a single show. I would be walking paintings around for two days from one place to another until the whole room looked right and then we would start hanging. And then there were catalogs and listings."

The gallery, which is actually a group of galleries occupying 2,900 square feet fronting the courtyard, is central to Westbeth's sense of itself as a home to the arts. Every year it hosts several independently curated shows, including the one the Whitney holds for the artists on its staff, but its primary role is as a showcase for Westbeth artists. Being selected for a show means something. So does which gallery your work is shown in and what work is hung alongside it. When designing shows, Dowling tried to visualize "a person coming in—a complete stranger—to the gallery, and how do you lead them through, and how do you encourage them to continue moving, and how do you get them to be engaged with what they're seeing, and how do you get them to move from one painting to the next in a smooth kind of way so that they are not suddenly stopped by something that's completely out of the message that's going along." He sought out the gallery's hot spots where work that registered clearly from a distance could be hung to attract passersby. While he often chose one painting for each painter, he felt photographers needed to have more work on the walls. "A photographer, usually you should have at least two so that you get a sense of where their head's at. Often with drawings, too. A single drawing is just a single drawing, but if you see three, then you have a sense of what that person is all about."

Sometimes he clashed "with people who felt that their work was bigger and better than it was. One year I put together two works on one wall. One was a lithograph and the other was a watercolor. One of the painters came in and yanked her piece off the wall, saying, 'You cannot hang me next to that woman. She slept with my husband!'"

I Like to Shock Myself

BARTON BENEŠ HAD COME INTO possession of a Picasso lithograph. It was an object of some worth, so you can imagine his chagrin one morning when he realized that the night before, lit up on coke or just in a very good mood, he'd defaced it with graffiti. "So, I thought, let me see how I can salvage this," he tells Joe Lovett. "I put the Picasso in the blender and chopped the whole Picasso up and put it in little bottles, and I sold Picasso by the gram." The bottles were the barrel-shaped vials carried by head shops. It was a way of making the most of a mistake. In 2015, a 1 *Gram of Picasso* sold at auction for $313, about three times the going price for the same weight of coke. According to one chronicler, the first lot of pieces sold out so quickly that Beneš had to "cut" others with ordinary shredded art paper.

It was during this period that people started bringing him things to use in his work. When he let it be known that he was looking for items associated with various contemporary artists, he got a paint-spattered scrap of one of Rothko's neckties and a shard of crockery that had fallen off a Schnabel at a museum. He asked Susan Weil, who had been married to Robert Rauschenberg and was still friendly with him, to bring back a crayon from his studio. She brought him three. Beneš's pieces were taking on a new characteristic form: multicompartmented wood and plexiglass cabinets housing thematically linked objects. They were mostly larger than Cornell's boxes and less mysteriously arranged. He called them "reliquaries" or "museums." There was the *Artist Museum*, whose eighty chambers seemed to house the ephemera of nearly every major American artist of the second half of the twentieth century. You could see it as a kind of imitation magic—if you take objects that belonged to the great, some of their greatness may transfer to you—or as an outsider's revenge. You could imagine it as an artifact of a fallen civilization. There was a *Hair Museum* and a *Foot Museum*, one of whose exhibits was a mummified human toe that someone had found under the Williamsburg Bridge; another chamber contained a thread from Mikhail Baryshnikov's ballet slipper. A food reliquary included a crumb from Prince Charles and Princess Diana's wedding cake and a drinking straw that bore a red smear of Monica Lewinsky's lipstick.

The works recalled eighteenth-century *wunderkammers*, the collections of exotic oddities assembled by naturalists, explorers, and archaeologists and treasured by kings and merchant princes. Peter the Great was a connoisseur of them. Beneš's wonder chambers were notable both for their content and their masterly execution. The boxes were arrayed in a perfect grid, every item was elegantly mounted; often he placed objects at a slant, which created a sense of streaking movement inside the static frame of the box. A friend of Lovett's probably had the reliquaries in mind when he said of Beneš: "He's genius in concept and genius in design, but he's also a genius in craftsmanship. And he's obsessive. He could do it forever." Beneš's longtime assistant Nicholas Cirabisi says that the artist would have him execute a pattern and then vary it to "make it less perfect" but "far more interesting." Hoarders, too, are obsessive, and Beneš justified his acquisitions the same way hoarders do: You never know when this—*this* being a snip of linen from a mummy's wrappings or some gallstones scooped out of the abdomen of Larry Hagman when the actor, a longtime friend, was getting a liver transplant—will be useful. Unlike most hoarders, Beneš used his piles of *this*. Actually, *used* is too passive: Beneš *crafted* his finds. He set one of Hagman's gallstones in a ring that Hagman later gave his wife; another found its way into a reliquary. "That's how I got into the celebrity thing," the artist explains. "And they're good sources for relics." Hoarders are people who try to master chaos but succeed only in bringing it into their homes. Beneš took chaos and imposed order on it; what's more orderly than a grid? To one degree or another, this is what all artists do, recreating what the god of Genesis did when he parted light from darkness. They do it with greater or lesser workmanship, with greater or lesser refinement of their raw, acrid *prima materia*. If you looked closely enough at Beneš's reliquaries, the rawness of their primal matter became evident: the stale crumbs of a wedding banquet, a drinking straw discarded by a reluctant actor in the biggest sex scandal of the 1990s, a severed human body part, leavings, castoffs, detritus, garbage.

"I like to use materials that you wouldn't consider art materials," he tells Lovett. "I like things that are taboo. It's not so much to shock other people. I like to shock myself."

On Becoming the Work of Art

IN THE WINTER OF 1991, Lorraine O'Grady took a black-and-white photo of the windows of her studio in Westbeth's A building—the windows rather than the view out them, since the latter is barely visible because of the angle and the light, the flat white glare of a winter afternoon above the half-frozen river. In the foreground are a window seat covered in a floral print with matching cushions, a low table with a female figurine holding what may be a pair of very large feathers or lotus blossoms, some shelving made from wire grocery crates, a white basin, a cutout of a palm tree that might be a piece of stage set. But the focus is the white glare of the river and the blurred silhouette of a finger pier whose decrepitude is apparent even beneath a light powder of snow. You can see the spaces where planks are missing, the splintered pilings jutting from the water that is almost indistinguishable from the sky.

That winter, O'Grady had her first solo show, *Critical Interventions*, at the INTAR Gallery. She was fifty-five and already known in the New York art world for her performances, notably the dreamlike, autobiographical *Rivers, First Draft*, which she'd staged in 1982 at the secluded northern end of Central Park; the setting would have been perfect for an alfresco production of *As You Like It*. In it, a dozen-odd performers played white Debauchees, a loft full of snobbish Black Artists, a Woman in White silently grating coconut, and three female figures who represented the artist at different ages: a Child in a Pink Sash, a Teenager in Magenta, and a Woman in Red. In its hypnotic slowness and arresting visual compositions, the characters performing a single action with obsessive attention, *Rivers* owed a debt to the theater of Robert Wilson. But its theme of reconciliation—the reconciliation of opposing origins and fragmented, split-off selves—was as ancient as Sophocles.

O'Grady grew up in Boston, where her Jamaican mother raised her in an atmosphere of propriety and striving. From early on she understood that she was expected to excel and bring credit to herself and her family. Her first rebellion was to throw her mother's clothing out the window. "I always experienced my family as a unit that was trying to ignore me as much as they could," she told an interviewer. "And I was pretty unignorable . . . I began sort of defining myself against my sister, my family, almost immediately. I didn't feel I was nothing. I felt I was something. But I was not what they were."

After graduating from Wellesley with a degree in economics, she became a defense analyst for the Departments of Labor and State. The job required reading as many as ten national and international newspapers a day, and during the leadup to the Cuban missile crisis the brief expanded to three complete daily Spanish-language transcripts of Cuban radio stations. "At a certain point in the day," O'Grady said later, "you could watch language melt away." Among her earliest art pieces were poems she composed out of words and phrases she cut out of the Sunday *New York Times*. It was better to dissect language than to watch it melt away.

She had aristocratic cheekbones and humorous eyes. After leaving government work, she'd gone to grad school at the University of Iowa Writers' Workshop, briefly taught fourth-graders in Chicago, volunteered for Jesse Jackson's Operation Breadbasket, and done translations (from Spanish, French, Portuguese, Italian, Danish, Swedish, and Norwegian) for clients that included *Playboy* and the *Encyclopaedia Britannica*; years later, she would supervise the translation of the text on ATM screens into multiple languages, including Japanese, which she didn't speak (she was so visually discerning that she could compare three different translations by three different translators and locate their errors just by focusing on inconsistencies in the kanji characters). She wrote rock criticism. When she arrived in New York, her charisma and erudition got her a job at the School of Visual Arts, where she taught a course on the Dadaists, Surrealists, and Futurists. "It was the opposite of everything I had experienced in education. It wasn't Girls' Latin, with its two-hundred-year history. It wasn't Wellesley. It wasn't any of that. It was bombed out. They had just one building, and it was a mess. And yet the energy was so great. It was still the era where all the students came from the five boroughs. It had not been internationalized—it was dominated by Italians from Brooklyn. How come these working-class kids were able to think of themselves as artists? That's really just because the Italians had such a long tradition of art in their culture. The father of some crazy kid going to SVA could boast about his kid, and people would say, 'Oh, so your boy is going to be Michelangelo!'"

Somewhere during this period she came upon a copy of *Six Years: The Dematerialization of the Art Object*, Lucy Lippard's groundbreaking book about the conceptual art movement. "By the time I finished it, I thought, 'You know, I can do this. I have ideas like this all the time. I just didn't know they were art.'"

O'Grady began her career thinking of herself as a "post-Black" artist who was free to make work that ignored race. But in 1980 she saw the white avant-gardist Eleanor Antin perform in blackface at a show at the New Museum and changed her mind: she decided that she was Black after all. She adopted the persona of Mlle. Bourgeoise Noire, a figure of regal provocation in a gown and cape made from 180 pairs of white gloves who declaimed poems while thrashing herself with a white cat-o'-nine-tails she called "the whip that made plantations move." She was a windup version of the Black Boston Brahmins of O'Grady's youth but one who was intent on burning down the temple. When she crashed art openings—including one at the New Museum, which invited white artists to perform (in blackface, if they wanted) but had no place for Black ones—she demonstrated that what people called "The Art World" was barely half of one. Her performances were directed simultaneously at Black audiences and white ones. She told the first, "Now is the time for an invasion!" Her message to the latter was, "Now is the time for you to be invaded."

"I was coming into the art world," she explains, "because I was convinced that this was where I could make my argument." What was the argument? Her abiding interest was hybridity or, as she sometimes put it, *miscegenation*. This made sense in view of her mixed ancestry, her multiple professions and métiers, her polyglot, polymathic brilliance. Beyond that, however, she was impatient with the binary, the idea that one could be either Black *or* white, male *or* female, subject *or* object, viewer *or* viewed. What she wanted was both/and. (Fittingly, that was the title she gave her 2021 retrospective at the Brooklyn Museum.) The signature pieces in her 1991 show were the photomontages she called *Body Is the Ground of My Experience*. As a form, the photomontage is itself hybrid, bringing the documentary authenticity of the photograph into play with the flagrant artifice of the collage. Sometimes the images were found, as in a piece that placed old photos of O'Grady's mother and maternal aunts above the gables of a New England mansion like the ones where they'd once worked as ladies' maids. Sometimes she photographed each object separately and then meticulously intercut it with others. In the left panel of the diptych *The Clearing*, naked lovers—a white man and a Black woman—cling to each other as they float above an idyllic landscape where two children play on the grass. In the facing panel, the woman lies on the ground, arms rigid at her sides, while her lover has given way to (or metamorphosed into) the figure of Death, Death in torn chainmail with a proprietary white hand on her breast. The surrealists juxtaposed images to subvert the rational consciousness and place a higher reality—a sur-réalité—above it. O'Grady wanted to return the image to the realm of private significance and signification, a sous-réalité in which there was space for the perspectives of excluded others.

An older term for this might be Keats's negative capability: "When a man is capable of being in uncertainties, mysteries, doubts, without any

irritable reaching after fact and reason." When an artist is capable of enter-
taining two opposing ideas at the same time without declaring either one
more truthful than the other. The diptych draws the gaze back and forth
so that even as one focuses on the lovers blissfully twining in the air above
their possible future children, one also sees the prostrate woman and the
gloating skull. Both/and. When *The Clearing* was accepted for a show
meant to foreground women's—and implicitly white women's—sexuality,
the curators only hung the left panel. "Because this show was about, you
know, sexuality as an uncomplicated, positive blessing," O'Grady explains.
"Not sexuality as a complicated life issue or even sexuality as an issue far
more complicated for women of color than for white women, none of the
modulations of sexuality were to be present in the show. And I said, what
have you done, you've put my piece up and it's not my piece."

O'Grady also offered the piece to North Carolina's Southeastern Center for Contemporary Art (SECCA) for a show on Black women. The
horrified curator told her, "That's not what sexuality is, or at least that's
not what it's supposed to be."

"But well," the artist demurs, "that's what it is."

On Becoming a Mark

"IN THE EIGHTIES IT WAS a very gay neighborhood," George Cominskie
remembers. For many years he was president of WARC, but he now just
serves on Westbeth's board of directors. "Except for Westbeth. I mean
Westbeth was pretty straight, and there were a lot of kids here. And then in
the nineties, between the double whammy of the AIDS epidemic and the
crack crime epidemic, it was a very sketchy neighborhood. People thought
it was dangerous." Some people—Cominskie implies that they were mostly
straight—thought it was dangerous because of the trans prostitutes and gay
leather bars, and it goes to reason that if some people go out of their way to
cultivate a look of sexualized menace complete with zipper-mouthed leather face masks, other people will take that menace at face value. Cominskie
didn't. Of the sex workers and leather-folk, he says, "You left them alone,
they left you alone. But in the nineties people were assaulted."

This was probably because of the street kids who'd gravitated to the piers over the preceding decade, some to sell ass, some to roll the men who were buying it; the latter, whatever else they might be, being men with money who lacked the social protections that accrued to white men with other preferences or with the same preferences but in better parts of the city—that is, they were less likely to call the cops. The streets around Westbeth had become as dangerous as they'd been twenty years before, more dangerous because the sex workers who'd once made their living giving blowjobs and rolling the occasional john were now smoking crack and doing stickups in the building's courtyard. Even the cops were a little scared of them: at a public safety meeting a police spokesman said that crack made users "violent, even superhuman." This was the era when that woman on the fourth floor was not just mugged at knifepoint as she stepped out of the elevator, but also then doused with lighter fluid, presumably so that her assailant could set her on fire.

By the nineties, many tenants were visibly aging, a few were frail. It made them easy targets. It was a strange thing to have moved into the building as a pioneer and wake up one morning as a mark.

What Memory Changes

"In any commercial sense I'm a total failure." Simon Carr sounds oddly jaunty about it. In his early sixties, he's still boyish looking, with a full head of silver hair, and he has the energetic briskness of somebody setting off to do work he loves. "Let's be frank. I show in a gallery, but it's a co-operative gallery. It's hard to get into, but I fork up a hundred and seventy a month and I show there every two or three years. I'm happy to be there, I respect the other artists who show there, but it's a venue. All my life I've tried. I take work to galleries, I had a commercial gallery for a while, but it went out of business. I've shown in every kind of place from libraries to churches to people's houses. Academic, a lot of academic venues."

Some of Carr's problem may be that his paintings look as though they could date from the nineteenth century. His views of the Hudson riverfront recall Seurat in their sensitivity to the interaction of light and solid surfaces: a line of buildings on the horizon, a woman sitting on a park bench, a man in a green jacket and straw hat holding a dog on a leash, all variously lit or shadowed by the late-afternoon sun. His studies of a West Village farmers market have the naive charm of Utrillo's compositions. His misfortune is that he's doing the kind of work he does in a place and time in which charm has fallen into disrepute, been denounced as a shoddy player's trick. New York collectors "like to collect what they don't think likes them," Adam Gopnik has written. "The prestige lies in showing that you don't need to be flattered by the art you own." Carr's art isn't exactly flattering, but it doesn't kick the owner in the shin.

"I have very rigorous training in plein air painting, but the stuff I do now and the stuff I've done for a very long time is done from drawings and even more done from memory. Memory colors everything, memory changes everything. So I think there's a sense of getting a more profound insight into what you're seeing." One of his recurring subjects is the farmers market in Abingdon Square, which he portrays at different times of day and from different perspectives. "If anybody came who was [one of the market's organizers]—in fact they have—they'd say, 'Oh that's not *there*, that's over *there*!' And they'd miss the whole point: I do it from memory, I'm drawing from a lifetime of looking at it, and that seems to influence the emotional impact of the work. It comes more from memory than anything else."

Carr is one of Westbeth's newcomers, although *newcomer* means something different in Westbeth than it does in most communities, apart from small towns in New England and the Deep South. "We get on the elevator and conversation stops because people don't know you." The Carrs came into the building in 1990. "We were living in a tiny little tenement apartment in the East Village for many years and began having a bunch of kids, and it was really difficult. I didn't think the world had anything else, but my wife, luckily, had more ambitions. She discovered Westbeth, did all the applications. And I was," a dismissive wave of the hand. "'I don't want to live with artists.' But it really made a huge difference."

"We had three kids, and the list at that point for people with a lot of kids was really short. They called up—and now I know what it is—Westbeth calls and people are very picky and very choosy, 'I only want *this* and I only want *that*, I have to have *this* view and not *that* view'—and they called, and my wife just said, 'We'll take it.' There was no argument. So we were on the fourth floor for a long time, and now we're on six, and I've got a studio on twelve. It's embarrassing how supportive it is. I could basically go to my studio in my pajamas, though I told my kids that if I do that, they have to commit me. Because some tenants do that. They wander around in the halls looking for their studio." His voice takes on a high-pitched quiver. 'It's here somewhere.'" He laughs.

The laughter of older people is often a response to misfortune, up to and including the grand misfortune of death. Some of that laughter is at the misfortune of others, some at their own, and those misfortunes may be divided further into the misfortunes to which they reckon themselves immune and those they understand may one day, time and luck running out, befall them too. Carr's laughter is the last kind.

He grew up downtown, not far from Westbeth, and comes from a family that could be called illustrious. Lucien Carr, his father, occupies an outsized role in the history of the Beats, first as a louche, brilliant college friend of Allen Ginsberg's and Jack Kerouac's and then for the 1944 killing of David Kammerer, whom Lucien stabbed during a drunken struggle in Riverside Park after he rejected the older man's sexual advances. His defense attorney presented the crime as an act of manly self-defense against a homosexual predator, and Lucien ended up serving only eighteen months in the Elmira Reformatory. Following his release, he worked as an editor at United Press International, where he was revered as the "soul of the news service." According to a tribute in *Columbia* magazine, the elder Carr "rewrote, repaired, recast, and revived more big stories . . . than anyone before or after him." As a father, his legacy is mixed: he took his sons to Sunday worship at St. Luke in the Fields on Hudson Street and enrolled them in the St. Luke's School, where Simon later sent his own children. But he cruelly abused Simon's younger brother, the writer Caleb Carr, who even before he began to speak about the abuse in interviews hinted at it in his historical crime novels (the best known is 1994's *The Alienist*). They often hinge on the theme of child-murder.

By the time Carr moved into Westbeth, most of the children of the first generation of tenants were away at college or living on their own, so

164 I THE TWILIGHT OF BOHEMIA

the Carr kids didn't have many friends in the building. "When they made a movie [*Westbeth: The Next Generation*] about kids who'd grown up in Westbeth, they forgot to ask us. It was really sort of a home movie for everybody to ogle their kids in. My guys wouldn't have wanted to be in it. But they got the benefits of being there. They really got the benefits of being in that neighborhood, of being close to the school, and we continued to be involved with that church. They got an experience growing up in New York that's really rare now. It was a rough neighborhood when I was a kid, we used to get beat up on occasion. It really was a different kind of growing up."

In 1990, the neighborhood was still rough. "It was still the meat market, and as soon as the weather got warm, the meat market would begin to stink. There was a lot of prostitution, a lot of drugs along the river. It was still a little bit scary. West Street at night, I wouldn't let the kids go out there alone. I was nervous enough with my wife going out to walk the dog. But we'd just come from the East Village, so it didn't really seem like a big deal. Cars were getting trashed. Our car got broken into."

Still, it wasn't the hellscape that so many accounts of the period shudder over. As he and his children drove back from weekends in the country, Carr remembers, the car would be thronged by prostitutes at every traffic light. They'd "come up to the window and say, *Hiii!*"—he imitates a street hooker trying to imitate Marilyn Monroe—"and then they'd see these cherubs in the back and go, 'Oh, sorry! Sorry!'"

Carr's children are grown now. Two became writers, one is an architect, the fourth a scientist. None has gone into the visual arts. Carr is philosophical about it. "You read about the Wyeth kids. N.C. used to put the kids in the studio and say, 'Today we'll have an art lesson, and that's how you do it.' I never wanted to do that. So they spread out. But compared to other—and this is a nasty thing to say—compared to a lot of Westbeth kids' stories, they did really well. I mean we made friends with a few families. But there's a whole social world there, people constantly walking down the hallway with a casserole on their way to somebody else's house for dinner. We were never involved with that."

Like many working artists, Carr supported his family by teaching. For many years he worked at Parsons, where one of Barton Beneš's instructors once warned him against pursuing a career as an artist. Presently he teaches three days a week at the Borough of Manhattan Community College. It leaves him ample time in his studio. "It's a little bit of a trap," he acknowledges. "Some people think it's a huge trap—but I like teaching. I like teaching what I do, sharing the thing that I do, and that's what I'm able to do at BMCC. So it's not a bad thing. I don't resent it, I enjoy it. But it also takes the edge off of being a starving artist. Maybe you don't push as hard with commercial galleries. But whatever the secret is, whatever makes it work, my friends in commercial galleries made it work. I never figured it out. I never could. I'm not good about going to openings and things like that. The compulsion is to work in the studio, and that's the thing that has to be balanced with everything else, and that often, often, takes away from participating in the art world."

The Carrs arrived in Westbeth twenty years after its opening, when it was already an established community. During those twenty years it had evolved rules—not the rules envisioned by Joan Davidson's experts or spelled out in the lease, but rules that were unstated, picked up by osmosis, and as essential in their way as paying your rent promptly on the first. Asked what the most important of these was, Carr said, "It's social stuff. People don't talk to you, or if they do talk to you, you have to keep a distance. There are people who'd *like* to talk to you and who'd like to get right into your apartment with you. Discovering who the crazy people were and how to deal with them and how the building dealt with them. There are a lot of crazy people. There was a guy down the hall—they eventually got him out of the building—attacking people with hammers. That was horrible and compared to what Westbeth is now, a world away. But we had come from the East Village, on Second Street and First Avenue. So the idea that it was dangerous to be in the hall or dangerous in certain areas of the building wasn't unacceptable. It was worth it for the apartment we had. They called it a three-bedroom, but it was just one long loft with a bedroom at one end and the other end had been split into two bedrooms. We were HUD then, and HUD housing meant you had to have separate bedrooms for boys and girls. So it was me and my wife at one end and the boys and the girl at the other. The reason nobody wanted the apartment was because it had five big windows but they looked onto the courtyard so there was no view out and no cross-ventilation. But it was fine. We were happy to be here.

"Westbeth is kind of an anomaly. I think the thing about the neighborhood is that there's a whole veneer of young people who look exactly the same. Scratch through that and you find the old people, the people who've lived there for forty years. There's still a lot of cranky neighborhood people who haven't been chased out. There were always people like that whom you never socialized with but whom you knew from the elevator or the hall and who knew your kids and watched the kids grow up."

On the Loneliness of Godzilla

WHEN SHE WAS WORKING FOR the Parks Department, Christina Maile once got an emergency call from a crew that was supposed to demolish an old, disused rec facility on the Lower East Side. She went down to the site. Inside, the building had fallen into ruin. But on climbing up to the roof, she saw that it was a riot of wild grasses, herbs, and flowers: bluestem, liverwort, purslane, coneflower, morning glory, prairie smoke, purple loosestrife. "It was a paradise," she wrote, "an enormous, secret wilderness stretching in every direction, so complete and perfect it was as if the world below did not exist." The paradise had one resident: an enormous turtle at least two feet in diameter, its shell scabby with moss and algae. It stood balefully regarding the demolition crew, which regarded it. Who knows how it had gotten there. Maybe it was a child's pet that had been discarded and against all odds found shelter and sustenance on what back then had been bare brick and asphalt, baked by the sun in summer and scraped raw by the winter cold. It had survived. Over the years the barren world in which it had arrived became lush and overgrown. Now the turtle was too big and heavy and sullen to be easily removed. Some of the crew wanted to kill it for meat, and Maile had to remind their foreman of the likely penalties for killing a representative of an endangered species on city property. Thrashing and snapping, the turtle was packed into a rubble-bag and lowered from the roof by pulley, then loaded into her car. Maile and an assistant debated where to take it and eventually settled on a wildlife sanctuary in New Jersey. On arriving, they prodded the turtle out of its bag and watched it trundle into the brush. It may still be alive out there.

A MAJOR PART OF MAILE'S work as a landscape architect was drawing schematics for clients and community groups to show what a completed project would look like. This kind of drawing is functional—*applied art*— and governed by rigorous conventions. Trees, footpaths, berms, terraces are represented in a particular manner so as to be immediately legible. They're like the characters of a written language. Over time Maile realized that she could make renderings that were less alphabetical, more interesting and fanciful. As children, she remembered, she and her sister would "make these sculptures to scare each other, go in the backyard and weave together grass or nail together some wood or carve something out of a broken two by four . . . So making art was a part of my life."

Another landscape architect, especially one working for the sprawling, torpid bureaucracy of New York City, would have seen the roof-turtle as an inconvenience to be gotten rid of with a forklift or turned over to the construction crew. Maile saw its singularity, its nobility, its loneliness. She described them in an essay titled "Regrets":

> Between the few remaining patches of asphalt and the burgeoning wilderness were the evidence of the turtle's incomprehensible days which had turned into years, following one upon the other, in which the turtle in his vast solitude had watched a barren world grow from the individual solitudes of everything that had landed on the roof around him.

She saw the way an artist sees. So it's not surprising that in time she began to make art. Maile started out painting, but one day George Cominskie mentioned that there was a printmaking studio in Westbeth's basement that was practically unused, and she went downstairs to look at it. The abundance of space and equipment was thrilling. "It was like coming into Tikal just after the Mayans abandoned it." As a landscape architect, her job was to make nature compatible with the needs of the humans who passed through it: to make nature enjoyable. In the basement studio she approached nature differently. She wanted to show "nature when man's hand is not on it. I thought that would be really a nice thing for people to have instead of everything being so designed and cosmetic and not threatening. Because nature *should* be threatening and surprising and unexpected. And we should feel it."

Perhaps this sentiment is what she tried to express in *The Red Bear's Dream*, a polyester plate lithograph dominated by the figure of a gigantic bear with fur the color of a dying coal standing on the edge of a lake in the middle of a dense forest. The trees that crowd overhead cast trembling reflections in the water. Both the trees and their reflection are black and white. Apart from the bear, the only spot of color is a tiny woman in an orange dress who confronts the animal from atop a rock or hummock. Bears' faces are notoriously inexpressive; it's part of what makes them dangerous—you can't necessarily tell when one is about to break your neck with a swipe of a paw. But this bear looks perturbed. Maybe it's thrown by the sight of another point of color in its newsprint wilderness.

Maile often represents nature as a monochrome backdrop for brilliantly colored human and animal figures, as well as for hybrid ones: women with the heads of birds ("Birds have seen everything! They've flown over oceans, they've dived into valleys"); mothers and children you might see in any park in New York if not for the Baluba masks that cover their faces; a tree that grows from the hips and legs of a naked woman alongside a row of saints that might have been copied from the dome of Saint Mark's Basilica. She likes multiples of things: gemlike dead hummingbirds that recall the ones John James Audubon killed by the hundreds and then reanimated in his paintings; Dayak children posing for a photograph beside a terrifyingly robust white priest, the children anonymized by the yellow skulls painted over their faces; soldiers and toy soldiers; bombs tumbling down a waterfall to be collected by faceless men in white hazmat suits. The duplicates might be inspired by the Xeroxed band posters that colonized New York's streets in the seventies and eighties, when you couldn't walk down Bowery without seeing the Dead Boys, Mars, and the Contortions layered on every wall and lamppost, each image multiplied hundreds of times. Though duplication occurs in nature, it's mostly thought of as an industrial process, executed with molds and stamping machines and, lately, 3D printers. In Maile's work, duplicates signal man's hand on nature, leaving its greasy fingerprints on it. If you didn't know better, you'd think nature was man-made.

Maile's mother was Trindadian, her father an indigenous Dayak from Sabah on the island of Borneo. They met in New York and raised Christina and her sister in Bedford-Stuyvesant. The family was poor. "I think a lot of my work is basically storytelling," she says. "I've been deeply influenced by my father's stories about growing up in Sabah and my mother's and grandmother's stories about their life in Trinidad. They share the same British colonial attitudes towards the world. My father's was much looser. But my mother and grandmother lived both in a supernatural world and then the natural world. Part of it, I think, was that they had not fully assimilated being in the US. So some of their stories were really kind of training for how you deal if you happen to meet a ghost on a lonely road. Or in my father's case, if you happen to meet a giant boa constrictor, don't mistake it for a log. This was their way of [alerting me to the] kind of dangers of what could happen. Just didn't apply that well to New York.

"My grandmother, especially, told stories about ghosts and spirits and love potions and secret gods doing things to people's destinies, and then my father told stories about surviving in the jungle. So there was a lot of stories about quicksand and boa constrictors and . . . and . . . actually murdering someone; they probably would call it involuntary manslaughter. But the story was so vivid the way he told it that it didn't strike me as terrible. It just struck me as being another colorful part of his life. My father really wanted to become American, and how he got introduced to American culture was that he listened to baseball constantly, so that he could kind of be part of whoever he was working with, they would share something."

In another lithograph, period photos of three Dayak women are placed against a tinted backdrop of tropical brush. Two women have brassieres painted over their breasts; the third is bare-breasted, with a pair of oversized, blood-red cupped hands lying at her feet. The work is titled 2 of 3 Dayak Women Convert to Christianity. Maile went to a Catholic school for twelve years, "so I was really invested with a lot of religious imagery and symbolism. I understood why the missionaries felt a need to convert 'the natives,' quote, unquote . . . So I don't just feel a terrible sense of imposition but, much more, I feel a loss of that culture that then got so intertwined with not only the Christian religion but also Western colonialism.

"My parents—yes, both of them—really felt a need to deny everything about themselves. Except my grandmother held true. But then when she went back to Trinidad, she'd been away for about thirty years, and when she went back her farm was gone and the whole city of Port of Spain had been very urbanized. She was quite old by then. And when she went back for her first and last visit, she never talked about any of that again because everything she'd known had been totally erased. And so part of my work is that joy of her telling those stories and living that life. As a child growing up, even though she was surrounded by all these spirits, a lot of them were protective. And that's what I really want to show: that something mysterious is also something that's beneficent."

Maile's art has been shown at the International Print Center and the Feminist Artists Collection of the Brooklyn Museum; she's been awarded a Pollock-Krasner Foundation Grant and a Joan Mitchell Studio Grant. The diversity of her output suggests the excitement of someone trying out different methods and technologies of visual self-expression: paintings, sculpture, monoprints, lithographs, linocuts, varying degrees of realism and abstraction, varying intensities of color, references to fairy tales and industrial safety posters, Dayak murals, Hokusai and Hiroshige—everything up for grabs. Birds and animals are everywhere. In *Picnic with Nuclear Butterfly*, there's a monster: Godzilla with two pairs of butterfly wings roaring down at the shadows of some very scared-looking humans and what appears to be a nuclear reactor.

"Godzilla is this thing that's one of its kind, melancholy and lonely," Maile says. Godzilla is a monster, but it's also us, *homo faber, homo manufactus*, man the maker, man the made, frantically excising ourselves from the web of organic existence even as we set it on fire. "We are creating ourselves as a monster that has no connection to anything."

When asked to account for the breadth and variousness of her career, she becomes contemplative. "I grew up very poor and with very limited access to the outside. I went to Catholic schools and was taught that everything was on one journey, and that was the journey towards God and marriage and nothing else. So when I began writing plays and moved into Westbeth, it wasn't that I wanted to be a playwright, I just wanted to experience every single thing because I had never done this before. That's why playwriting to me was the same as being a carpenter. And then being a carpenter and a playwright, and being involved in theater was how I got into landscape architecture. So it wasn't that I wanted to be a playwright, or a carpenter or landscape architect, I wanted that experience of manifesting, of saying things or creating things out of nothing. Other people probably have different reasons. But that was my reason, just the lure of expression."

Westbeth allowed her to follow that lure wherever it led her. When she was made a Westbeth Icon in 2022, Maile described her home as "a modern-day utopia that would provide happiness around a certain idea: a community of artists." Still, she added, "Any utopia takes a lot of effort."

On Putting In and Taking Out

EDWARD FIELD BEGAN WRITING POETRY long before there was an entire ecosystem of MFA programs, at a time when one learned to write poetry on one's own, trying a line, a phrase, a word, an image, and discarding it, trying another, maybe changing a word or putting a break in an unexpected place. An advantage was that he was spared the group-think that's a pernicious feature of most MFA programs, where one of the first things one learns is which writers are worthy of being read and which are not.

"Greenwich Village poets were never considered quite up to the mark, for some reason," he says. "There were famous Greenwich Village poets like Maxwell Bodenheim, but they never quite made it in the modern poetry world. Except Edna St. Vincent Millay, but she was a little special, a very good poet in an old-fashioned way. You couldn't dismiss her, but she did write heavily romantic verse. That was considered unacceptable." When Field says *modern*, he's speaking of poetry that is now old. Who today thinks T. S. Eliot is cutting edge? Of course, Field knows this. "Everything in modern poetry was hard-boiled. The language had to be tough. I remember once I showed a new poem to May Swenson. She said, 'Soul? What soul? Where is it?' You couldn't use words like that anymore."

What makes a poet different from a non-poet, the Field who wrote about his plane going down in the North Sea different from the Field who barely escaped with his life? "You learn to use words plastically," he explains. "That's the hard thing to do. When you're first writing poetry, it flows out of you. All of that is suspicious in modern poetry. What flows out of you has to be worked on, looked on with a cold eye. You keep finding a stronger language and discovering your form. That was a big thing that happened in poetry. You poured out your heart in the beginning, but by the end of the revising it was somewhere else."

"The first time you write a poem, you tend to leave out some very important material that you meant to say. I like to enlarge, I'm a fairly wordy poet. At the same time, you have to know how to cut out everything unnecessary; adjectives are mostly unnecessary. By now all this stuff is built into me. I don't really work the same way anymore. It's now all instinct, it's gone into my bones. If you study a poet like Yeats—after he got monkey balls transplanted into his scrotum, he became virile again, he had a resurgence of energy and his writing changed tremendously. When he was young, he wrote romantic poems like 'The Lake Isle of Innisfree.' When he got old, his writing became gritty and concise. It's so tight and digested, it's really a different thing." Field is fond of lurid sexual gossip, so it isn't a surprise to hear him casually drop a reference to monkey-ball implants into a conversation about poetry. He once recounted a story about accompanying a revered artist to shop for butt-plugs before a date with a hustler known for his formidable cock. Yeats evidently did receive a transplant of monkey's testicular tissue when he was sixty-nine. In the 1930s the procedure was popular among aging men of a certain financial or intellectual status: another recipient was Sigmund Freud.

Field often quotes a phrase attributed to Allen Ginsberg (though it was coined by the Tibetan Buddhist teacher Chögyam Trungpa): *First thought, best thought.* "The first words you put down when you get an idea are always very valuable. You'll never get those words again. They're really the heart of the poem." This jibes with the straightforwardness of Field's poetry, its almost ethical refusal of artifice. "Free verse doesn't mean 'free,'" he cautions. "It means you have to work very hard. Poets don't talk about it that much anymore, but in the old days poets used to brag about how many drafts they did. They'd say, 'I wrote a hundred and fifty drafts of that poem.' Then Ginsberg came along and said, 'Just put it down.' The Beats changed everything. They were what poetry needed because poetry had gotten so fucking high-falutin'."

A moment later, he became wistful. "But at the end, Allen Ginsberg was rewriting his poems too. Because of course it's fun. You don't want to give it up."

On Sustenance

FOR A LONG TIME, THERE were very few restaurants in the neighborhood. There was a diner where the meat cutters went for lunch (which, given how early they came to work, was at eight or nine in the morning); the Bonbonniere coffee shop on Eighth Avenue and Twelfth Street, which always had a crush of customers in the doorway waiting for a table to open up. El Faro, the first Spanish restaurant in New York City, was on Greenwich Street. On Ninth Avenue, the Old Homestead Steak House, which had opened in 1868 as the Tidewater Trading Post, now served young financial workers from Wall Street happy to spend more than $100 for a cut of Wagyu, the luxuriously cosseted Japanese beef the restaurant introduced to the United States early in the 1990s. The owners went so far as to work with Japanese farmers to bring their facilities up to American health code.

You couldn't get Wagyu at Florent on Gansevoort Street, just a perfectly nice hanger steak frites at a fraction of the price. But since its opening in 1985 the French bistro cum vintage American diner had established itself as the hippest and most soulful restaurant in lower Manhattan. It had a pink neon sign in the window and a quilted steel backsplash behind the long Formica counter, and it served meals round the clock to meat cutters, drag queens, sanitation workers, club kids, artists, and AIDS activists. Jack Dowling described it as a place where there was "a lot of uptown-downtown action." More vividly, the actress Jackie Hoffman called it "the halfway house of restaurants." After learning he was HIV positive and being warned not to let word get out lest it put a crimp in business, the owner Florent Morellet started chalking his T-cell count on the specials board every day. When Roy Lichtenstein, a longtime regular, died, Morellet hung a map of Lichtenstein near the table where he used to sit. Florent had the vibe of a workingman's (and woman's) place, though work could mean driving a truck or designing dresses (Calvin Klein and Diane von Furstenberg were frequent customers) or doing S and M shows at the Vault—and this made it an egalitarian redoubt in a city that was becoming a showpiece of inequality.

Another customer remembered the first time he stepped inside: "It was one of those rare times when you walk in a place and think, 'Gosh, I could come here twice a week. I belong here.'"

On the Uses of Unwanted Things

THE WORK THAT MADE BARTON Beneš famous outside the art world— *notorious* is probably a better word—began with a kitchen accident. "I was in the kitchen cutting parsley one day, and I cut a piece of my finger and blood went everywhere. And I freaked out. 'Oh my god, I'm going to get AIDS!' So I ran for the bleach and the rubber gloves, and I put on rubber gloves, afraid of my own blood. And I'm cleaning it with bleach and freaking out." But as the shock subsided, he remembered that he was already HIV positive.

He may have contracted the virus from Howard or from one of the men he'd had sex with in the trucks back in the seventies. The drug AZT had been found to slow the disease's progress and extend the lifespan of people who had it. But AIDS was still a death sentence, and one measure of the horror it inspired was that someone who was already infected and presumably beyond further harm freaked out at the sight of his own blood.

"I thought, 'This is nuts. This is my blood. My kitchen.' And I'm going through all this craziness. And that's when I thought, 'If I have this fear, you can imagine the fear that other people have.' Then I realized, this is scary stuff. It's powerful. And I thought, 'I may start making weapons out of it.'"

Some people are paralyzed by fear, and some are galvanized by it, provoked to run or fight. Beneš chose to fight: to seize the thing he was afraid of and point it the other way. He took various objects, most of them innocuous, some even a little silly—a kids' squirt gun, a perfume atomizer, a holy-water bottle, a joke-shop lapel flower designed to soak the patsy who leaned in for a sniff—and filled them with some of his contaminated blood. He turned them into weapons. That's what he called the pieces: *Lethal Weapons*. Of course, one wouldn't know they were lethal unless one knew something about the blood they contained. Seen purely as objects, the pieces were delicate, decorative, finely finished—even a poison dart fashioned from a hypodermic syringe had its menace offset by the neatly clipped feathers attached to the base. Beneš mounted the pieces in shadow boxes sealed with wired glass, which simultaneously protected the viewer and reminded them of the danger sealed inside.

Beneš's New York gallery wouldn't show his new work—no commercial gallery would. The venue that finally took it was the North Dakota Museum of Art in Grand Forks. It's small but artistically ambitious, thanks in large part to its curator, Laurel Reuter, who until her retirement in 2021 finessed a taste for aesthetic risk-taking with a local's understanding of North Dakotan mores. Born on the Spirit Lake Tribe reservation, she's lived in North Dakota most of her life. "The people who came to the museum were used to seeing work that one wouldn't expect to see out here. And don't ask me to tell you why that was, but it was normal for us. And we would also make sure that the artist spoke and that they had an opportunity to hear the artist talk about what the work was. As long as they don't use art-speak."

By all accounts, Beneš spoke to the people he met at his 1993 opening the same way he would to his Westbeth neighbors. At one point Reuter introduced him to a woman who'd been offended by the invitations, which came stamped on nitrile examination gloves. "She had a fit that we were mistreating the medical field. And then Barton came, and I called her and said, 'Why don't you come over and meet Barton.' She came over, and of course he just made her swoon. He took her through the show and explained everything. He was very good at that. And when she left, she made out a check for $500, and she said, 'Don't you dare tell anyone I gave this to you.'"

Elsewhere the response was less generous. Following the show in North Dakota, *Lethal Weapons* traveled to Lund, Sweden, where within a few days of the opening authorities ordered the gallery to close as a threat to public health. Newspapers reported that it was selling HIV-infected blood "by the liter." In England, the tabloids shuddered over an "AIDS Horror Show." Eventually, the gallery director and the health authorities agreed on a compromise: any piece sold would be heated in a hospital oven at 160 degrees for two hours to deactivate the virus before being released to the buyer with a certificate attesting to its safety. *Safety* was a relative term: although the lethal weapons were rendered virus-free, they remained disturbing, even queasy-making. As Joe Lovett put it, "When you look at Barton's blood pieces, whether they're AIDS blood or not, they're still blood. It's tinkering with a life force." Prankster that he was, Beneš enjoyed the scandal: "I never thought that I would become a terrorist."

But as stories about *Lethal Weapons* started hitting the American press, he began to worry about having his health status made public. Warren Beneš recalled getting an anxious phone call from him one morning. "He said, 'Warren, is mom still getting the newspaper delivered?' I said, 'Yes.' 'Warren, get the Sunday paper. Do not let her read it! Mom doesn't know I'm gay.'" Beneš decided he had to come out to her, and he asked Warren to go with him for support. Warren recounts the conversation in a husky voice; at times he seems to be fighting back tears. "'Mom,' he says, 'I want you to know that I'm a gay man.' She says, 'I know.' He says, 'How did you know?' She says, 'Barton, I knew from the time you were crawling.'"

He didn't want to be labeled "an AIDS artist," but for different reasons. While in much of the country people with AIDS were still being demonized, by the nineties, in certain quarters they were objects of somber veneration: they had become a cause. You couldn't go to an opening or awards ceremony without seeing people wearing the little red lapel ribbons designed by Patrick O'Connell, the director of Visual AIDS (Beneš sat on its board). There were "ribbon bees" in which thousands of the emblems were cut and folded, sometimes by crews of homeless women, to be given away as high-minded party favors. The designer Isaac Mizrahi explained their popularity: "If you can't do anything big about AIDS, second best is to appear to do something." And maybe because one measure of a cause's seriousness — or the seriousness of its adherents — is how much they're willing to spend promoting it, or maybe because cloth or paper ribbons are sort of flimsy, someone began making designer red ribbon lapel pins. Soon they were as ubiquitous as American flag pins on the floor of Congress. The one that set Beneš off was jeweled and worn by a presenter at the Oscars, who may have gotten it at Tiffany's. It made him furious. "Why the hell didn't he wear a paper ribbon like everybody else and take that $80,000 and give it to an AIDS organization?" he complained to Warren.

Among the many unwanted items that had been sent him over the years were the ashes of a friend's sister. Her name was Brenda Woods. She'd been sexually abused as a child, and as a young woman she'd fallen into drug addiction and the kind of life that went with it. She might have contracted AIDS from a dirty gimmick. She died of it in 1989, the same year as Howard Meyer. She was forty-two. Her family had her body cremated but didn't know what to do with the remains. Beneš liked to say, "Everybody has something they don't know what to do with."

The night he saw the ostentatious pin at the Oscars telecast, he cut two hundred ribbons out of heavy paper. Then, as Warren recalled, "He dipped the ribbons in glue, and just like you were putting flour on a piece of meat you were going to fry, he dipped those ribbons in Brenda's ashes and he had two hundred ribbons with Brenda's ashes." Years later, Laurel Reuter showed them at the North Dakota Museum, mounted on a wall in uniform gray rows like the gravestones at a military cemetery. When visitors entered that room, they almost always fell silent.

Brenda didn't create the same sensation *Lethal Weapons* had, but it launched a trend. More and more people started sending Beneš the ashes of loved ones who'd died of AIDS; a few who had the disease willed him their own while they were still alive. In 1996, he mixed together the ashes of Noel McBean and James Barden, lovers who'd died three weeks apart, and decanted them into a large hourglass, an early device for keeping time housing the dust of two men who had run out of it. The piece is called *Hourglass*. "I have all these friends' ashes, and they're all different colors," Beneš mused to his brother. "I must be one of the few people in the world who knows that ashes are different colors. Is it temperature? Diet? It's something in the bones."

✹

On Second Chances

I DON'T THINK GAY MILIUS knew Beneš or was even aware of him other than as someone who got on the elevator at the ninth floor. But Beneš
was the one artist in the building he would have envied.

He would have envied the expansiveness and weirdness of Beneš's
collections and the meticulousness of their organization, and he would
have envied the profitable use he made of them. For a while, Gay had
an entire pantry filled with recalled products: a bottle of Tylenol from
the batch some sociopath had poisoned with cyanide in the early eighties,
ominously bulging cans of tainted Bon Vivant vichyssoise. But the soup
cans sat there until he threw them out for fear they'd explode on the shelf.
No doubt he could have made art from them—he could have mounted
a single can of Bon Vivant inside a clear plastic cube and trained a video
camera on it so viewers could watch it inching toward detonation and a
lethal spray of botulin. He just didn't. Maybe it was laziness. Or a lack
of interest. Maybe it was because his sensibility remained the sensibility
of a painter, attentive to shape and color, the distribution of light and
dark. And maybe it was because, for all his love of jokes, Gay treated art
as something fundamentally serious, even exalted, and when he made a
work that was clearly a joke, like the painting of an empty frame festooned
with price tags, it was a tacit admission of failure.

Midway through the eighties, I left New York and moved to Baltimore
for what I thought would be a little while but turned out to be seven years.
In retrospect, I think I meant to end my life, either by a definitive act or by
attrition. So I know only some of what happened in my friend's life during
those years.

I visited Gay and Molly just after Christmas of 1985, got fucked up on
the drugs and alcohol I had at the loft on top of the drugs and alcohol I'd
had earlier in the evening, and then rode back to the apartment where I
was staying with a woman friend of theirs who drove a cab. I was attracted
to her, or maybe just to the novelty of her profession, but had to keep
asking her to stop along the route so I could open the door and be sick in
the street, and I guess I still had enough of a reality sense to see that this
foreclosed the potential of the night ending more rewardingly. When she

dropped me off, I paid the fare and tip and apologized for making her stop so often. "No, no," she said, with emphasis. "I'm glad you did."

After I got sober in 1986, Gay scoffed at any mention of my drug use. He said it had been an affectation, especially the needles. What kind of Jew shot heroin? I once made the mistake of saying Lenny Bruce. He snorted. Lenny Bruce was the Sandy Koufax of heroin addiction. Sometime during the first year of my changed life, he asked me to dog-sit while he and Molly were away on a trip; I drove up to New York, grateful for the use of the apartment and the implicit trust behind the invitation. Still, when I entered the loft, I noticed that one of the autodial buttons on their phone was labeled JUNKY, and when I pushed it the line rang and rang until I got the outgoing message of my answering machine in Baltimore. If somebody else had done that, I would've been devastated. Back then I slinked through the world like a bad dog with a mean owner, always waiting to have my face shoved in my mess. But I understood Gay was being funny. For all I know, he'd changed the label just before he left for the airport. He knew I wouldn't be able to resist finding out who JUNKY was.

He met Karen diving in the Caribbean; she was a diver too. It was something that set her apart from Molly, who didn't enjoy it, though that may be just another of the things Gay started accusing her of when he passed into that stage of disaffection where the partner becomes a lint roller for grievances. Scuba diving isn't especially dangerous; in a given year more people are hurt swimming, fishing, bowling, or playing golf. Still, you could conceivably die doing it, and it can be hard on the sinuses, so who would blame Molly if she really didn't want to? Karen had blond hair that she wore in a seventies shag and the rosy cheeks of a Campbell's Soup twin. She was sort of a sexual buccaneer, or that was what Gay told me. He was both aroused and abashed by it. Meeting her, you could imagine that someone might break up his marriage for her. It was harder to imagine that one day she'd be stricken by mysterious painful and disfiguring illnesses that sent her blindly stumbling through a labyrinth of doctors, support groups, and alternative healers until she emerged years later and some two thousand miles away in a desert town in New Mexico By that time Gay was dead.

Almost as soon as they met, they started an affair. He broke it off. They picked back up. The sex was potent and adhesive, and Gay said that every time he tried to leave, Karen would start crying. He commemorated the entanglement in one of his few self-portraits. The backdrop is a tropical beach: white sugar sand, green palms. A blond woman in a bathing suit and sunglasses sits reading in a beach chair. Gay occupies the foreground; it couldn't be anybody but him. Everything in the painting is more or less realistic, but Gay's head sprouts from an impossibly long brontosaur's neck, the features distorted in a yell of anguish and frustration; maybe he was referencing Munch's *The Scream*. The image is grotesque, yet the effect is comic. The figure's body is outside the canvas; there's just an anxious head hollering at the end of the rope of flesh that yokes him to a body we can't see—not a bad metaphor for the distance between conscience and concupiscence, the fact that one part of you can be knotted with guilt while the other is led around by a hard-on. It's the Yiddish saying *Ven der putz shteht, ligt der sechel in drerd*, only turned upside down: When the head rears up, the prick goes somewhere else.

Some men would have broken off the affair. Others would have kept it going as a side thing, lying about it with such fluency that they barely thought of it as lying. Gay couldn't do either. At a certain point Molly found out, or else he told her. She filed for divorce. She did it matter-of-factly and, as far as I could tell, without real anger. She even ceded the loft to him. Probably she knew he'd never be able to afford rent anywhere else in the city, and where else could he live, really? One of the last times I spoke with her, she asked me to stay friends with him. Maybe she worried I would judge Gay for cheating on her. I did judge him for cheating on her, though I could hardly hold it against him, having done the same thing more than once myself. For all he'd complained about Molly in the years before their divorce—she wasn't fun, she knew nothing about art, her friends were assholes—the moment they separated he was sick with remorse. He'd fucked up. He was no good. "I know what I'm like," he said. I heard him say it many times in the years that followed, as the preamble to any number of confessions: *I know what I'm like*. But another thing he said all the time was, "You don't understand."

Molly moved to eastern Pennsylvania, close enough to the city that she could still commute to her job by bus. To Gay's horror, she got involved with Chris Harms, who left his girlfriend and moved in with her. Gay warned her that Harms was only interested in her money. It didn't go over well. So in one stroke he lost both his wife and his best friend. Other friends had left town or become boring. Jonny Takami, photographer Bob Gruen's onetime assistant, moved to Maine. Mark Sloan, the head shop owner with Prince Valiant hair who may have coined the slogan "Frodo Lives!" or at least been the first person to print it on a button, was felled by a heart attack behind the counter of his store on MacDougal Street. Gay's old roommate Larry suggested they have buttons made that read "Mark Sloan Lives." Gay thought that was genius. On consideration, such a button wouldn't have been that different from the sign Christina Maile displayed in her window during the rent strike: "Nothing Lasts Forever." A statement whose power lies in its resistance to interpretation.

In 1992, Gay traveled to Indonesia with me and another friend. The ostensible purpose was to keep me from being ripped off by the thieves and con artists who would swarm a soft-headed American the moment he stepped off the plane. But he also wanted items he could resell in New York. In Jakarta I saw him communicate with magical ease with the vendors at the flea market on Jalan Surabaya, easing his passage down the thronged aisles with a fistful of dollar bills that he held aloft like the torch of Liberty. Along with the usual masks and shadow puppets, he bought antique brass diving helmets and toy boats made from hammered tin with motors that ran on vegetable oil. He bought more than he could carry, but thanks to those dollars he drew an army of small boys to serve as porters. One of them held an umbrella over him when it started raining. I was mortified to be seen with him; I think this heightened his pleasure. He had a good time until we got to Kalimantan, the Indonesian portion of the island of Borneo. It was hot and damp, and it took days of traveling by riverboat to get anywhere, and none of those anywheres held anything of interest to him. Days of staring at the coffee-colored Mahakam River and the unending scroll of tropical foliage until you got to a village where boys rode their motorbikes in circles around the *alun-alun*, stirring clouds

of dust that settled slowly in the thick air. The community houses painted with indigenous murals where everyone gathered at night to watch
TV, the popular favorite being an Indonesian sitcom whose principal
laugh-getter was a sassy drag-queen-next-door.

In Samarinda, Gay got fed up and caught a flight to the coast. He
found a diving spot where he could go out with a hookah rig. This apparatus replaces the diver's scuba tank with a gas-powered compressor that
pipes air down from the surface through a hose. The place's remoteness
appealed to him. None of the divers he knew had even heard of it. In a
nearby village someone offered him a small skull inlaid with beadwork,
and he bought it for not very much money. Only when the skull was
impounded by customs at JFK did he discover that it was an orangutan's.

On returning to New York, he sold his purchases at the big flea market
on Twenty-Sixth Street. From then on, this was the main source of his
livelihood, though his margin tightened when the Indonesian merch ran
out and he had to replace it with items he picked up at sidewalk and garage sales; sometimes he had to drive as far as the towns along Chesapeake
Bay. For extra money, he supplied macabre props to some of the neighborhood's S and M clubs. These had largely supplanted the old sex clubs
because of the risk associated with penetrative sex, and in spaces along
Greenwich and Washington Streets ceremonial whippings and piercings
of nipples and genitals were performed before rapt audiences that gathered like religious congregations. The spectacles satisfied people's appe-
tite for the *appearance* of risk. It was in those years that the BDSM floats
at Gay Pride started displaying a sign that read WE USED TO BE SICK,
NOW WE'RE SAFE. One chilly October night after I'd moved back to the
city, I helped Gay deliver a coffin to the Vault. We walked up Washington
Street with the thing balanced on our shoulders, our eyes slitted against
the wind. The streets were almost empty; I don't remember anybody looking at us. And when we entered the club, the customers paid us no more
attention than if we'd been delivering beer.

By the mid-nineties the first protease inhibitors had become available
to AIDS patients, and people had stopped dying in such numbers. The Far
West Village was no longer a queer neighborhood: that is, queer people lived
there, but they were no longer the prevailing demographic. People who

could afford $2,500 one-bedrooms (today it would be $3,500 studios) were the prevailing demographic. Like other disasters before and since, AIDS had been good for gentrification. Karen moved into Gay's loft with him. For a while they got along pretty well. She made her living as a photo retoucher, which in those years before Photoshop was an exacting and well-paying craft that shared certain features with medieval manuscript illumination. She set her own hours so they could go out at night. She introduced Gay to swing dancing, and he turned out to be surprisingly good at it, performing its steps, turns, and swingouts with rangy, straightforward grace, his face as impassive as Buster Keaton's. Every once in a while, he'd crack a shy smile of enjoyment. He was a physical person. He liked swing's formality, its well-delineated steps and gestures, and he liked that you mostly held your partner by the hand instead of dry-humping her in front of the whole room.

Still, there was tension. Some of it arose from the gap between what Gay made at the fleas and the cost of living in the city and some of it from Karen's desire for more of a commitment. At length they got married; it was another thing Gay said he agreed to do just to stop her crying. A while later they announced that they were leaving the city for a tiny, historic village on the Eastern Shore of Virginia. It was called Wachapreague, and it was situated on marshland by the ocean. There were only three hundred residents, most of them old, and a lot of gnats; in the summer you walked through clouds of them. They bought a house whose mortgage wasn't much more than the Westbeth rent. When Gay asked me if I wanted to sublet, I was happy to pay him an extra $900 a month. I'd dreamed of living in the loft from the first time I stepped inside and looked out the tall windows at the twilit dream of the river.

Gay drafted a simple contract, handwritten in ballpoint pen. I still have it:

Peter will take occupancy June 15 1995 at a rate of $1400 a month, Pro-rated, to reside there untill [sic] *either side shall give 3 months notice as a desire to quit the relationship.*

The sublet, of course, was illegal; hence Gay's insistence that I keep a low profile. And one of the terms of our informal lease was that he could stay whenever he came up for the Twenty-Sixth Street flea market, his van stuffed with old clam baskets and oyster rakes, refinished chests of drawers, and sun-bleached rocking chairs he'd bought off porches where they'd been sitting for fifty years.

Peter shall also pay first $100.00 of any repair— & secure repairman himself. This is of any repair not covered by insurance or not caused by negligence on his part. Any negligence repairs Peter shall pay for himself.

Maybe that was why I continued to see the loft as Gay's home and myself only as a sort of caretaker. If he were alive to read this, he'd note that most caretakers don't take the liberty of slapping a bunch of six-by-eight decking on the roof so they can grill out there; it's true I did that, and he might have thrown me out for it, he certainly threatened to, but he got distracted by the two kittens my girlfriend and I brought down with us from the country after we'd found them in the shrubbery near her apartment. The moment Gay saw them peeping out of the box, he forgot he was angry at me. "Do you have food for them?" he asked suspiciously. "What about toys? They need toys." Evidently, he'd forgotten that there were two adult cats in the loft, both very spoiled, with more toys than they could use in a lifetime, all suitable for kittens. Whenever my girlfriend at the time, who is now my wife, wants you to know what Gay was like, this is the story she tells.

Gay & Karen shall have access to stay in the alcove sleeping area when he needs to work or show in NYC. He shall give respectable notice as to his intent to do so. Peters [sic] defined relationship as far as the building goes will be one as roommate.

Interlude: On the Beauty of Zero

NICOLINA TYLER ARRIVED IN NEW York in January of 2002, when even on cold days lower Manhattan still sometimes smelled of the auto-da-fé it had been four months before; it's disquieting to realize how many acts of faith involve killing. If she'd applied for an apartment in Westbeth then, by the time I met her in the summer of 2020 she might have just moved into one, having finally reached the head of the building's Kafkaesque waitlist. But she hadn't even heard of Westbeth. Instead, she did what artists in the city have always done, seeking out undeveloped spaces in undeveloped neighborhoods or in ones that had once been developed but subsided back into neglect. One of these was the apartment in Bushwick she'd found some four years before. It was long and narrow, almost a hallway, with her roommates' bedrooms opening off of it. The main room was subdivided into a kitchen and sitting area and had exposed brick walls that were twelve feet high. One was hung with musical instruments, including a baroquely curled sousaphone that looked like a giant cochlea. The facing wall had a loft big enough for two people to sit on it like spectators at a circus. And, really, the whole space suggested a circus, a small, rickety one that travels from town to town in horse-drawn caravans.

"I was traveling in India and I had all my stuff in storage, and my friend Jade had found this space and was like, 'Come move in with me!'" On returning to the city, Nicolina moved into one of the bedrooms. There were two roommates, who eventually moved out. The rent was $3,400 a month. "My first vision for it was actually more of an art hotel. But I'd always wanted to create a space that was full of color and artwork and plants. I decided to take over the lease myself and build this loft and strip it down to zero and then start from scratch. It's taken me about four years. I worked on it pretty fully for a couple years. In the beginning it was more of a construction site so anyone who was willing to live here and pay rent was great, but they had to put up with me building this loft.

"The frame for the loft is welded steel, it's really a glorified piece of furniture, only held in the wall by one screw. Everything else is shimmed into place. It's just very tight. At first I didn't know where I was going to put the ladder so I decided to build it without the ladder so that I could think about it, and my friends and I were talking and they said, 'Wow, if only it had a spiral staircase it would be perfect!' And I said, 'Yeah [sarcastically]. Spiral staircases are like $2,000, and I can't afford that.' And a couple days later I was walking through Crown Heights and I saw this disassembled spiral staircase in someone's front yard. I knocked on their door and they said it was a gift from a friend and they were going to put it up on their roof. And I told them if they ever changed their mind to give me a call, and I gave them my number. And they called me later that day and said, 'You know what? If you can come get it this weekend, it's yours.' They just gave it to me.

"Living in New York really expands your creativity, maybe because you have to figure out how to make things work. What's that phrase? Necessity is the mother of invention. That's how I feel in New York. I definitely figured out how to make things happen. Like I built this room to offset the cost of my rent so that I could live here."

By then two other roommates had moved in, and the loft created space for a third, which lowered the rent accordingly. For two years Nicolina kept the landlord in the dark. "I established this outside table as our meeting space, like, 'Let's meet at our spot.' Just to try to get him to always go there to meet instead of coming up here. I feel like I lucked out because he *did* eventually see this place. One of my roommates told me he'd walked in behind the electrician one day. I was on a job on the Upper East Side painting a window, and I freaked out, and then he called me later that day and I was so scared of what he was going to say. And I picked up the phone, and he said, 'I love what you've done with the place!'"

By inclination and aesthetics, Nicolina is drawn to the communal. The instruments on the wall were meant to be played; she regularly had friends over for jam sessions. Her own instrument is the accordion, which she plays with a dreamy pleasure, swaying a little as she works the bellows. "That's in a way the point of creating this space: to be a magical-looking space whose magic enhances everything that takes place here. We usually play just for each other. Sometimes we do little shows, and every year I do a gingerbread village building weekend spectacular. We put together two long tables and build a little gingerbread village, and then we march it off to my friend's backyard when it's all finished. And afterward—there's nothing really good to do with that gingerbread village. It's not good to eat, obviously; it's not good enough looking to donate to some kind of children's hospital or something. And we don't want to throw it away. So we blow it up with fireworks. Usually in our neighbor's backyard. It's quite a scene, this postapocalyptic gingerbread village burning."

Like most artists in New York—like most artists in any of America's late-capitalist urban centers—Nicolina has had to do other things to support herself. In her case, it's been painting murals in restaurants and, more recently, signs. "The work that I do for money makes possible the work I do for myself. When you're painting for money . . . well, I've painted Santa Claus a million times. For an artist to survive, you've got to figure out how to, obviously, cover your bottom line, and sometimes I think that the best way to do that is find something that will make you as much money as possible without spending all your time doing it. You can't do something that kills your soul, 'cause that'll affect your art. If you can bartend or whatever and make a bunch of money and have four days off and make art, that's great. I think the important thing is just to make sure that you're making the art, 'cause just surviving in a city like this can take up all your energy."

Unlike most of her peers in the city, Nicolina didn't go to an MFA program. She just started making art. "I got fired from my last waitressing job, and I'd always wanted to be an artist, but I was always afraid that I would be a starving artist. I was afraid to just scrape by. I was living in the East Village on Second Street between A and B. And I was waitressing, and I was really depressed because I was doing nothing that I loved. I was living in the city, and everything was really expensive, I was taking all the money that I made and giving it straight to my landlord. I knew I couldn't go back to the service industry because I knew I could be there for the next ten years, and I wouldn't learn anything new and I wouldn't make any more money. It would just be this dead end, and I'd wake up ten years later and be in the same position. So I made this pact with myself that I wouldn't go back to the service industry. And then I was in despair because, 'What am I gonna do then for money?' I had this very pivotal thought. I imagined myself as an old woman looking back on my life and wondering what if I'd done what I really wanted to do, which was to be an artist. I recognized that if I tried and failed that I could live with that as an old woman. But if I never tried, I would feel it was a tragedy. So then I was left with no choice but to try. Because I was super scared about it, I was like I'd better just give this thing everything I have. Like a backflip, you don't hesitate with a backflip."

NICOLINA'S SPATIAL IMAGINATION AND GIFTS for construction allowed her to pay a fraction of what most New Yorkers pay, often for much smaller spaces, even in the most remote and sketchy neighborhoods across the five boroughs. It allowed her to make art that was gay, audacious, carnivalesque, often ephemeral: the elaborate "portals" that she painted in vacant doorways, whose pulsing detail included a QR code that led viewers to instructions for tasks that when properly performed led them to another portal and then another in an antic hero's quest across the Lower East Side. The floating gallery of fishing boats moored in Rio de Janeiro's Quadrado da Urca harbor whose roofs had murals that when seen from above coalesced into a shimmering whole. The angel—she looked like a more severe version of the Torch Lady in the Columbia Pictures logo, only with wings and a Sacred Heart—painted on the wall of a pizzeria on Sunset Boulevard, surrounded by a swarm of spacecraft, rockets, airplanes, butterflies, and a flying pig.

The work was part painting, part public monument, and part performance, its performative aspect heightened by the presence of the artist, who looked like a circus acrobat beaming atop a tightrope. (In fact, she is an acrobat, in the sense of someone who often works at a height. She used to paint murals on the upper stories of apartment buildings while hanging over their roofs.) The art was meant to involve the communities around it, especially communities of the street and waterfront. For the boat project in Rio, Nicolina began by persuading one fisherman to let her paint his vessel. Another captain was so impressed by the result that he asked her to do the same with his boat. Then others signed on. The only holdout was a woman captain who was afraid the art would make her look weird. But as the project drew in more and more of her neighbors, she came to feel it would look weird to have the only boat that was undecorated.

Sometimes the art involved children, like the free art workshops Nicolina and local collaborators taught at schools and community centers in Brazil, India, Mexico, and Haiti or the one she led at a girls' club on the Lower East Side. You could easily picture her teaching kids at Westbeth, maybe getting them to paint a new set of murals in the hallways that they would race past during those sprawling building-wide games of tag. It was art that couldn't be purchased. The only income it produced came from grants, most of which went for materials and labor. However, the art could be stolen, as happened to two of the East Village portals; one was taken less than twelve hours after it had been unveiled. I don't know if they were resold on the underground market or if the thieves just enjoyed looking at them, picturing the invisible worlds onto which they opened. "That's the nature of art on the street. When you make art for people, they can do what they want with it."

For all the joy she took in her work, it was hard to keep up in one of the most expensive cities on earth. When I met Nicolina, she was moving to New Orleans, where she'd bought a four-bedroom house in the Bywater district for less than what she'd pay for a studio in Crown Heights. "I got the house, I built a kitchen, and I turned two of the four bedrooms into its own private little unit, so now I get to live alone in the back with the garden, and my mortgage with all the insurance and property tax and stuff will be five hundred bucks a month. But I was worried I wouldn't be able to do that because I was, 'Are people even going to be able to pay rent? Will it take me a year to find someone to rent this place?' But I did it and it worked great. That's applying what I learned living in New York: surviving."

Still, it was painful to leave the city where she'd spent her youth and the enchanted dwelling she'd built within it. "I was dismantling everything, and I took this one frame off the wall that had a beautiful poem by a friend of mine, and I read it and started to cry. And I thought, 'Why am I destroying this beautiful space when I could give it to a friend of mine?'" The friend was a musician who plays the tuned percussion instrument called the handpan; it looks like a miniature flying saucer with rings of portholes around the circumference. He gave one to Nicolina when she passed down the apartment's lease. It was a kind of payment, a version of what back in the sixties and seventies, when artists were first moving in to disused industrial and manufacturing spaces and trying to recoup some of what they'd spent making them livable, was called *key money*.

Chapter Six

2002
$76,529,059 | Peter Paul Rubens *The Massacre of the Innocents*

2004
$104,168,000 | Pablo Picasso *Garçon à la pipe*

2007
$71,720,000 | Andy Warhol *Green Car Crash – Green Burning Car I*

2010
$106,482,500 | Pablo Picasso *Nu au plateau du sculpteur*

2012
$119,922,496 | Edvard Munch *The Scream*

2015
$170,405,000 | Amedeo Modigliani *Nu couché*
$179,365,000 | Pablo Picasso *Les Femmes D'Alger (Version O)*

2017
$450,312,500 | Leonardo da Vinci *Salvator Mundi*

2018
$157,159,000 | Amedeo Modigliani *Nu couché (sur le côté gauche)*

On Catastrophe
2001

WHEN PETER RUTA MOVED INTO Westbeth in 1970, he was immediately taken with the views from the roof of his studio, and he began bringing up his paints and easel to work in the open air. His eye traveled the rooftops of lower buildings, their hatches, air vents, water towers and smokestacks, the edges where light met shadow, sharply or in soft mutual interpenetration. He watched the two towers of the World Trade Center rising to the south. Against the stepped silhouettes of the older office buildings beside them, their shape was as simple as that of cigarette cartons, not streamlined but blandly functional, their function being to contain thousands of workers performing mostly mental labor stacked floor upon floor into the sky. Ruta went up almost every day. His canvases, with their soft slate blues, cadmiums, and ochres, are a visual document of the transformation of the New York skyline. There are no people in them, and this makes them even more austere than the cityscapes of Edward Hopper, to whom Ruta is often compared. They might be studies of a city emptied of life.

He was born in Germany in 1918 to a Jewish mother and a Protestant father. After the Beer Hall Putsch in 1923, the family moved to Italy, only to see their adopted country descend into its own opera buffa brand of fascism. In 1936 he immigrated to the US, arriving almost penniless. He studied drawing, sculpture, and fresco at the Art Students League. "I evolved more and more into the art world," Ruta told an interviewer many years later. "As a painter, as a student, and so on, and suddenly you can call yourself an artist. For a long time, it sounds presumptuous, naturally." He'd just won a scholarship when he was drafted into the army, and although he was offered a position as a division artist, he asked for combat duty and was sent to the Philippines. During the 1945 Battle of Bataan, he was shot four times in the abdomen at close range. Seeing the severity of his wounds, the men in his unit put him in a tent to die. He recalled:

"Nero, when he died . . . he said, 'What a great artist is dying in me!' When I was lying there dying, I said, 'Here's a painter dying in the Philippines. If he could have five years more or ten, I'd be happy, or twenty.'"

He got another seventy. In the course of those years, Ruta lived in several countries and knew many of the emblematic figures in the arts of the twentieth century. In Mexico he boarded with Siqueiros; in Venice he was the extra man at Peggy Guggenheim's dinner parties. His work was shown at the Uffizi, the Leipzig Stadtgeschichtliches Museum, and the Museum of the City of New York. In 2000, in recognition of his sustained attention to the World Trade Center, the Lower Manhattan Cultural Council awarded him a studio on the ninety-first floor of the North Tower through a program that matched artists with temporarily unleased office spaces. At eighty-two, he was the program's oldest participant. The new studio gave him an unequaled panoramic view of Manhattan. If Ruta and his wife hadn't decided to stay a while longer on Cape Cod at the end of the summer of 2001, he would have been working there on the morning of September 11; when American Airlines Flight 11 struck the North Tower at 8:46 a.m., he was on a Metro North train into the city. None of his paintings explicitly reference the terrorist attack. In some of his later work, however, still lifes are placed against slices of the lower Manhattan horizon, the verticals of skyscrapers mirrored by those of a milk bottle and a jar of cooking utensils, the mass of a warehouse condensed into some loaves of bread on a table. By this time, he may have been too old to comfortably take his materials up to the roof every morning. And he may not have cared to look too long at the skyline he'd painted almost every day for more than thirty years, which was now irreparably altered, some would say gone.

THE PLANES STRUCK THE TOWERS in full view of Westbeth, and between the time of impact and the time the buildings fell, the entire community was transfixed by what was happening 2.4 miles to the south. Everybody saw it. Everybody heard the continual whoop of sirens and the slow, titanic rumble of the buildings' collapse. Everyone smelled the stink of burned metal and concrete and all the other substances that had been turned to vapor at temperatures approaching one thousand degrees centrigrade; it lingered in the air for weeks. Everybody had a memory.

"At 8:45 a.m. on September 11, 2001, I was writing thank you cards for a recent birthday party. A morning news program was droning in the background when the first news of a plane hitting one of the World Trade Center towers was broadcast. I quickly grabbed a few rolls of film and my camera and went to the [Westbeth] rooftop . . . When I first saw the huge holes in both the north and west side of the North Tower, I knew that it had been hit by a large plane. The few of us that were on the roof thought it had been an accident, although someone wondered if it was the work of a terrorist. I decided to head downtown on my bike, had walked about ten steps when someone cried, 'Oh my god. Another plane.' I turned to see the second tower get hit. I froze. I couldn't move. Couldn't shoot."

—DAVID PLAKKE, photographer

"And all of a sudden there's a second one, and we just stood there and watched it *melt*. Just like when you put sugar in your tea and it just melts down.'

—EDITH STEPHEN, dancer and videographer

"There's that smell again . . . That acrid burning steel smell has traveled all the way up here, about a mile and a quarter, and here I am down on Washington Street, having that same strange experience of looking down a very familiar site down south and there's something missing from the sky. It must be like someone who's lost a loved one and they come home and they're not there anymore. It's the absence that's strange, not being able to see those familiar tall towers. Not the sight, the absence. The aftermath signs: the orange parking cones all along the street, security people that didn't use to be here. And that strange smoke, which is kind of like its skeleton."

—SUSANNAH KELLY, visual artist

"I didn't at first know what I wanted to say or do, but I lived it . . . Walking the streets, not seeing too many cars. The bridges were very carefully watched. Everything was being watched. The overhead flight of the jets. We were constantly bombarded with the realization that 9/11 [had] happened and could happen again. And of course there was the terrible sorrow of all those lives lost, and knowing how they were lost. And for me the firemen. I couldn't believe that many firemen went with those buildings . . .

"When you lived on the West Side of Manhattan below Fourteenth Street, you began to smell every day the World Trade Center. The electric, the smoke. I knew every time they found bodies. Even in February and March of the following year, I knew every time. I could walk down to West Street and wait for the ambulances being escorted by police cars because they found bodies."

—THERESA KING, photographer

"After 9/11 I just wanted to do pretty pictures of flowers or something innocuous. Something that wouldn't have any emotional content or that could possibly be visionary. I thought, 'Yeah, I'll do decorative work or something.' So I just didn't work."

—JOAN HALL, collagist

"All artists felt, having seen the horrible sight of the people jumping off of the building—that was the—one of the most painful things: our helplessness when we were up on the roof of Westbeth. And the artists extended their arms out, screaming, an attempt to stop the people from jumping. But we were too far away. We couldn't prevent them."

—KAREN SANTRY, painter and illustrator

On Quality

THE PIECES JACK DOWLING HUNG with such care in the Westbeth gallery had very little in common with the art you'd see in the galleries that began opening in Chelsea in the mid-nineties. Over the next decade those galleries advanced west into the shadow of the High Line, the casually lovely walking park built on the remains of the old elevated railroad that had once transfixed the third floor of Westbeth's A building like a tunnel from the past into the future, a future that by the turn of the new century was just more of the past. In 2014, the small, independent galleries would be joined by the Whitney when it moved from its location on Madison Avenue to Gansevoort and West Streets, confirming the Far West Village's ascendence as a showcase for new American and international art. At the 2019 Whitney Biennial, the last before the COVID pandemic, Dowling came upon a wall hung with clocks set to different time zones (Agustina Woodgate's *National Times*, a closed-circuit network of clocks synchronized directly by the power grid). "I thought, 'Okay, that's nice. I could have done that in high school.'" His voice has a shrug in it. He may or may not have noticed that the minute hands of some of the clocks had sandpaper affixed to them so that with each revolution they ground down the numerals on the faces until they would finally be erased.

"I still see Westbeth as the last bastion of the easel crowd, and that's more or less vanished from the art world," Dowling says. "Once Warhol came onto the scene and paintings became museum-sized, and collectors like the Sculls came in and gallery owners and auction houses started driving up the price of art, it ended the small intimate work. There are some extraordinary painters in Westbeth who have always continued to do the work they wanted to do, and they intellectually understood that this was what they had to do. They just couldn't adopt a new style."

In the catalog of the 2012 Whitney Biennial, the last one held during Dowling's tenure as director of Westbeth's Visual Arts Committee, is a sculpture by Cameron Crawford called *making water storage revolution making water storage revolution*, a cumbersome frame of struts, panels, and folded muslin that was deliberately constructed as an embodiment of useless labor—work, in the artist's words, "that does not benefit the body, be it one's own body or the larger social body." It's ugly, but the ugliness is a secondary condition of uselessness, since labor that produced something of beauty couldn't really be said to be useless, could it? There's a piece by the artist K8 Hardy that appears to be an ad in a fashion magazine but one in which the model is obscured by fragments of other photos that were layered on top of her in a shimmering palimpsest. Another entry was Michael Robinson's *These Hammers Don't Hurt Us*, in which footage of Michael Jackson dancing in a gilded halter and a black Egyptian wig segues into scenes from Elizabeth Taylor's 1963 epic *Cleopatra*, a movie whose ruinous expense made it that era's embodiment of useless labor.

The catalog for Westbeth's holiday show that same year featured a colorful linocut of a red SUV parked on the edge of what might be a barge or one of the piers that served as stages for the queer sexual utopia of twenty-five years before. Some gulls swoop and strut in the foreground, and Westbeth's silhouette can be seen at the upper left. In holiday shows from previous years, there's work that is less illustrative, including an explosive abstract titled *Red Earth* by Dowling's friend Beverly Brodsky, done almost entirely in reds and oranges.

Language often fails when we attempt to explain visual art or even describe what it looks like. "The hardest thing in writing about painting is just how do you describe it," Dowling says. "Beverly did not set out in this painting to title it, say, *Forest Aflame*. You don't want to lead the viewer down the wrong path but allow them to take in the work on their own terms.

"But there are times that that slight suggestion will connect with the viewer's reaction and engagement. It is really important to see the actual work before making comment on it from a photograph. All of my life I had seen photos of *Sunflowers* by Van Gogh. I always responded in a positive way. *But* when I saw the actual painting, the photos became pieces of paper with color on them. The paint strokes, the carving out of the surface to enhance light and shadow in a normal day are all missing until you stand in front of the real thing.

"*Red Earth* would be Beverly's way of leading the viewer with the slightest of hints away from a confused reaction. The surface of her work, as in the Van Gogh, is extremely important because you see and engage with brushwork; the slightest tint of a color lost in the photo but glowing in the original."

It's true that even in the photograph, if you look at it long enough, you become conscious of the brushstrokes, some of which sweep horizontally across the canvas, though most of the movement is vertical or diagonal. You see where the red and orange darken or pale and also the places where those colors are overlaid with sinuous twists of greenish black that could be seen as smoke or veins of some mineral.

If you compared the art at the Whitney Biennial to that in the Westbeth holiday show—in 2012 or any other year—which art would you say was better? Maybe "better" ought to be in scare quotes. Put another way, which art would give the viewer more pleasure? Which art would speak to the viewer more urgently, challenge them more profoundly? Could one even assume that the creators of these works had the same viewers in mind? Judged strictly in terms of their aesthetic appeal, Brodsky's paintings were probably more pleasing to look at (probably "pleasing," too, should be placed in quotes). But the pieces from the Whitney were more exciting, more immediate. No need to track brushstrokes like the spoor of some elusive forest creature or the microtonal variations in a field of color. Here were self-annihilating wall clocks, and a doggedly overbuilt monument to uselessness, and a processed photo that portrayed fashion as the delirium of desire and disgust it really is. To become exciting, familiar things were knocked off axis: clocks turned from instruments for recording time into instruments for erasing it, the fashion photo revealed as a stylish prank on the viewer who expected to see objectification and got it in spades.

Of course, terms such as "pleasing," "exciting," "illustrative," and "abstract" all require context. The print of the SUV on the waterfront might be apprehensible as iconography but have associations that would be apparent only to longtime Westbeth residents. For one thing, in 2012 a visitor from outside the neighborhood probably wouldn't realize that it had been many, many years since any of the nearby piers had been sound enough to park a vehicle on: in 2012, even a Mini Cooper would have plunged through their rotten planks. This meant that the image either harkened back to a vanished past or referenced an alternate present in which New York has been spared the decay that until recently was the city's signature. (Of course, today you could land a small aircraft on those piers, as long as you took due diligence to clear them of pedestrians, dog-walkers especially.) An image that seems apprehensible might turn out to be more opaque than a self-referential abstract painting.

Another measure of an artwork's quality might be how much one was willing to pay for it, that "one" sometimes being an individual buyer, sometimes a government or a foundation or a corporation, the purchases guided by a credentialed art consultant or two. The few K8 Hardy photos I saw listed at auction or on dealers' websites have prices in the $1,500 range, while a selection of Beverly Brodsky's paintings on the website of Saatchi Art are priced from $20,000 to $25,000; *Red Earth* is listed at

$23,750. Van Gogh's ineffable *Sunflowers* sold for close to $40 million in 1987. Of course those prices also depend on the condition of the art market, and that can be unstable. With the market's major downturn in 2023–2024, a painting by Allison Zuckerman that had sold for $212,500 a few years before resold for only $20,160, a 91 percent drop in value; she learned about it from an Instagram post while she was on her honeymoon. The bust has been especially hard on younger painters that the industry categorizes as "ultracontemporary" and mostly reflects the misgivings of collectors who paid large sums for their work during the earlier boom and now fear they won't recoup their investment.

So it makes sense that some artists balk at letting this abstract thing called "the market" determine the value of their work. At the 2021 Frieze fair in New York, the Argentinian conceptualist Agustina Woodgate, whose clock installation at the Whitney Jack Dowling dismissed as high school, sold prepared one dollar bills with their markings sanded off so that they were essentially ghost money. Each bill sold for $200. The price was debited from the buyer's bank account when they inserted their card into an onsite ATM—it was labeled ADM for "automated dealer machine"—that then dispensed the currency. To complete the transaction, one paid an additional $1,800 for a certificate of authenticity; this step of the sale was executed by an actual dealer. "The artist works with theories of value, and the idea of creating new value," Woodgate's gallerist explained. In a final coup of value-creation, the artist offered three of the ADMs themselves for $35,000 apiece. The project was called *Don't Trust, Verify*, which happens to be a slogan used by Bitcoin.

On Catastrophe
2012

IN THE COURSE OF ONE week, the tenth hurricane of the 2012 Atlantic hurricane season ripped through Jamaica, Haiti, the Dominican Republic, Cuba, the Bahamas, and Puerto Rico before making landfall near Brigantine, New Jersey, on October 29. Most of the people who lived through it refer to it as Hurricane or Superstorm Sandy, but at the time it struck the Northeast it was technically a post-tropical cyclone with hurricane-strength winds that at times reached one hundred miles an hour. The storm flooded the New York subway system and all but one of the tunnel roads leading into Manhattan; the Battery Park station was submerged beneath eighty feet of water. The storm sent parked cars bobbing down the streets of the financial district and the Lower East Side. It cut power to 2.2 million customers. It destroyed thousands of homes and a quarter of a million vehicles and caused some $32 billion in damage. It caused the deaths of forty-four New Yorkers.

On the West Side, the Hudson surged over its banks and across the highway to pour through the windows of Westbeth's basement with such force that it burst interior walls. The boiler and oil tank were destroyed, the power went out, and with it the elevators, heat, and water. Some tenants didn't get their electricity back for two weeks. The building stank of unflushed toilets and rotting food. Black mold blossomed on the walls. The studio spaces in the basement were submerged for weeks, and much of the work inside them—paintings, sculpture, photos, prints—was destroyed. Film and recording studios were destroyed. The sets and costumes of the Martha Graham Dance Company, which had just moved into the old Merce Cunningham space, were destroyed, at a loss of $4 million.

"If they didn't have insurance, it was gone," says George Cominskie. "There was nothing we could do for that. Some of the art we could bring up. We had it drying out in the courtyard. The gallery, we canceled the show there, and we were putting art in there to dry out. And then we made arrangements with art conservators to come in and give people tips on what they needed to do and, in some instances, actually do it for them. And then we arranged for a warehouse in New Jersey to store the art until they could find some place to put it."

At the time Sandy hit, Cominskie was in Ohio volunteering for the Obama campaign, so he organized much of Westbeth's relief efforts remotely. No one in the building had working phone or internet, but every day the resident committee's vice president would travel uptown to where she could get cell service and call Cominskie with any messages that tenants wanted to get out, then he'd post them on social media. In this way people in the building were connected with friends and relatives who could take them in or send them needed supplies. In a gesture of solidarity with his childhood neighbors, Vin Diesel paid for hot meals and water to be delivered to elderly tenants stranded on the upper stories. Isabel Borgatta, a sculptor in her nineties who lived on the eleventh floor, remembered, "I would be in here, lying in bed, and a flashlight would shine in my face—suddenly someone who had been looking for a person in an open apartment. And they'd have a supper."

Not everyone who got help was grateful. Roger Braimon, who would become WARC's president after Cominskie stepped down in 2017, had a neighbor yell at him because a little water sloshed out of the bucket he was hauling upstairs. Braimon is a sweet man with the shy decency of Jimmy Stewart. But at times his sweetness gave out. "There was one bakery open, I want to say on Twenty-Eighth Street and Ninth Avenue, a bodega. I walked all the way there, got two dozen donuts, walked it up to the ninth floor and started to give them out to the tenants. And the first one I gave some to said, 'Do you have any blueberry? Can I take three for when my husband comes back?' I said, 'You know what? Just take them all.' I didn't want to deal with that."

The basement was inaccessible. Artists who tried to check on their studios were threatened with arrest. This may have been for their own protection. The stagnant water that filled the basement was a reeking stew of heating oil, solvents, and sewage. The only people allowed below ground were FEMA workers whose hazmat suits, Christina Maile wrote, made them look "like giant earless bunnies."

Still, at least one artist wouldn't get with the program: Karen Santry, a painter and illustrator who taught at the Fashion Institute of Technology (FIT). Santry applied for an apartment at Westbeth when it opened in 1970 but had to wait twenty years until the Admissions Committee found a space for her in 1990. Now in her early seventies, she's a petite, energetic woman with a style that's part goth and part Dr. Seuss; she looks like an exclamation point. Her eight-hundred-square-foot jewel box of an apartment has a wraparound sleep platform and tall windows that give her an uninterrupted view of Manhattan from the Empire State Building to the Lower East Side. The decor includes a taxidermy swan that used to be an exhibit at the American Museum of Natural History; she keeps it beside the sofa. "I'm not a wanton person," Santry says with ironic understatement. "Just a nice teacher, a quiet little person."

While studying for an MFA at the University of Pennsylvania, she was hired to accompany David Bowie on the Ziggy Stardust tour of the East Coast and make drawings of him and his band. "He was extremely nice, and I was so blessed that I didn't understand who he was or that he was so famous or what was going on. Because I just acted naturally with him. He was the nicest. He was staying at the Bellevue Stratford, so I would come in the morning and draw as they practiced and rehearsed. And Mick Jagger and Bianca were with them, and they read me the riot act. They said, 'There's no hanky-panky here, there's no fooling around. We lie about drinking and drugs and alcohol, and we trash the hotel afterwards just to make it look like we're out of our minds. But we want to get ahead of everybody else, so we're very strict here. And you better be on time.' So I said, 'Oh, absolutely, such a privilege to draw you all.'"

Jagger later arranged one of the first gallery showings of Santry's work.

While still in her twenties, she got a teaching job at FIT, a state university that serves as a feeder school for much of the city's fashion industry. A mentor advised her to tell her mother it was the school with a "gold-lined coffin," and her mother was ecstatic, understanding that he was referring to its excellent retirement plan. "I just walked in all dressed—high heels, long black velvet dress, jet-blue-black long hair, long nails—and ended up in the Illustration department," Santry recalls. In the beginning, the job paid so little that she had to waitress at Max's Kansas City. Eventually, she started a company that licensed fashion illustrations. This necessitated renting two studios in Westbeth's basement, one for the company and its ever-growing archive, a second for her own work. The commercial space held thousands of dollars' worth of drawings and a mannequin that cost $4,000. In the second studio, she was painting a series of life-size portraits of famous Kabuki actors on wood cutouts. The project had been approved by the Japanese embassy, which regards those actors as national treasures. Both studios were flooded when Sandy hit on October 29.

At first, Santry didn't realize the extent of the damage. Only a few people in Westbeth seemed to have understood that the building was at risk and moved their work out of the basement. Santry's apartment was on the tenth floor, and like many of her neighbors, she spent the first two weeks after the storm marooned. "We lived days and days and days upstairs, never going anywhere for days and days. Luckily, we didn't know what had happened because the impact of it probably would have wiped us out. We couldn't imagine how long it would last. We had no idea because there was no television and there was no radio, no electricity. We just stared at the ceiling and cleaned up our apartments. And then we'd try to sneak out in the hall to talk to people. 'Have you heard anything? Have you seen anything?' And then the rumor started that became very unnerving: 'You know, the sculpture studio's all underwater.' And I said, 'Oh, that's not possible, of course it's not underwater.' I was in denial for a long time.

"It was George [Cominskie] who slowly began telling people, letting them know in small, delicate doses, in the nicest way: 'Karen, we're very concerned about your studio.'

"And I said, 'Oh, it can't be because we've got nice walls and everything. No, I don't think so. I think you're wrong.' So there's a complete denial, total denial, until finally George took me and said, 'Karen, I think you need to come downstairs.'"

He took her to one of the windows on the street that looked down into the basement. Cominskie warned her of what she was about to see. Santry interrupted him. "Wait a minute, I've got all these drawings that were supposed to go to the Whitney Museum!" Cominskie asked her, "Now, where would those drawings be?" and she replied, "Don't worry, George, they were in my studio." She remembers that he winced. He told her, "You're going to have to take a look at this." And so he held Santry's hand and said, "You have to be very brave."

"And I looked and there were big paintings, absolutely huge: a knight in shining armor that was done in the style of the old masters, huge, and it came up and spun and then went under. I went, 'Wait, what's it going under? What is that?' And George gently said, 'That's water.' But I said, 'Why is water in the studio? I don't get this.' See, my brain couldn't even understand. Everything was just churning around. I said, 'Where are the walls? Something's wrong here.' And little by little they broke it to us."

Santry ran into an artist she knew named Charlie. He was crying. "I said, 'Charlie, what's the matter?' He said, 'Our studios don't even exist.'"

More time passed. Some two weeks after the hurricane, she was visited by a friend named Richard Holly, a large man—she describes him as "portly"—who was popular at FIT as a character model. "He was the ideal person to hire to be with, let's say the mermaids, and he'd be a sea captain, and the girls would have on their mermaid costumes and the whole bit, and we would be drawing that." She persuaded him to go downstairs with her to check on the state of her paintings. They crept down at night. The guard manning the Washington Street exit was dozing in his chair.

As a teenager Santry had been a practiced swimmer, good enough to have tried out for the 440-meter butterfly in the Olympics. She decided that with the proper protective gear she could swim into the basement. She took Holly with her to Paragon Sports, and together they purchased two wet suits, along with fins and full face masks. She told a sales clerk: "'We want to get in that water, and we've got to swim.' They said, 'What place has water in the basement?' And I explained, and then somebody else yelled out, 'Oh, everybody's got water in the basement!' And the guy yelled back, 'These two want to go swimming in it!' And they said, 'Well, of course! Go get your stuff.' Nobody at Paragon thought this was weird."

Santry, small and wispy, and the three-hundred-plus-pound Holly stuffed themselves into their formfitting wet suits and fins.

"So, Richard and I are upstairs. We get completely dressed. The elevators don't work so we go down. You know how you do, you're thinking but you're not thinking? The stupidest things we did! We should have carried the fins under our arm! We had them on and we went [she makes flopping sounds] all the way down, holding on to the rails. Why didn't I take them off and just walk down the stairs? But that's what we did. And we went down the stairs, the full ten flights. There was nobody at the front desk, not a soul. So, we went [she mimes tiptoeing] *doo-doo-doot*! And then we waited, and sure enough the guard was asleep, so we simply walked by him and went down."

The water was lapping against the stairs. They waded into it. It was jet black. Westbeth had been without power for fifteen days. At a certain point the floor dropped away beneath their feet and they began to swim. "We weren't dirty because we actually had masks and scuba things. It smelled horrible, but we didn't care. We wanted to see, and we can see a little bit because—this is very, very bad, what we saw, but we didn't know it was bad."

There was a buzzing sound overhead. Something sparked in the gloom.

"All of a sudden, we heard screams, extreme screams. Screaming, screaming, screaming coming from outdoors. Then the guard yells, 'Oh my god, oh my god!' What happened was they turned the lights on! So, the electric was going through, and we're going into the water that was hitting all this stuff. And we realized: 'Oh my god, we gotta get out of here because it could catch on fire or explode!'

"And so we quickly went as fast as we could. I had to swear for the rest of my life never to say the name of the guard. He saw me, he said, 'I'm gonna kill you, Santry!' As we were walking up the stairs: 'What the fuck did you do, you're gonna get me fired!' I say, 'I'm sorry, I'm sorry.' 'Take your stupid things off your feet! Get out of here, run!' And water was all over the place, it smelled awful. He whipped his jacket off, trying to clean the floor. He said, 'Get out of here before the building explodes!' So we ran up the stairs, hysterical, took our wet suits off, just left them on the floor inside the apartment, and I said, 'Quick, we got to get out of the building. It could explode.' We run down the stairs and we run up the street to—what is the exact address of that wonderful photography store on Ninth Avenue? B&H. We were so scared we ran to B&H!" It was more than a mile away.

A few days later she began to feel dizzy and went to an emergency room, where she was told that her heartbeat was erratic. At her doctor's urging, she was fitted with a pacemaker. But she never regretted her brief secret dive. "I just wanted to get my work back more than anything in the world. I felt like a mama, like, 'Give me back my work, my babies!'"

Ten years later she was still restoring the damaged Kabuki paintings, each five to six feet tall, mounted on rosewood cutouts that make them larger than life-size. The figures enact the *kata* and *mie*, the stylized gestures and freeze-takes that actors traditionally strike at the end of a scene. The folds and contours of the cutouts' garments are rendered in voluptuous detail; one can almost feel the weight of layered silk.

Santry pointed out a mannequin head on which she had draped a shaggy crimson wig; the red was so intense that it seemed fluorescent. Shortly before his death in 2016, David Bowie had come to visit her in her studio. He'd recognized the wig. "He said that's what he'd [used] to design his Ziggy and the Spiders from Mars outfit."

After Sandy, the federal government awarded Westbeth a $40 million Build It Back grant that paid for new boilers and electrical panels and helped replace much of the century-old plumbing. The courtyard that had flooded with such alarming speed had been excavated and shored up with new beams. But the grant was running out, and a lot remained to be done.

"I kind of sneak around and hide that I'm still working on [the Kabuki], because they take so long to fix," says Santry. "I want to fix them. And it's been years, but they are getting fixed. If it's the last thing I do with my life, I'm going to fix [them]."

EDWARD FIELD AND NEIL DERRICK were in Berlin during the storm and didn't return to the building until the power was back up and the elevators were running again. The most visible evidence of the catastrophe was the wet artworks that had been rescued from the basement and laid out in the courtyard to dry. "They were all moldy," Field says, "and our windows were open because it was warm. The building was full of mold spores, you couldn't escape them, so it wasn't such a great idea to come home." Derrick had eczema in his feet, and the mold spores got into the rough, irritated skin, which opened up in lesions, and the lesions turned into—or maybe turned out to be—a rare type of cancer called cutaneous lymphoma, which led to his death in 2018. "The doctors I don't think ever understood," Field says. "They'd say you can't get [lymphoma] that way, but I did research, and a dermatologist in Brazil says, yes, you can. So, I know that Hurricane Sandy killed him." They'd been together more than fifty years.

On Catastrophe
2012–2013

BARTON BENEŠ DIED IN MAY of 2012, before Hurricane Sandy was even a corkscrew of warm air over the Atlantic. Smells and inconveniences aside, he might have actually enjoyed the homely and bizarre flotsam the storm cast up that could be used in future reliquaries. The North

Dakota Museum of Art had once commissioned him to design a donor wall, for which members sent Beneš objects that commemorated the devastating Red River flood in 1997. There'd been a collar belonging to a cat that had died trapped in a heating vent, a tire from a capsized truck: Beneš cut it into slices like a pizza.

He'd been sick a long time. He took so many medications for AIDs and AIDS-related conditions that he started using them in art pieces, the way he'd used his infected blood. He glued the pastel pills and capsules onto an artist's palette, where from a distance they looked like daubs of paint, and loaded them into the chamber of a gumball machine that spat some out when you put in a nickel. He strung capsules on a cord made of tightly rolled dollar bills and called the resulting piece *Talisman*. What killed him, however, wasn't AIDS but COPD, chronic obstructive pulmonary disease, which he'd had since he was in his fifties. When *The New York Times* identified AIDS as the cause of death in Beneš's obit, his brother made the paper print a correction. Bob Brier recalls, "Barton made a very big point when he was dying, to all of us, 'I'm not dying of AIDS. It's the COPD.' That's what he said always. He somehow felt it was better he was dying of that." Someone might interpret this as evidence that, all his art to the contrary, Beneš still saw AIDS as shameful. But you could also take it to mean that he saw the disease as an ordinary misery, something you could live with until you died of something else. Which by 2012 was what—assuming one had access to decent medical care and the wherewithal to pay for it—AIDS had become.

Beneš had a vexed relationship with his oxygen tank. It kept him alive and gave him an excuse to leave a party that was starting to bore him. But he often got tangled in the oxygen hose. Once, in a fit of rage, he cut it into inch-long pieces only to realize he had no spare. With his remaining breath, he had to call up a hospital or all-night pharmacy and ask for a new hose. When asked what had happened to the old one, he explained, "My dog ate it." He used the sections of rubber tubing in one of his last pieces. Somewhere you can hear Tosca singing "Vissi d'arte."

In 2006, Beneš had a double lung reduction that he hoped might give him another five years of life. "He always had a philosophy," Warren says. "'The longer that I live, the longer that I hang on, the more and more things will be found that will make things better and allow [me] to live a little longer.'" Still, eventually he was back in the hospital. Usually it was Joe Lovett's job to take him; as a doctor's husband, he understood how to speak with other doctors. "I remember once, he was being wheeled out and the doctor asked [irritably], 'Well, what do you want me to do next time?' And I realized that he just saw this very old man in trouble." Lovett called a meeting between the doctor and Beneš's close friends and executors and urged the doctor to help get his patient home to Westbeth to make art in the time he had left. "If something happens and he's going to be on a respirator, don't do it. But if you can pull him through for a couple of months, he's ecstatic."

Beneš's friends rallied around him. "He had a gift for friendship—more than a gift," says Lovett. "He was brilliant at friendship." For decades they'd phoned each other every morning. "We would tear each other *apart*, viciously. One of our routines was to be as cleverly mean as we possibly could, and we loved it. You'd make a remark and he would go"—Lovett closes his eyes and shudders theatrically—"'*Ooooh-ooooh-ooooh!*' And then he'd come back. Barton used to complain that whenever he was on the phone with an operator, they'd think he was a woman and call him Miss." He laughs. "It upset him terribly."

Brier says, "Even when Barton was in the hospital, there was always a party going on, so to speak, a bunch of us hanging out and having a good time, even though he was dying. I remember him saying to me when we were at the hospital, he looks at me and says, 'I'm okay with this. I'm ready to go.'"

In the last month of his life, he arranged for the full group of *Brenda* ribbons to travel to the North Dakota Museum of Art. Warren went over to the apartment to lay out the pieces for shipping, but he could only find 199; the two hundredth ribbon was missing. Beneš thought he might have loaned it to someone, but illness was affecting his memory and he couldn't say who had it. He instructed his brother to cut out an extra ribbon and roll it in some ashes he had in a closet—not Brenda's ashes, but someone else's, maybe even those of a stranger whose friends or lover had sent them to Beneš to turn into a memento mori. "That's the two hundredth ribbon," Warren says. "It's a slightly different color than the others."

Maybe because of that show or because the museum had been the only venue in the US that had the audacity to display the *Lethal Weapons*, Beneš agreed to donate his apartment to it. "I've got all this stuff," he once complained to Laurel Reuter, the museum's curator. "What am I gonna *do* with it?" Reuter remembers telling him, " 'Oh, give it to me. I'll make a twentieth-century period room, an artist's studio as a period room.' And that was it. We never had a contract. We began going in and photographing. A couple-three times I had people photograph it as it was, and then a couple staff members saw it and that was what we used when we built it here." The apartment was dismantled and brought west in two twenty-four-foot trucks, then reassembled with exquisite care. Only the kitchen and bathroom are missing. The exhibit is called *Barton's Place*. There was some dispute between the curator and Beneš's family as to whether the bequest is supposed to be temporary or permanent and whether it includes the entirety of the artist's vast collection of African, Egyptian, and Amazonian art or just the pieces he kept at Westbeth. At this writing, *Barton's Place* is still housed in the museum, on the campus of the University of North Dakota. "The apartment embodies all the quirks and the interests of someone who's very involved in the popular life," Reuter says. "It should be preserved as an actual work of art." It's like a mini Temple of Dendur, housing the relics of a figure many Dakotans (and not a few New Yorkers) would find as exotic as Tutankhamun.

For all its fidelity, the exhibit contains one item that was placed there only after Beneš's death. This is a small pillow covered in kilim fabric. It rests on a Chinese opium bed facing a television set, and it's filled with Beneš's ashes, mixed per his instructions with those of his mother, who died in 2006. The TV plays a loop of episodes of *Law & Order*, and although Beneš watched the show, it wasn't the one he stipulated in his instructions to Reuter. That would have been *Judge Judy*, which both he and his mother adored. The museum couldn't get permission to use it.

The opening of *Barton's Place* in November 2013 was also a memorial. Most of the people who'd loved him came. His Westbeth neighbor Joan Hall flew out to Fargo and was then driven to Grand Forks with some of his other friends in a limo provided by the hotel. "It was one of those disco limos with the chandelier and unlimited champagne for an hour and a half as we rode to the opening. We were all pretty drunk by the time we got there. And then when we got there, of course, they had the room. It was just as if I'd walked into Barton's room, I couldn't believe it. Uncanny. Everybody always sat at this table that he had, this long table, after the entrance. It was beautifully finished. And I remember that at the memorial I sat at the table and I had my drink . . . it was champagne, not a martini . . . and I was fine. But all of a sudden I hear this voice over my shoulder, and it sounds just like Barton, and it's saying," she imitated his rasp, "'Use the *coastuh*!'" She laughed. "He did that when you were at the table. And I lost it. That was it, the flood thing. I sat there and I just wept. And Warren came over and held my hand and he wept as well."

Everyone left to go on to the memorial. Hall lingered in the room. "So I went to the bed, and I picked up that pillow, because I knew what pillow it was, and I just hugged that pillow. That was my goodbye."

On Trying to Say Something

TO MAKE JUDGMENTS ABOUT THE quality of a work of art, don't you have to know what art is for? Is it supposed to be beautiful? Is it supposed to be new? Is it supposed to make a statement, even if that statement is just about itself? *I am a bunch of paint brushed onto a piece of canvas hung on a wall. Look at me!*

Of course, what art is for would be different for a painter in Florence in the high Renaissance and one in Montmartre in 1915 or one hanging out at the Cedar Tavern when Jack Dowling was studying at the Cooper Union in 1953. It's probably different for Cameron Crawford, the creator of the prodigy of useless labor that was shown at the 2012 Whitney Biennial, and for K8 Hardy, whose artist's statement announces, "I think of my basic gesture as the American middle finger flying in the air of defiance." Saint Augustine thought that all created things had been placed here to reflect the glory of their Creator. The Romantics may have had this in mind when they began to speak of art as an expression of the artist, who imposed their will on sluggish, inchoate matter like a rider bridling a stubborn horse. But artists were signing their work as far back as the early

Renaissance. "Albrecht Dürer made this," or "Giotto di Bondone painted me." That, too, was a statement. It may have recorded the moment when Dürer or Giotto was struck by what in Italian is called *la prima idea*—the first, or original, idea—like a tree by lightning, with such violence that he had to make some visual notation of it in the instant and affirm that the inspiration had come to *him*, to him alone, it had been aimed at him by whatever god transfixes human beings in that manner. Or the point of that signature may have been no more exalted than that of a dry cleaner's ticket. Without a name, what was to keep some other, inferior artist from getting the commission?

Five hundred years later, the authentication would eclipse the work when the NFT *Everydays: The First 5000 Days* sold at auction for $69 million. This sum didn't represent the value of the artwork, which Beeple assembled from parts of previous compositions in his *Everyday* series. It represented the value of the files, recorded on blockchain, that verify the work's authorship and provenance. In theory, at least, the artwork could be duplicated. The artist's digital signature could not. Supposedly, that was what made it valuable.

I HAVEN'T SEEN THE CATALOGS of all the Westbeth holiday shows. I'd guess they have one thing in common with the catalogs of every Whitney Biennial, back to when the museum was located on the Upper East Side within a short walk of Dolce & Gabbana and Max Mara, which made it convenient to do some shopping on one's way home, and back before that, to when it was housed in some converted row houses on West Eighth Street.

All the art is attributed to specific artists.

A big difference between those catalogs is that the artists who showed at Westbeth were a lot older than the ones at the Whitney. Even in 2009, 60 percent of Westbeth's tenants were over sixty years old; 30 percent were over seventy. The median age of the artists in the 2019 Whitney Biennial was thirty-seven, one year younger than at the previous exhibition. Are younger artists better than older ones? If only by virtue of physiology— those elastic muscles and purring nervous systems, the metabolisms that barely pause as they alchemize food into energy—they are likely to be stronger and more vital, more eager, more adaptable. They're more ambitious, they have something to prove. They can code and build robots. And in an arts system where the vapor barrier between artist and artwork has all but vanished, young artists make hotter commodities because along with everything else their stories are fresher. Barring some catastrophic bust of the market as a whole, their prices have nowhere to go but up.

One problem with old artists is that we already know their stories. If we don't know them, the assumption is they weren't worth knowing in the first place. Which, from the perspective of the market, makes their art less desirable. When he was directing the Westbeth gallery, Jack Dowling would always buy some of the work at the holiday show "just to get a red dot on the wall." Some pieces he'd keep, some he'd gift to friends. The walls of his tenth-floor apartment were almost entirely covered with paintings, drawings, and lithographs he'd purchased over the years. "In my early years there were people who'd come to an artist's studio with a little money. They'd buy the work as part of their cultural development. But there's a whole shift in who buys unknown painters, painters without a name." Part of his vision for the gallery was to keep "older artists engaged with their creative selves," to give them the assurance that even if they no longer had gallery representation, their work would still be seen. "Without the idea of being able to show your work somewhere, you don't have a goal."

On the internet one morning I watched an adorable video of an elderly Indian flying fox that has reached the advanced age of thirty-three. It can no longer fly, but its caregivers at the bat sanctuary regularly walk it around the premises, holding it up so it can flap its wings for a while. Afterward, it gets a treat of fresh fruit. A caption says something like, "This old bat is still living his glory days." I don't want to see the Westbeth gallery as a sanctuary where old bats are held aloft by other old bats so they can revisit the sensation of being airborne. (I'm allowed to say this because I too am an old bat.) But it's hard not to see it in those terms as long as one thinks of art as an arena of purely individual achievement. In that arena the artist stands alone on their pedestal, arms lifted in triumph, the kind that's measured purely in sales and commissions, in residencies and shows, in *Artforum* cover stories.

Of course, this is how we've seen art for centuries, at least since its practitioners started signing their canvases, then measuring themselves by the patronage of the rich and highborn or by a place of honor above the altar. "My pure intention . . . has been not to gain praise for myself as a writer but as craftsman to praise the industry and revive the memory of those who, having given their life and adornment to these professions, do not deserve to have their names and their works wholly left, even as they were, the prey of death and of oblivion." So Giorgio Vasari addressed his patron Cosimo de' Medici in the original dedication to *The Lives of the Artists*, making a claim for his subjects as individuals deserving of honor in their own time and remembrance after it.

For thousands of years before that, however, art was mostly a collective or communal enterprise. Certainly this was true of those works so massive or intricate that they required the labor of entire kingdoms: the great pyramids, the Gothic cathedrals of Reims and Chartres or the Byzantine church of Hagia Sophia, whose immense gilded vault so overawed the delegates of Vladislav of Kiev that they "no longer knew whether we were in heaven or on earth," and on hearing their reports the king converted his nation to the Orthodox faith on the spot. But even pieces small enough to be fashioned by a single person, a length of dyed cloth or a wooden statue with cowrie shells for eyes, reflected communal standards of beauty, common notions of what the work of art was *for*. Ogotemmêli, an elder of the Dogon of Mali, explained his society's aesthetics for a French anthropologist: "The mat . . . on which the woman works is a symbol of that of the first human couple. The craft of pottery is like a person on a mat. In moulding the clay the woman is imitating the work of God, when he modelled the earth and the first couple. She is creating a being, and the round pot is like a head resting on the mat, a head or a womb. A pot without ornament symbolizes a man, a pot with two small breasts a woman."

As a consequence, such art—the art of the Dogon or the Kwakiutl or the Maya and Olmecs or the art of medieval Europe—may seem to lack originality, but in sacred art originality is beside the point. It may even be blasphemous. It was for the gods to be original. The artist's—that is, the human artist's—charge is to be accurate or, a slightly different word expressing the same general idea, *faithful*.

I don't know if any of the artists Dowling selected for the Westbeth holiday shows was trying to reenact some primal instance of creation. I recall nothing to that effect in any of the artists' statements. The work I saw didn't seem archaic; some of it might have been called old-fashioned. A lot of it, like Beverly Brodsky's *Red Earth*, was abstract expressionist. For a long time abstract expressionism was considered the first authentic American art, though surely this reflects a limited idea of America. More than any art that had come before, it was concerned with freedom. In his essay "A Kind of Sharing," the great art writer John Berger points to a line in a catalog statement from the 1940s: "Only now has there been a concerted effort to abandon the tyranny of the object and the sickness of naturalism to enter within consciousness." He takes the thought further: "Entering into consciousness—an obscure phrase—meant trying to be oneself on canvas, without the props of a single familiar reference, and thus to be free of rhetoric, history, convention, other people, safety, the past." Much of the art of the communitarian past, whether in Western Europe or Africa or East Asia, referenced nature, but when Jackson Pollock was asked about nature's significance for his art, he replied, "I am nature." The sovereign individual artist had taken nature's place: I want to say usurped it. This wasn't too audacious a thing to imagine when just a few years previously, human beings had succeeded in making a bomb that in a matter of seconds destroyed a city and tens of thousands of its inhabitants.

Westbeth's holiday shows thus embodied a peculiar irony. The works expressed the self-assertiveness of a postwar America that had elevated individualism into a national cult. Their makers had striven for originality, and Dowling had arranged the pieces to emphasize their variety. At the same time, the shows' overall ethos was communal, like that of the markets where artists sold their work in the Middle Ages, the kind you still see today in Africa and Southeast Asia, where works of a common type are displayed together in seeming defiance of the laws of marketing. Some of this reflected the fact that the artists on display were members of a single community who had lived alongside each other for years and sometimes for decades. But it also reflected Dowling's vision, which was radically democratic: "I wanted to be sure that the gallery did not become something exclusive, where somebody—not myself, but anybody—would decide what could be shown and what could not be shown. I never refused anybody's work. Sometimes there were pieces that were maybe not quite up to par. We don't always know exactly what's our best thing. So sometimes somebody would bring something down that they were all excited about, and I'd seen their other work and realized that maybe that piece is not going to serve them well, that there might be another piece that would serve them better. I had that happen with one artist who brought down three paintings. Two of them were very much alike and not terribly interesting, and the third one was terrific. I said, 'I really can't take the three.' And she said, 'Then put those two in because they're my favorites.' And I said, 'No, we're going to put this one in because that's the best. That represents your work better than the other two do.' And she said, 'Really?' I said, 'Yes.' When the show opened, she came to me and said, 'I'm so glad you picked that painting because everybody is coming up to me and telling me what a marvelous painting it is.'"

His generosity and discernment made him a beloved figure in the building. "Jack changed the whole feeling of the gallery, from a feeling of 'It's good enough' to 'It has to be the best,'" the painter Sheila Schwid said. "Artists who had not been painting for years went back to their studios and made the best work of their lives."

In 2017, Dowling became the first Westbeth Icon. At the ceremony, a younger painter named Joe Cannon remembered putting together his first solo show in the gallery while Dowling was out of town. "I laid out my work along the gallery floors in what seemed like a logical arrangement, and then I panicked. I didn't have enough work. I'd have to leave two of the rooms dark, and that was extremely depressing. The day before the opening, Jack came back. He sized up the situation, told me to trust the strength of my work, and spread it out. He then deftly rearranged everything, allowing each work to breathe and command its own space while simultaneously making each work seem to lead inevitably to the next and to play with and against works in other parts of the gallery. All the rooms were filled. I was amazed at how good he made everything look, seemingly in five minutes."

✳

On Catastrophe
2021

WESTBETH WAS MAKING PREPARATIONS FOR its fiftieth anniversary in May of 2020 when COVID struck New York. The public libraries shut down on March 14, the public schools on March 16, theaters, music venues, and night clubs a day later. On March 22, all nonessential businesses were closed under a PAUSE (Policies that Assure Uniform Safety for Everyone) order from the governor's office. Despite this, the city's infection rate was five times that of the rest of the country; one-third of the nation's recorded cases were in the five boroughs. By the time Westbeth's actual anniversary came around, fifteen thousand New Yorkers had lost their lives to the disease—many bodies were still being shelved in refrigerated trucks since the morgues had quickly become too full to receive them. As befitted a naturally occurring retirement community with a highly vulnerable population, Westbeth was shuttered. Visitors—mostly deliverymen from the supermarket and NYC Fresh and local restaurants—were admitted only as far as the guards' station, where they dropped off food and picked up the money their customers had left for them. The art galleries were empty. The elevators were silent. Most tenants stayed in their apartments. Still, every morning after his yoga practice, Edward Field walked out into the neighborhood and did a mile loop up to the Chelsea Market on Fifteenth Street and back to the building. His legs hurt the whole time. "I went to my vascular doctor, and he said, 'You're too old for treatment, but you'd better keep doing what you're doing. The nursing homes are full of people who can't walk.'" Of course, it was in the nursing homes that people were dying fastest.

Field saw few other pedestrians on his route, not even the young ones who only a few months before had been romping through the Meatpacking District like reality-TV shoppers admitted into a luxury store before opening. He may have walked past the high-rises that had risen along West Street, including the matching slivers of glass, sleek as credit cards, that faced each other on the north and south corners of Perry. They'd opened in 2004 and by now were a familiar part of the scenery. They too were homes to creatives. Lou Reed and Laurie Anderson had lived in them, along with Vincent Gallo, Calvin Klein, Nicole Kidman, and Jean-Georges Vongerichten. And they too had been designed by Richard Meier, now one of the most revered architects in the US. But the buildings were anti-Westbeths, constructed virtually without constraints from the ground up, every tile and plate of glass brand new. There was nothing repurposed about them and nothing remotely meant to instill a sense of community. Every apartment had been built to its owner's specs, and if any two tenants discovered that their flats looked remotely similar, they would probably have a word with their architects.

"Nobody lives there," Field said with certainty. "All those towers along the river are empty. They're for investment purposes only. All the foreign billionaires have bought apartments, but they've never lived in them. It's real estate. *Westbeth* is fabulous real estate. The Meatpacking District is the most expensive real estate in Manhattan."

Like many longtime residents, he and Neil had changed apartments over the years, moving from the one whose radiators used to clang with their neighbor's outbursts of anger or exuberance or whatever it is that moves one to smash golf balls across the room, to one on the fifth floor that was larger but dark and, finally, to his present apartment on the third. The living room was filled with light from the windows that overlook the courtyard on Bank Street. "There are trees outside the window," Field said. "It's simply a wonderful apartment. And the neighbors are dead quiet."

Many things had changed since he moved into Westbeth in 1976. Some hadn't. "It really isn't *that* different," he decided. "The only thing was that everybody got old—the ones that haven't *died*. I'm 95 and I'm one of the oldest people in the building, of the men. There's always a woman who's older. Edith Stephen just turned 101. I saw her on the street a couple of days ago, somebody took her out. So, she can still move. [Stephen, a dancer and choreographer who studied with Martha Graham and José Limón, died in March of 2021.] It is very strange to be this old. Neil died a little over two years ago, so now I'm alone. And that is a *big* difference. You wake up to absence. And the apartment is empty. And you don't have the work to do, it was *a lot* of work taking care of a blind man. I was very good at it.

"The thing is, when you get to my age everybody's dead. I came to realize that when I was interviewed by somebody for a book about May Swenson, who was a very prominent poet in my day, and we talked and talked about all the people who were in the poetry world of that time. And when the interviewer left, I realized that everybody we talked about was dead."

IN THE FALL OF 2020, Jan Harding was visiting Black-Eyed Susan in her apartment in a rare break from the social isolation that was still in force.

"Look at this neighborhood," Susan complained. "It was once so full of artists, who lived in these old houses and rented by the floor. I had a friend who lived on the third floor of one across from us. He loved it because he could put a mural up on the wall and start painting. It was wonderful. But then they kicked all of those people out and they sold those homes for millions of dollars to one family each."

Once a week she went out to buy groceries at a health food store on Seventh Avenue. In the past, her regular market had been the one beneath the old Integral Hatha Yoga studio, one of the first in the city back when yoga was a pursuit of beatniks and religious crackpots. But that store was gone; it had closed even before the pandemic.

The theaters were still dark. Both artists were getting by on government assistance and, in Susan's case, social security. Neither was in imminent danger of losing her home. Mostly they were bored. "I don't know what to do with myself," Susan said. "I always had wonderful eyesight, better than 20/20 vision. But it's going now. I try to read, but the print is too faint. So I do a lot of crossword puzzles."

Harding is in her early fifties, a full generation younger than most of her neighbors. She came in as an actor, supporting herself between shows with restaurant jobs, but in recent years she's begun making sculpture. "I don't sell my sculpture. I've been shown in galleries, but I don't sell it. It's usually very personal, and I'm not trained to be a visual artist." She speaks with the rivet-gun speed and emphasis of a thirties character actor. "Now my acting is a whole other thing. I worked in the avant-garde downtown for next to no money, but I also was a member of Ensemble Studio Theatre, I did Shakespeare at the Public, I did a lot of regional theater. So, I was able to make a living."

This was no longer the case. "The performing arts, we're in trouble," Harding said. Many of the show people she knew had moved up to the country or to other states, even abroad. "Not only for us performing, but for the audience, period. I'm at a loss. They say you can do it on video. No, live is live. When I was visiting my daughter in Chicago, I was driving and I heard live music. And as I passed this house, on the front lawn there were three musicians, and there were about six people in lawn chairs [listening], and I just pulled the car over and rolled down the window and listened, because it was live. When they finished, I clapped. I went off, but then I had to do a loop and I came back. They were packing up, and I said, 'That was beautiful.' 'Yeah,' they said, 'Yeah. We saw you stop.' And I said, 'Just live music.' We're screwed. Anything live, we're screwed."

BY THE TIME JACK DOWLING stepped down from running the Westbeth gallery, the old Superior Ink factory on the corner of West and Bethune had been demolished—over the resistance of much of the neighborhood—and replaced with a seventeen-story condominium building and nine Georgian revival townhouses: the realtor's catalog called them "townhomes." In a gesture at community outreach, representatives of the developer had made a presentation to the Westbeth Residents Committee. They were confused when the artists objected to the green glass tower that was part of the original plan. Dowling explained that the sun bouncing off the glass would flood Westbeth's north-facing studios with green light, making it impossible for the painters to judge their colors. In a small victory for the tenants, the green glass was eighty-sixed.

As far back as his time at Cooper Union, Dowling had been writing notes and brief observations. In the nineties he began writing stories, and over years of patient application, he began publishing some of these in small magazines. All of the work was fiction; he was insistent about that. A story called "John's Trip to Coney Island," begins with John, a sixteen-year-old kid from New Jersey, traveling into New York and ending up at Coney Island. Standing by one of the rides, he is drawn to a tough-looking older boy named Billy, who invites him to come down and visit him. "Come on the el and we can have a beer and then fool around or something." The invitation thrills and frightens him. *What does fool around mean?*

Looking back on this incident as a grown man, the narrator realizes that Billy was his first crush. But a later meeting with him ends badly. It happens at the Astor Bar, where Billy is now a hustler with "a sad aura; a vacancy to his eyes." When John introduces himself and confesses that he once thought he loved him, the older man snaps, "Nobody ever loved me. Fuck off, fairy."

The story is set at least fifty years in the past, and it expresses a vision of homosexuality—not queerness but homosexuality—that is similarly dated, at best a condition, usually a curse. "We have civil rights now," Dowling said, "and hate-crimes laws that aren't always enforced. The bars aren't raided anymore, but there aren't any bars anymore. Nowadays you've still got Boots & Saddles and Stonewall, which is not the Stonewall I went to. It's the Disney version of gay New York. It's not destination time. For the young kids, the internet is destination time. One thing I will say, though: They finally got around to giving gay bars decent bathrooms. They used to be absolute cesspools.

"During the epidemic, gay men started going to gyms to show they weren't sick, and then the marriage thing happened. It completely changed the gay community. There's no cohesiveness anymore. Years ago, somebody standing in line at the ferry asked me, 'Where do the gays go?' And I said, just joking, 'They all go to Montclair, New Jersey.' And that's becoming true."

Much the same thing, Dowling felt, had happened to the New York art world. The obvious culprit was the city's relentlessly climbing real estate prices, which over the past fifty years had driven artists out of SoHo, Tribeca, the East Village, Williamsburg, and Bushwick like game animals harried by beaters from one covert to the next. COVID completed the process. Jack said that 2020 was the fiftieth anniversary of Westbeth's opening. "And we had all sorts of events planned, and they've all been scuttled because of the virus. We can't gather in the lobby or the mailroom, which we always used to do. You see a friend from six feet away, all you can do is wave to them."

Did he think the lockdown was excessive? He shook his head. "If I ever got the virus, it'd be the end of me." He returned to his earlier subject. "In the seventies, if you lived in the creative world of New York City, you'd know everybody. Now you can walk around the city and never see anyone you know. There was a wonderful mix between artists, writers, and theater people. They had a communal bond because they were making things. And if someone had a better gallery or was getting higher prices for their work, it didn't matter because you were all making something. You were making something from yourself."

I SPOKE AND CORRESPONDED WITH Jack over a period of almost a year, and toward the end I felt I had come to know him pretty well, his ambition, his tetchiness, his discernment, his good manners, his love of family, his long-held grudges, his adamantine aloneness. Still, there was a question I felt I ought to ask him. It had to do with Westbeth's criteria for admission and its stipulation that applicants have to be "working artists," artists for whom art-making is an ongoing and primary occupation. When Jack served on the Admissions Committee, he told me, "We'd get artists applying, and I'd look at the dates of their shows and they could be really far back. If it's someone who's seventy years old and they're pumping out art and have shows everywhere, that's fine. In the case of somebody who's sixty-five and they haven't painted since they were forty-five and that's the only reference, or when their last exhibit was twenty years ago . . ." He raised an eyebrow.

But by his own admission, Jack stopped painting around the time he moved into Westbeth: fifty years ago. Would he be admitted if he applied today? It wasn't a question I wanted to ask him. I dreaded asking it. I considered the coward's expedient of asking a third party, Roger Braimon or George Cominskie, who'd known Jack for many years and had served with him on one committee after another. But I figured they'd refuse and would probably tell Jack I'd been asking questions about him behind his back. Moreover, I could imagine what they'd say, and really, it wasn't very different from what I believed myself. Jack described curating as a creative enterprise, involving judgment, composition, and a sense of visual narrative that allows one to assemble works by different artists into what might be called a story. In that respect, it invites comparison with directing a play. Joseph Chaikin had been a director, and nobody would have disputed his right to live in Westbeth.

Theater directors work with companies. Some directors see those companies, or the companies' individual members, as their instruments; some see them as collaborators. Jack worked with other artists. This put him at odds with what most of us—contemporary Americans indoctrinated by popular biographies and movies from *Lust for Life* to *Amadeus, Basquiat, Shirley*, and *Born to Be Blue*—think of when we speak of art: the solitary individual straining at their creation like a strong man lifting barbells over his head. His talent was for combining, arranging, showcasing, counseling. "You see something in people's work that they're not even aware of, but you find it extraordinary, and you tell them, and they may disagree with you, but it may start them thinking."

I ended up posing my question to Jack directly, in an email that in retrospect seems more than a little obsequious. "I don't intend this as a gotcha question and indeed can think of many reasons why you are (and would be) a vital member of the community. But since I'm trying to tell this story as much as possible through your eyes, your words on this subject would be worth a lot more than anything I could say."

This was on February 18, 2021. Two weeks passed without my hearing back from him. His silence was unusual. I worried that for all my assurances, Jack felt that I *had* asked a gotcha question. I wrote an apology, then deleted it, then wrote another and trashed that too. To apologize would be to admit I shouldn't have asked the question, and I couldn't *not* ask it. He might be so offended that he'd retract his permission to use his words, even his story. Early in March, I mentioned him in passing to someone else I was interviewing and was shocked when that person texted me later to tell me that Jack had died on February 4, of COVID-19, as he'd feared he might.

✷

On Catastrophe
2006

EDWARD FIELD WASN'T THE FIRST person to tell me the Meatpacking District is the hottest real estate in Manhattan. We can't know whether its hotness is the result of its loss of function or the cause of that loss. From a practical standpoint, why should a leasing company rent a building to meatpackers—or, in other neighborhoods, ships' chandlers or wholesale florists—when it can get ten times the income renting the same property, cleaned up a little, the brick whitewashed and the floors made skiddy with polyurethane, to artists or hedge-fund managers who want to live like artists, who won't violate noise statutes and stink up the property with blood and offal? Regardless of what initiates it, the process by which a neighborhood becomes fashionable mirrors the process by which an industrial economy gives way to a postindustrial one, the production of things yielding to the stringing together of ones and zeros. When this happens, some of the old, ponderous but useful things become useless but also oddly charming. The maul, the anvil, the two-man crosscut saw, the waxed canvas chore coat, the hand-pulled freight elevator. The three-thousand-square-foot factory loft whose floors still bear the footprint of machines whose names you don't know. Absent their former use, these once-useful things become more valuable.

Sadly, this does not happen to formerly useful people.

DURING THE FIRST YEARS I lived in his apartment, Gay came up from the Eastern Shore every two or three weeks. Apart from the fight over the decking I'd installed on the roof, we got along well, though it often involved yelling at each other. We yelled not out of anger but out of an enthusiasm for disagreement. Gay liked to tell people what they were doing wrong. He once told Edie Vonnegut that she didn't deserve to own anything—*not a single thing*—because she'd forgotten to put oil in her moped; it also bothered him that she didn't know who'd been president during World War I. He thought my politics were dopey and naive. He thought I didn't have enough appreciation for *stuff*. He thought the twelve-step program I went to was a cult, the one saving grace of which was that I appeared to be one of the cult leaders, a conclusion he came to because he often found me taking phone calls from people as broken and needy as myself or going out to meet them for coffee.

As time went on, we argued about Gay's marriage but without enthusiasm. It was clear the marriage was a mistake, as any enterprise is that was embarked on chiefly to stop one of its parties from crying—that was why Gay said he'd embarked on it, and though he was probably half joking, that he was saying it only weeks after the wedding didn't inspire confidence. He could be generous to Karen, especially just after they moved down to the shore. He'd bring her a bouquet of fresh-picked wildflowers or cook her a dinner of bluefish he'd caught on the water only hours before, its eyes still shining with life. But he'd stopped loving her, if he ever had to begin with, and the dominant notes of the marriage were obligation and resentment. Karen made most of the money and paid most of the bills. He knew he owed her; he said she wouldn't let him forget it. And in turn he made it clear that whatever he did for her he did because he owed her. He was repaying his debt. This got harder when he stopped bringing in money.

He'd begun writing a novel. I don't recall feeling surprised when he told me this. Even if he couldn't spell, Gay could read, and apart from his sniffiness about Nabokov, his taste in literature was pretty good. I'm still grateful to him for turning me on to Kem Nunn's great surf noir *Tapping the Source*. Gay's book was set on the Eastern Shore and was called *Box Lot*. This is an auctioneers' term for miscellaneous items that are put up for bid as a group, usually in an actual box, and sold for a single price, as is, with no guarantees that any of the contents are even functional. One bids on a box lot at one's own risk. As Gay put it in the novel's prologue: "Box lots are the bottom of the antique trade—odds and ends the auctioneer feels aren't strong enough to bring a bid on their own . . . Most often it is what it is supposed to be: junk."

The novel's central character is a raffish, good-natured antique picker named Benny; he was Gay's idealized vision of himself, less neurotic, more suave. The story is a bric-a-brac of random narrative threads, much like a box lot itself. It spins around a box lot that may contain a rare, unauthenticated drawing by Salvador Dalí. The latter is pursued by, among others, a pair of popinjay antique dealers who may be the only people on the Eastern Shore who know who Dalí was; a diminutive Mayan detective searching for children who've been spirited away from his village in the Yucatán; and a hulking biker-preacher named Otto DeFay with a racket in counterfeit Beanie Babies. For all its exaggeration, the book was true to its milieu. The characters connive over the cast-iron skillets and dog's-head-shaped cuff links that showed up at every auction in Accomack County. The dealers' patter is just like the patter I heard when I came down to visit. *Lot twenty-six. Let's see. Uh, yeah, first one's got what looks like a lunch pail on top of some pens, pencils, and one of them long shoehorns. Hey, I see a glass water pitcher covering a real big spoon and it looks wooden to me. Maybe real old, I'm guessing. And some dining utensils and, ah, an ashtray.*

Box Lot is often laugh-out-loud funny, if you're not bothered by jokes about male homosexuals, exploited children, and Mayan people, not to mention rednecks. It couldn't be published today. It probably couldn't have been published in the early 2000s either, mostly because the delirious turns of the story didn't actually advance it. Gay's narrative method was the one Dr. Seuss employs in *The 500 Hats of Bartholomew Cubbins* and *On Beyond Zebra!*, a method of unending sumless addition (though I guess in *500 Hats* it's endless difference-less subtraction). Each new letter was followed by another new letter, and when you took off one hat, there was always another hat beneath it.

He kept sending me installments, ten, twenty pages at a time; his productivity made me sick with envy. "What happened to that Dalí?" I'd ask him, and he'd tell me, "I'll get to it. Don't be so fucking impatient." Of course he was irritated. He didn't want to be told to cut to the chase, he wanted to be told the pages were great and he should just write more of them. If I'd been a better friend that's what I would have told him, especially if I'd kept in mind that literature has its share of inconclusive, accretive masterworks, from *Tristram Shandy* to *Life: A User's Manual* and *If on a Winter's Night a Traveler*. However, those works belong to the avant-garde, and Gay wanted to write a bestseller. Or, anyway, a good-seller.

As so often happens when you start writing about something you love, he had fallen out of love with his trade. With each new twist of plot he spent less time at swap meets and estate sales, less time cleaning his finds with steel wool and mineral oil, less time sanding, painting, and refinishing, less time driving the merchandise up to New York to sell at the flea on Twenty-Sixth Street. Soon Gay was making only a few hundred dollars a month. In time this would bring about what was probably the worst business decision of his life. But before that, it brought about many fights with Karen. They were ugly fights, their cruelty equaled only by their pettiness. Once he put her on speakerphone so I could hear her screaming at him. "Screaming" was his word: to me it sounded more like she was moaning, as one might moan in pain. A shameful thing to eavesdrop on. What kept you from yelling at him was his readiness to admit fault. "Look, I know there's something wrong with me," he'd begin in his aggrieved squawk of a voice, and wipe his face as if mopping off sweat. You lost some sympathy for him when he added that Karen had something wrong with her, too, she was no saint. Still, he was so transparently miserable there was no point in yelling at him; he would have borne your yelling in silence, the way a dog does, looking down at his feet.

During his visits to Westbeth, he stayed in the guest room by the entrance. In the past it had been where I slept the nights I was staying over. The room was barely wide enough for a foam mattress and a pair of shoes and would have been claustrophobic if not for the double-hung windows that opened onto the roof, allowing whoever was staying there to step outside to smoke and gaze at the night sky and the dark river below. We called it the dog room: it was a room only a dog could be comfortable in, every inch of it itchy with dog hair: Cracker's hair, Crumbs's hair, Wheatie's hair, and the hair of his successor, another Airedale named Grits. Also that of the ferrets Pretzel and Croissant. In a departure from the pattern, Gay's next dog was named Razz. He was a magnificent, deep-chested husky that he found tied in a yard on the shore and bought from his owner out of pity and indignation. This was in 2002, when the marriage—and really Gay's entire life—was coming apart. A dog, especially a big, energetic one bred to drag a sled hundreds of miles across ice and snow, was the last thing he needed. He just couldn't stand to leave him tied out in a yard next to a bowl of hot, scummy water and some unplayed-with toys.

For a long time, I saw Gay's marital problems as funny. He presented them as funny, the ancient, joyless Jiggs-and-Maggie comedy of a scrawny guy who just wanted to fish (and paint—and now write) and an ill-tempered wife who wanted him to bring home the bacon. I'm not sure when my attitude changed. It may have been the time he put Karen on speaker. It may have been when he told me she'd brandished a gun at him because she suspected him of cheating. After that was the time he told me *he'd* fired a gun into the ceiling during another of their fights. I guess it says something about Wachapreague that none of the neighbors called the police. The way Gay put it, he'd done it out of exasperation and immediately was mortified. There was a thunderstorm that night, and he walked out into it, hoping to be struck by lightning. For a moment, the impotence, both of the violence and the attempt to atone for it, seemed almost funny again. That was the last time. "This is crazy," I yelled at him. For once I was yelling for real. "Just get out of there. Get the fuck away from each other. This is how people get killed." He said he couldn't get out of there. If he left, she'd take everything. I asked him what he thought he'd have if he killed her. He told me not to be ridiculous, he wasn't going to kill her. He'd never laid a finger on her.

That must have been June or July. In August I learned he was in the jail over in Accomack for violating a protection order Karen had taken out against him. I guessed it was for the incident with the gun, in which case it shouldn't have come as a surprise to him. But evidently it did, and on finding the order posted on the front door when he got home from fishing one afternoon, he proceeded to rush around town looking for someone to explain it to him and finally went to the home of one of Karen's friends, not realizing that Karen had taken shelter upstairs. The next he knew he was being arrested. He should have been out in a few hours; instead, he was in county a month. The reasons were never clear to me.* He didn't struggle with the deputies who arrested him, but he was mouthy with them, and then with the judge at his hearing. His old college friend and roommate Larry had gotten a summer house a few towns over and was

---

* In his will Gay accused Karen of having set him up "with the hope that I'd be murdered in jail or kill myself."

able to find him a lawyer, but the lawyer was incompetent. Gay sat in jail. He was beaten by the other prisoners and maybe by guards; he may have been sexually abused. He tried to hang himself with his bedsheets, and the authorities put him on an antidepressant that made him drool uncontrollably. He was still drooling when he moved back to New York three years later. Every so often he'd realize he was doing it and wipe his mouth and look at you to see if you'd noticed. You'd pretend you hadn't.

This was in the fall of 2005. He still had Razz. It couldn't have been easy having a large dog to care for in the city. Still, I hoped Razz would give him something to live for at a time when he had little else. Put another way, a dog might not give him a reason to live, but it might give him second thoughts about dying. He was staying in the loft while I spent most of my time up in the country, but I continued to pay the rent. Every month I'd tell him I couldn't keep paying it—I was having money trouble of my own—and he'd say he understood. Then the next month I'd numbly write another check. I knew he couldn't come up with the $575; he could barely buy groceries. Whenever I came down, I'd bring him bread from my town bakery. I didn't like coming down much. The train was expensive, the loft was dirty and cluttered, and Gay was exhausting to be around. He'd chain-smoke discount cigarettes and rant about Karen and Larry, whose attempts at help, he'd decided, were purely self-serving. He'd rant about the fascist police. I'd agree, but he'd yell that I didn't know the first thing about fascism. He did: the cops really were fascist; the whole country was fascist. This conviction had been inscribed in him as if by an awl. Jail had inscribed it in him. If he saw a black-and-white behind him while he was driving, he'd start shaking so badly he had to pull off the road.

For as long as I'd known him, he'd threatened to kill himself whenever he was unhappy—when Wheatie died, he'd cried out, "Now I can finally kill myself!"—but he had begun saying it more often and with greater vehemence. He said he'd kill himself if Larry tried to take the loft from him. Larry might do that because in 2001, in a jaw-droppingly stupid and shitty business decision, Gay had sold Larry his lease for $40,000. Actually, he'd sold it to an entity called 'Gay Milius Productions,' of which Larry was the director and sole proprietor. We were made to understand that this was chump change for him. At the time, it looked like a shitty decision on

Larry's part—among other reasons, because in New York City one cannot legally sell the lease on a rental apartment to another person, at least not without permission of the actual landlord; this is still more problematic when the building's mortgage is held by an entity of the United States government. Even Gay had qualms about it. Underneath his signature on the sale agreement he'd written, I AGREE TO THIS BUT HAVE RESERVATIONS AS TO WEATHER [sic] IT WILL WORK.

For a long time, Larry took no advantage of the agreement, and you might easily have assumed it was a tactful way of giving his friend some cash. It was only after Gay moved back that he started to act as if he'd actually *bought* something. He'd made a lot of money in tech; now he wanted to be an artist, to resuscitate the creative partnership he and Gay had had thirty-some years before when they'd messed around with the Baba Ganouj story. He had an idea for a series of animated children's "learning modules" featuring a character named Mr. History, and he wanted Gay to help develop it. He was coming up a few weekends a month from his home in Philadelphia, sometimes with his wife Nancy, sometimes by himself. I always kept away during these visits and would come back to find the loft littered with the cheap electronics Larry appeared to buy in bulk: three or four DVD players with their clocks reproachfully blinking at 12:00; TVs; cordless phones. Gay complained he was treating him like a flunky, making him park his car for him and sending him out at all hours on humiliating errands. And Larry had disfigured the loft with some flimsy drywall partitions that then had to be torn out when the building discovered them and said they were against code.

Still, I told Gay, that didn't mean he was planning to take the loft from him. He couldn't take it from him because the loft had never been his to sell. Anyway, Larry was his friend. If he hadn't bailed him out, he'd still be in jail. He said, "You don't know Larry. He let me rot in that place a whole month." I asked him if he was talking about this with his shrink. A friend of ours had found a therapist who was willing to see Gay for practically nothing. He said of course he hadn't told her; she'd think he was crazy. He laughed. I let that reassure me. I told him anybody had the right to kill himself. I thought it would be insulting to lie to him. Immediately afterward, I lied: "But you have to stay alive to finish your novel." He looked at me sourly. He knew I didn't believe it could get published. So I said, "You have a dog to take care of!" As stupid and desperate as it was, the gambit seemed to quiet him. Razz was undemonstrative as dogs go. He didn't bark in greeting, he didn't lick you, he accepted petting without gratitude or evident enjoyment. Instead of looking at you like most dogs do, he gazed off at the horizon as if seeking a destination there, a point to run toward. Still, he was a dog, and I knew how Gay was about dogs.

The dog was the first sign that something was wrong.

On the morning of January 18, 2006, Razz appeared on the roof outside the office window of the Bruces, who lived next door, and butted his muzzle against the glass. It wasn't unusual to see him out there; Gay always left the window to the dog room open so Razz could go out on his own when he didn't feel like taking him downstairs for a walk. Rocky, the Bruces' assistant, thought he looked hungry, and she put out some food for him, which he ate before disappearing back inside Gay's apartment. He showed up again that evening. Again she fed him. Afterward Rocky followed the dog across the roof, but seeing a light on in Gay's loft and knowing he kept odd hours, she decided he was just sleeping. Maybe she actually saw him lying on the sofa; if his back had been turned toward her, she might not have noticed the bag. All these years later, I'm no longer sure what she told me. It was only when Razz reappeared the next morning that she became concerned enough to enter the apartment. Did she call out a hello? It was Thursday, January 19, 2006. That's the date on the death certificate. But Gay may have died as many as two days earlier. The autopsy report speaks of "advanced putrefactive changes."

Gay had run a long hose from the propane tank of the gas grill he kept on the roof and fed it through a hole he'd cut in the side of a white plastic garbage bag, then pulled the bag over his head and tucked its open end under the neck of his sweater. He'd gone to the trouble of sealing the hole with tape to make the bag as airtight as possible. The autopsy report notes that his hair was wet from condensation. He may have modeled the apparatus on the hookah rigs he'd sometimes used when diving, which provide the user with an almost limitless supply of air, though of course they limit how far he can swim. His death was probably painless, even mildly euphoric. In his last moments, he may have had the illusion he was on a dive: the quick backward drop over the side of the boat and the silent plunge through the darkening water in which the sun got smaller and dimmer until it was a small silver bubble floating in darkness and then was gone.

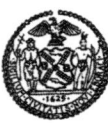 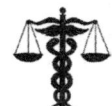

OFFICE OF CHIEF MEDICAL EXAMINER
CITY OF NEW YORK

REPORT OF AUTOPSY

Name of Decedent: Gay Edward Milius III   **M.E. Case #:** M06-00392

Autopsy Performed by: Mary Fowkes, M.D.   **Date of Autopsy:** Jan. 23, 2006

FINAL DIAGNOSES

I.   INTENTIONAL INHALATION OF PROPANE GAS WITH
     A. ASPHYXIA

II. ADVANCED DECOMPOSITION

CAUSE OF DEATH: **ASPHYXIA DUE TO INTENTIONAL INHALATION OF PROPANE GAS.**

MANNER OF DEATH: **SUICIDE (PLASTIC BAG OVER HEAD ATTACHED TO PROPANE TANK).**

THIS IS A TRUE COPY
Office of Chief Medical Examiner
This record cannot be released without
prior consent from the office of Chief
Medical Examiner, New York City, N.Y.

A. Constante *AC*
5/11/06

I'm not sure who called to tell me Gay was dead; it was either Rocky or one of the building staff, maybe Matthew, the manager. I don't remember the drive down from the country, just standing in the driveway of our

OFFICE OF CHIEF MEDICAL EXAMINER
CITY OF NEW YORK

REPORT OF AUTOPSY

CASE NO. M06-00392

I hereby certify that I, Mary Fowkes, M.D., City Medical Examiner - I, have performed an autopsy on the body of **Gay Edward Milius III,** *on the 23rd day of January, 2006, commencing at 10:30 AM in the Manhattan Mortuary of the Office of Chief Medical Examiner of the City of New York. This autopsy was performed in the presence of Dr. Hayes and Dr. Prial.*

EXTERNAL EXAMINATION:
The body is of a well nourished, well developed, average framed, 5' 11", 143 lb White man whose appearance is consistent with the given age of 59 years. The curled brown hair measures up to 2". The nose and facial bones are intact. The eyes have cloudy corneas with indistinct irides and the conjunctivae are clear without hemorrhage, petechiae or jaundice. The oral cavity has rare natural teeth in good repair and an atraumatic mucosa. The torso is unremarkable. The extremities show no needle punctures, scars over subcutaneous veins, or injuries. The fingernails are short and do not extend beyond the fingertips. The external genitalia are of a normal circumcised man.

POSTMORTEM CHANGES:
There is no rigor mortis of the upper and lower extremities, neck, and jaw. Lividity is posterior, purple, and fixed. The body is cool. There are advanced putrefactive changes manifested by green skin changes, bloating, mummification of the fingertips, foul odor, purge from the mouth, and skin slippage.

CLOTHING:
The body is clad in one brown sweater, one brown belt, one pair of blue jeans, two black and red socks, one gray pair of underpants, and one tan shirt.

INJURIES:
There is a 27 x 22" white plastic trash bag over the head and is tucked securely under the neck of the turtle neck sweater and no marks around the neck. There is a 4" circumference hole cut form one side of the bag which is rimmed by black tape. The hole is 14-1/2" from the sealed bottom of the bag. The tape is 3/4" in width. (Comment: Per police report, the black tape and hole were connected to a tube which was then attached to a propane tank). The scalp hair is wet and matted with condensation. The cervical vertebrae, hyoid bone, tracheal and laryngeal cartilages, and paratracheal soft tissues are without trauma. The upper airway is patent. The tongue is unremarkable.

These injuries, having been described, will not be repeated.

rented house beneath the bare branches of the maple in the front yard and then getting out of the car on West Street two hours later, zipping my coat against the wind from the river. For all the years I'd lived there, I passed myself and then myself and my wife off as Gay's roommates. Now, however, the loft was a potential crime scene, and I was a sort of docent charged with walking some detectives from the Sixth Precinct through the premises and pointing out anything that seemed out of place. Everything seemed out of place. The suddenness and ambiguity of Gay's death made even the most ordinary possessions seem like evidence: the atoll of dirty dishes in the sink, the overflowing ashtrays, the plastic totes filled with the kinds of things he'd sold at flea markets strewn across the floor. On one wall were the last of his art pieces: a pair of ghosts he'd made years before from bedsheets stiffened with rabbit's-foot glue. They weren't the cute phantasms of *Ghostbusters*; they had gaping, silently shouting mouths, and they were furred with dust. Everything was inundated in the fierce golden light of a winter afternoon. Usually that light showed the apartment to its best advantage. Now it seemed to indict it, its dirt, its wear, the cheapness of its fittings, its conquest by crap.

Why hadn't anybody cared for it?

There was a note on the dining table.

I identified the handwriting as Gay's, then the cops dismissed me. That the loft was my home, or had been, didn't much concern them. Homes are for the living, and what they cared about was death.

Another three weeks would pass before the medical examiner ruled that my friend hadn't died by foul play, and I was allowed back in. I went over to the apartment of Gay's friend Denise, and for the rest of that first afternoon and evening I made calls to people who knew him. Only three of those conversations stay with me.

Larry was shocked into a brittle formality. He'd been formal the few times I'd met him at the loft, but back then his formality had been genial, the formality of the master of the house admitting an unfamiliar guest, and now it was the formality of a butler in an Agatha Christie novel telling the authorities that the deceased had always been regular in his habits. This was before I came to hate Larry. At one point I hated him so much that I dreamed of killing him twice in succession, once by shooting him, then by heaving him over the roof. But at the time I was merely suspicious of him because of what Gay had told me. Given what I came to feel, it may be beyond my power to be fair to him, but let me at least be factual. The one thing I would swear he said that evening was, "I've got to figure out what to do with my life now that my best friend is dead." Reading those words now all these years later, I'm filled with pity for him. Why I should feel that is mysterious to me. Maybe it's because I always thought Gay was *my* best friend.

Karen expressed no shock at the news. She may have expected Gay to kill himself one day; she just wanted it known she hadn't driven him to it. She'd always been practical, meticulous—fitting traits for someone who made her living as a photo retoucher—but she'd had an adventurous streak that drew her to painting and scuba diving in remote places and eventually to Gay. The streak had run out. She'd been ill. There was no money. Her voice was dull. What had happened couldn't make her any sadder than she already was. She just wished Gay could have realized—I forget whether she said *realized* or *admitted*—that he loved her and allowed himself to be happy with her.

The third conversation was with Karen's sister Pat, whom I'd once been friendly with. I didn't call her; she called me, probably after talking with Karen. She was angry, and she enunciated her words with such icy fury I could hear her teeth click. She wanted me to know why her sister had taken out the protection order three years before. Gay hadn't fired a gun at the ceiling, he'd pointed it at Karen's head. *At her head.* She kept repeating it. *At her head.* Maybe she thought I didn't believe her. Maybe she just wanted some acknowledgment of what a terrible thing that was to do to anyone, let alone someone you'd sworn to love and honor. *At her head.* It was; I should have said so. Instead, I inwardly rejected what she was telling me, not so much disbelieving it as refusing to hear it; entire nations have been known to do this. I wanted to tell her that Gay wouldn't point a gun at anyone, but already I was beginning to understand that you don't know what anyone would do. At length, I asked, with some exasperation, what she expected me to do with this information. Gay was my friend and he was dead. I couldn't change either of those things.

The next day I had to certify that Gay actually *was* dead, I mean that the body that had been found in the sitting area of the loft with its head wrapped inside a plastic trash bag was really his. My friend Sheila accompanied me to the Manhattan morgue. It's over on First Avenue, not far from where Jack Dowling's old loft building used to stand back when he was fighting over it with a remorseless city agency, which upon prevailing over him in court took possession and smashed the building to rubble. Before I went into the back room to view what I did not yet realize would not be a body but some photographs of one, small black-and-white photos you might get from a machine in a penny arcade, Sheila gave me some advice. Just look once, then shut your eyes. That will be enough. Of course she was right. I can't have looked at the photos for more than ten seconds, but I see them still.

THERE'S A VERSION OF THIS story in which I track all the maneuvers that Larry and I and various other parties performed during the next four months. He wanted to claim the apartment. I wanted to let the building have it back. He threatened to sue me. I hired a lawyer. Both of us made appeals to Gay's half-sister Mitzi in Aspen, who as his beneficiary had the final say over what would happen to the apartment, that is, if anybody had such a say apart from Westbeth's management or board of directors.

It's a long story, but it's not Gay's story. It's the story of people quarreling over his legacy, which was probably worth less than $5,000 unless you count the van he'd parked on Washington Street. By the time that could be legally claimed, it had a windshield impasto-ed with parking tickets and tires that someone had slashed with a utility knife until they were just puddles of black rubber.

The quarrel came to a head the day before Gay's memorial in April, more than two months after his death, when Larry learned—I'm still not sure how—that I'd turned the keys to the apartment over to Westbeth's management. Nostalgically, he'd planned to spend the weekend in the loft with a group of old friends he'd invited to the memorial: one was flying in from England. Now his plan was ruined. He asked me to meet him at the building. When I arrived, I found him standing before the doorman's desk inside the Bethune Street entrance, his bags strewn around his feet. He looked like a business traveler stranded at an airport—a tired, angry one deterred from making a scene by the hauteur of the agent at the gate. Jacaman, the doorman on duty, wasn't in the least haughty, but he was suave, a stocky gentleman with heavy eyelids and a pointed silver beard. You wouldn't want to lose your shit in front of him. His calm gaze would let you know it was *shit* you were losing and nobody was going to pick it up for you. He tipped his head in my direction, as if he'd conjured me out of the air. "You see, he comes." Since my key to the loft was now as useless as Larry's, Jacaman had to call the manager to let me in. He didn't look happy to see either of us. I mean, he sighed. He informed us that the building had taken possession of its property. As the deceased tenant's administrator, I was allowed to enter and exit the apartment for the purpose of vacating it. Apart from Westbeth staff, no one else would be allowed inside without my explicit permission. He looked at Larry and me in turn to make sure we understood. Larry turned to me and said we should talk upstairs. I refused. I didn't want to be alone with him. So our entire conversation took place in the lobby, in front of an exasperated building manager and a coolly amused doorman and the painters, sculptors, poets, novelists, playwrights, actors, dancers, and musicians who passed through it, most of them middle-aged, many old, bent, ponderous, spindly or thick-waisted, with bent spines and spotted hands.

I told Larry I wasn't letting him back in the loft. It was too bad about his friends. In the next moment, I had one of those perverse changes of heart you read about in Dostoevsky. I told the manager that Larry could stay in the loft that weekend; his friends could stay too. He just had to be out Sunday and leave the place as he found it. I smiled benignly, drunk on my chivalry. Everyone looked at me like I was crazy. Even Larry. He blinked rapidly behind his thick glasses, as if it were dawning on him that I might be smarter than I seemed and my generosity only a pretext for screwing him ingeniously. I thought I saw Jacaman shake his head. He didn't know me well, since all the years I'd lived in Westbeth we'd basically just exchanged greetings. But he knew me well enough to know I'm not that smart.

Looking back, I'm pretty sure that my change of heart was nothing but an inability to tolerate having the upper hand. The prospect of triumphing over an adversary flooded me with such anxiety that I had to foreclose it in the instant. Something like that used to happen to Gay at the flea market. A customer would ask him what he wanted for a clam basket that he'd diligently scraped and cleaned and painted and made into an object of beauty, and he'd say $200. The buyer would say that was too much. That is what all buyers say—I myself have said it many times. The standard response would be to knock the price down a fraction, maybe to $180 or $175. Gay couldn't do that. It was as if he had some impairment that made it impossible for him to deal in smaller fractions, even to enumerate them. His eyes would widen in fear. His forehead would knot dreadfully. At last he'd snap, "Okay, $50," and then shove the basket at the buyer, who in that instant had become his antagonist, his enemy, and destroyed him. Now Larry had destroyed me. No, that's melodramatic. He'd taken back the advantage I had stupidly, grandiosely given him. He'd have been a fool not to.

Mitzi had flown in from Colorado for the memorial and asked me to come see her at her hotel. I agreed because she was my friend's sister and because I hoped to somehow persuade her to approve my surrender of the apartment after the fact, or at least not side against me if Larry actually took me to court. I arrived at her hotel around seven. The hotel occupied the site of several of the old meatpacking plants that used to have carcasses hanging from hooks on their awnings; I could remember when the side-walks beneath them were dark with steers' blood. The view from Mitzi's room would have been as impressive as the ones from her brother's loft if three or four half-constructed high-rises hadn't been blocking the western horizon, their concrete subfloors hovering against the velvety night sky. Where had they come from? They hadn't been there a month ago.

As a young woman, Mitzi had turned men into idiots, myself among them. She was only in her forties now, but she had Stage 4 melanoma, and she was plainly dying. After leaving Wachapreague, Gay had spent almost three years caring for her in Colorado, driving her to chemo and doctors' appointments, trying to keep her from doing so much coke. In an early and unsuccessful attempt at treatment, doctors had inserted a seed of radioisotope into one of her eye sockets, pulling the eye out of the way to make room for it, then pushing it back in place. I kept thinking of that hot seed burning uselessly inside her. She was tiny and emaciated. She sat in bed, looking, in her quilted bed jacket, like a child's doll put on display. I sat down in an armchair across from her, but she patted the mattress by her side. "Oh, come on!" she snapped when she saw me hesitate. "Don't get ideas about yourself." Chastened, I joined her on the bed. "You and Larry, you're like little boys," she scolded me. "'He did this!' 'He said that!' 'He took my stuff!' Lay off that shit, will you?"

She talked about Gay. He'd been so good-looking and such a good dancer. All her girlfriends had had crushes on him. No one could wear an Oxford shirt like he did. She studied me critically. I ought to start wearing Oxford shirts, I'd look much better. I should take some of Gay's. I said that would be up to her. I'm sure I sounded priggish, but I disliked the impli-cation that I might just help myself to his stuff. Abruptly she said her feet were cramping, would I rub them for her? Gay used to do that, she added, she'd had to teach him how. For a sexy guy, he didn't have the first clue about how to touch somebody. Forget it if you wanted a hug.

It's true that in all the years I'd known Gay, we'd never hugged. I can't remember him giving me a compliment. My first indication that he even liked me was back in the late seventies when I went to see a writing doctor in Queens with the aim of bringing back a script for biphetamine but instead got shot up with vitamin B12 and a diuretic and out of sympathy or guilt Gay developed polyuria; all that afternoon he kept following me to the toilet in his loft and jigged outside the door while I rid myself of a pint or two of colorless piss. When I was done, he succeeded me and did the same, though probably not as copiously. In Banjarmasin he'd sung karaoke with a slouching, buck-toothed man who was probably an agent of the Indonesian secret police. He sang "Puff the Magic Dragon," and his voice was breathtakingly bad.

The whole time we exchanged these memories, I was rubbing Mitzi's feet. They were tiny and all bone, which made massaging them a little scary. They kept seizing in pain—it was as if they were trying to turn into fists—and she said she needed an OxyContin. She took one from a large bottle on the night table. Was I imagining, or did she give me a sideways glance as she swallowed? I couldn't take my eyes away. "I hope these last me through this trip." She unscrewed the lid again and began to count the pills. Either because of pain or the other drugs she was on, she kept losing track, but by the third repetition I knew she had forty-seven. It was a lot and it was not enough. In my memory, the dark eye Mitzi turned toward me was shrewd, assessing, gleeful. But I think it more likely I'd assigned her the role of temptress, and realizing she had no interest in tempting me sexually I decided she was tempting me to do the one thing I really wanted to do, not just then but always. Only an unexpected phone call from a friend kept me from doing it. Understanding that I was being rescued, I went into the bathroom to talk, and when I came out a half hour later, Mitzi was asleep. I was careful not to wake her as I slipped out.

In retrospect it's chastening that I didn't realize how foolhardy it was to see Mitzi that night. Even if I could have changed her mind, it would have meant nothing. But I was in the grip of a delusion, the same one that had seized Mitzi and Larry. It was the delusion that Gay's apartment belonged to us, that we had some say in its disposition, some power over it. We had none. We might as well have schemed and quarreled to reverse his death. In a sense that was what we were doing. And each of us was also claiming possession of him, who being dead was beyond anyone's possession.

✳

THE MEMORIAL WENT OFF WELL. The guests treated each other with courtesy and spoke of Gay with love. Edie said that during her divorce when she was drinking too much, Gay used to come over every day to wash her dishes. And Rachel and Emily remembered how he'd sat with them at the hospital while their mother was dying. He'd bring her fruit smoothies spiked with vodka, and in this way made her final days bearable. This had been barely three months before he took his life. My memories of Gay during that time are unhappy—the stink of cigarettes, the suicide threats, the rants—so it's some shock to realize he also knew pleasure then, for surely it must have given him pleasure to sneak doctored smoothies into the hospital and keep a straight face while his friends' dying mother sipped them under the eyes of her nurses.

Thankfully, neither Karen nor her sister came, and no one present brought up anything that disturbed the collective sense of the person he had been. Then again, isn't a wife, even an ex-wife, entitled to come to her husband's memorial? Molly had come, and I was happy to see her. And is there any rule that says everyone has to mourn without reservation? I don't know if Gay pointed a gun at Karen; I don't want to know. But even if he had fired the gun into the ceiling and then stalked out into the rain and lightning, hoping to be struck dead, it was domestic abuse, it was terrorism. So I have to ask myself what it means to love a friend who terrorized his wife. Would I love him if he'd shot her?

Larry had taken Gay's laptop on the pretext of making scans of Gay's artwork, and although I suspected this to be a ruse, it turned out that he had made scans. All afternoon the images were projected on the wall. They looked wonderful. In retrospect, the cartoonishness of some of them seems visionary. If Gay had lived long enough to finish his book about the secret society of pole-shifters, it would've been a graphic novel, and he might have published it serially and gotten rich. He died too soon.

The day I saw those photos of Gay at the morgue I had the thought that if this was what I'd gotten sober for, it would've been better not to get sober; it would've been better to die first. This shouldn't be mistaken for altruism. Not for one moment did I wish to sacrifice my life for his. It had to do with what I could bear or thought I could bear. It turns out you can always bear more than you think, if not in the moment, then over time. If you wait out the unbearable moments, you will arrive at others that aren't so bad. I often think that Gay killed himself because he couldn't envision a better moment or even a different moment, one in which his continued being wasn't a humiliation and a torment. Perhaps behind every suicide lies a defective apprehension of time.

On returning to the loft at the end of the weekend, I found Larry had left it intact. As far as I could tell, he hadn't taken any more of Gay's stuff, which lay in the same profusion and disarray in which it had lain for months. He hadn't returned the laptop, though.

Still, he'd left something else for me. I found it on the same dining table where Gay had left his suicide note. Because it also bore Gay's handwriting, I felt my skin prickle when I saw it. It was like coming across a postscript to the suicide note, maybe one that had been written beyond the grave. On a separate piece of paper Larry had written:

Peter, I'm afraid you don't know half of what my friendship with Gay was about. I don't usually talk about such things. But I think you are mistaking me.

The letter itself was dated August 22, 2002, shortly after Gay was released from county.

✳

22 AUG 02

GAY MILNS

DEAR LARRY,
FIRST OFF I WANT TO THANK YOU
FROM THE BOTTOM OF MY HEART FOR ALL
THAT YOU'VE DONE ON MY BEHALF THESE
LAST 30 DAY'S. YOU'VE MADE UP IN
SPADES FOR THE TIME 36 YEARS AGO
WHEN YOU AND THAT JUNKY ELBOW/ALBA/
WHO-EVER? MOVED INTO THE THOMPSON
STREET APARTMENT AND WOKE ME
EVERY MORNING WITH THE SIGHT OF HIS
HEROIN METH INJECTIONS.
    YOU, OF ALL PEOPLE, HAVE ALWAYS
TAKEN MY "HALF-COCKED" IDEAS WITH
AT LEAST A 1/2 DEGREE OF SERIOUSNESS
AND AFTER 30 YEARS OF HARDWORK
TURNED ONE INTO SOMETHING OF A
SUCCESS. YOU BOUGHT MY 1ST PAINTINGS
AND GAVE MOLLY HER 1ST JOB WHEN
SHE NEEDED IT MOST. YOU ALSO TAUGHT
ME HOW TO WATER-SKI AND DRIVE A
STICK-SHIFT (WHO ELSE WOULD HAVE RISKED
THEIR CAR DOING THAT ?!)
    I STILL MISS YOUR CRAZY MOTHER AND NUTTY
FATHER AND OF COURSE YOUR GENIUS SISTER
LAURA. IF THERE'S ANYTHING GOOD TO
BE SAID ABOUT OUR TIMES IT CAN'T BE

DENIED THAT THEY HAD TO BE THE MOST
EXCITING ONES IN HISTORY.
    AND I STILL THINK THE "MARK SLOANE'LIVES
BUTTON YOU MADE WAS PURE GENIUS.
I WANT TO BE WEARING IT WHEN I DIE!!

NOW FOR THE FUTURE:
    YOU OF ALL PEOPLE KNOW THAT NO MATTER
HOW OUT IN LEFT FIELD MY IDEAS MY
SOUND THEY DO ALWAYS SEEM TO WORK!!
WE HAVE 3 OR MORE IDEAS FOR BOOKS,
SCREEN PLAYS, ETC. YOU NO LONGER NEED
THE MONEY AND IT'S NEVER BEEN MORE THAN
A SECONDARY CONSIDERATION FOR MY-
SELF. I JUST WANT TO SPEND THE NEXT
YEAR GETTING ONE OR TWO DONE
SO WE'LL HAVE SOMETHING REALLY
WORTHWHILE TO LEAVE THE WORLD AFTER
WE'RE GONE. TIME IS GETTING SHORT BUT
I THINK OUR MINDS ARE PEAKING AT JUST
THE RIGHT MOMENT.
    MOST IMPORTANT IS TO FIND CONNECTIONS IN
THE PUBLISHING WORLD!!
    NOW THAT I'VE BEEN TO PRISON I CAN
SURELY GET SOMETHING PUBLISHED.
                        LOVE GARY

✳

NOT LONG AGO, I GOT an email from another friend of my youth in which she remembered our parents, who were difficult and eccentric and left marks on us that are barely distinguishable from scars. She wrote, "They were assholes and they were great." I'd say the same of my friend Gay Edward Milius III. He was an asshole and he was great.

Nearly twenty years later, I'm still sometimes angry at him. He killed himself in the apartment I shared with him and left me to identify his insulted remains and deal with his family and pay his parking tickets and the one for dogshit and sell what possessions of his I could and give the money and the stuff I couldn't sell to his heirs. For his sake, I had to spend a night helping his dying sister count her Oxies; it's a miracle I didn't take any. And I had to help find a home for poor Razz, who months later, when his new caretaker brought him to a nature preserve for exercise, broke loose and plunged into the forest and was found only after he'd come upon a rabbit hutch in someone's backyard and torn off the roof and killed the rabbit that lived inside in front of its traumatized owner, an eleven-year-old girl. The victim turned out to be a rare Hungarian rabbit that was worth at least $5,000. It seems somehow appropriate that a dog of Gay's would do that. I was paid a $1,000 administrator's fee, but the wretched business cost me much more than that and four months of my life besides. It made me crazy enough to want to kill somebody. What a torment it was to want that; and what a torment not to be able to kill him.

Still, I'd do it again.

Some six years ago I went to the building for the first time since I'd cleaned out the last of Gay's stuff. As I turned the corner onto Bethune Street, a gust of wind from the river slammed into me. I'd forgotten what that wind was like, how it could turn walking home into a test of strength and perseverance that brought tears to your eyes. A doorman I'd known let me up to the thirteenth floor. I found that the Bruces had done what Gay had always suspected they would and taken over his loft. Murray Bruce came out and met me in the reception area. He was in excellent shape, still tall and upright, his gray hair still thick and tied back in a ponytail, his eyes keen. He told me about the experiments in decay and about Gay's sorties along the ledge between their apartments. "You'd see him and say, 'Wait a minute, what are you *doing*? *You're outside the building!*'"

He invited me to look around. It was only then I realized we were in my—in *Gay's*—old loft. The familiar furnishings were gone, but the layout was the same, and when I climbed the shallow half-staircase I found myself on the same platform where decades before I'd watched an ocean liner gliding silently down the Hudson, its majestic length filling the horizon. Here too, some thirty years later, Gay had lain down on the sofa and taken his last breaths. Murray pointed out the window, beyond the smooth, clean expanse of the new park with its lanes for cyclists and pedestrians. "I love to take people up here and tell them, 'This is waterfront.' Because they don't realize it. It's all waterfront. There used to be piers down there." I remembered those too, and the men who vamped on them. All that was left were the pilings, the darkening river, and a thin band of scarlet light where the river ended and the sky began.

NOTES

Chapter One

Page 10, *The director condemned the piece*: Randy Kennedy, "Contrarian Stays True to His Cred," *The New York Times*, October 23, 2014, https://www.nytimes.com/2014/10/24/arts/design/hans-haacke-gets-establishment-nod-of-approval.html#:~:text=Thomas%20Messer%2C%20the%20museum's%20director,Haacke%20ohimself.

Page 12, *In 2006 the average rent in the*: Les Christie, "Rents Heading Up in '06," *CNNMoney.com*, April 21, 2006, https://money.cnn.com/2006/04/18/real_estate/apartment_rents_head_higher/index.htm.

Page 12, *Rents in Westbeth ranged from about*: S. Jhoanna Robledo, "Enforcing Utopia," *New York*, Nov. 29, 2010, https://www-proquest-com.pitt.idm.oclc.org/docview/807666540?accountid=14709&pq-origsite=primo.

Page 12, *which the building, through its Admissions*: For the first thirty-two years of its existence, Westbeth had an income cap for all residents; in 1970 it was $12,700 a year. In 2012, it had to drop the income cap as a condition of its new mortgage. No applicant can be excluded because they make too much. Almost all apartments of a given size now have the same rent regardless of whether the tenant earns twenty thousand dollars a year or two hundred thousand.

Page 12, *(By 2024 the average rent for*: "Rental Market Trends in New York, NY," Apartments.com, referenced August 30, 2024. https://www.apartments.com/rent-market-trends/new-yorkny/#:~:text=What%20is%20the%20average%20rent%20in%20New%20York%2C%20NY%3F&text=As%20of%20August%202024%2C%20the,an%20apartment%20in%20the%20US.&text=%243%2C158%2Fmo.

Page 12, *while that for a studio in Westbeth*: Tim Murphy, "Future-Proofing a Beloved Affordable Community for NYC Artists," *NYN Media*, August 2, 2024. https://www.nynmedia.com/personality/2024/08/future-proofing-beloved-affordable-community-nycartists/398542/.

Page 13, *When the Palazzo Chupi was finished*: Steffano Annovazzi Lodi, "Palazzo Chupi and the Story of 'An Exploded Malibu Barbie House,'" *Elle Décor Italia*, December 2, 2020, https://www.elledecor.com/it/best-of/a30896505/palazzo-chupi-new-york/.

Page 13, *At the unassumingly named Jeffrey*: Lauren Collins, "Soul Mate: Christian Louboutin and the Psychology of Shoes," *The New Yorker*, March 21, 2011, https://www.newyorker.com/magazine/2011/03/28/sole-mate.

Page 13, *Jeffrey folded in 2020*: Steff Yotka, "Another Retail Goodbye: Jeffrey Stores Close Permanently," *Vogue*, May 18, 2020. https://www.vogue.com/article/another-retail-goodbyejeffrey-stores-close-permanently#:~:text=The%20retail%20industry%20is%20being,stores%20will%20be%20permanently%20closing.

Page 15, *Now—and I think this started*: Janet Malcolm, "A Girl of the Zeitgeist," *The New Yorker*, October 27, 1986.

Page 16, *The buyer turned out not to*: Peter Lunenfeld, "Nothing for Something: Crypto, Cons, and Zombies." *Los Angeles Review of Books*, December 19, 2023, https://lareviewofbooks.org/article/nothing-for-something-cryptos-cons-and-zombies/?mc_cid=e89ba46af1&mc_eid=daec123a8a.

Page 16, *What was true for visual art*: Emily Temple, "A Brief History of Seven-Figure Book Advances from Tom Wolfe to Kristen Roupenian," *LitHub*, May 8, 2018, https://lithub.com/abrief-history-of-seven-figure-book-advances/.

Page 17, *I know what they say about*: Cora Peterson, Ph.D., Aaron Stussell, Ph.D., Jia Li, M.S., et al. *Suicide Rates by Industry and Occupation—National Violent Death Reporting System, 32 States*, 2016, Morbidity and Mortality Weekly Report, Centers for Disease Control and Prevention, January 24, 2020, https://www.cdc.gov/mmwr/volumes/69/wr/mm6903a1.htm.

Page 17, *"I imagined myself as an old*: Interview with Nicolina, June 27, 2020.

Interlude: Becoming Contemporary

Page 21, *"Looking into the future is not*: Joe Lewis, "About the Artist," Joelewis.art, https://joelewisartist.com/aboutthe-artist/.

Page 21, *The work is a kind of*: Tiernan Morgan, "35 Years After Fashion Moda, a Bronx Gallery Revisits the Landmark Space," *Hyperallergic*, August 6, 2015, https://hyperallergic.com/227683/35-years-after-fashion-moda-a-bronx-gallery-revisits-thelandmark-space.

Chapter Two

Page 25, *At the turn of the century*: Jay Shockley, "bell telephone laboratories complex (including the former Western Electric Company and Hook's

Steam-powered Factory Buildings) (now westbeth artists' housing)," New York Landmarks Preservation Commission, October 25, 2011.

Page 25, *Some thirty-four hundred people worked*: Ibid., pp. 5–6.

Page 26, *Their orientation made it possible to*: Phillip Lopate, *Waterfront: A Walk Around Manhattan*, New York: Anchor, 2005, pp. 16–17.

Page 27, *The railroad and the highway that*: Cited by Lopate, op. cit., pp. 61.

Page 27, *Someone who grew up in the building*: https://ephemeralnewyork. wordpress.com/2017/04/24/what-remains-of-theother-end-of-the-high-line/#comments.

Page 28, *To many of the people who*: Jon Gertner, *The Idea Factory: Bell Labs and the Great Age of American Invention*. New York: Penguin, 2012, p. 3.

Page 28, *One administrator made a point of*: Donald A. Yerxa, "The Idea Factory: An Interview with Jon Gertner." *Historically Speaking*, vol. 14, no. 1, 2013. pp. 19–21. Project MUSE, doi:10.1353/hsp.2013.0006.

Page 28, *The vagueness may not be so*: Ibid., p. 65.

Page 30, *In 1961, when the city announced*: Shockley, op. cit., p. 11.

Page 30, *Even cabinet secretaries spoke of building*: Jeanne Houck, "Ana Steele Clark: An Oral History Interview Conducted for the GVSHP Westbeth Oral History Project," New York: Greenwich Village Society for Historic Preservation, 2009, p. 18.

Page 31, *Under New York's housing code, it*: Jeanne Houck, "Richard Meier: An Oral History Interview Conducted for the GVSHP Westbeth Oral History Project," New York: Greenwich Village Society for Historic Preservation, 2009, pp. 2, 6.

Page 31, *"Today the foundation might be regarded*: Joan Davidson, author interview, July 2, 2020, Germantown, New York.

Page 31, *"He knew that my father was*: Jeanne Houck, "Joan Davidson: An Oral History Interview Conducted for the GVSHP Westbeth Oral History Project," New York: Greenwich Village Society for Historical Preservation, 2009, pp. 1–24.

Page 32, *"Here was this building essentially a*: Jeanne Houck, "Dixon Bain: An Oral History Conducted for the GVSHP Westbeth Oral History Project." New York: Greenwich Village Society for Historic Preservation, 2009, p. 4.

Page 32, *No other property offered so much*: Ibid.

Page 32, *With a population density of only*: Jeanne Houck, "Tod Williams: An Oral History Interview Conducted for the GVSHP Westbeth Oral History Project," New York: Greenwich Village Society for Historical Preservation, 2009, p. 5.

Page 32, *The amount later increased to $1.5 million*: Shockley, op. cit., p. 13.

Page 32, *"We interviewed him and we liked*: Houck, "Joan Davidson," op. cit.

Page 33, *And they had to get all*: Houck, "Dixon Bain," op. cit., p. 8.

Page 33, *"Why the hell are we doing*: Ibid., pp. 10–11.

Page 33, *Yet somehow, in just two years*: Houck, "Ana Steele Clark," op. cit., p. 15.

Page 33, *The total cost of construction was*: Grace Lichtenstein, "Artists' Housing, Like Art, Mainly a Matter of Taste," *The New York Times*, March 12, 1970, https://www.nytimes.com/1970/03/12/archives/artists-housing-like-art-mainly-a-matter-of-taste.html?searchResultPosition=18.

Page 33, *The structural engineer Nat Oppenheimer*: Nat Oppenheimer, author interview, New York City, December 18, 2023.

Page 34, *One of the early tenants recalled*: Terry Stoller, *Westbeth X Files, or How the Tenants Saved Westbeth*, https://westbeth.org/westbeth-x-files/chapter-1/.

Page 34: *Years later a new building manager*: Houck, "Richard Meier," op. cit., p. 7.

Page 34: *"Westbeth really was the pioneering project*: Houck, "Richard Meier," op. cit., p. 12.

Page 34, *In a roster of those first tenants*: Houck, "Ana Steele Clark," op. cit., pp. 15–16.

Page 35: *"These are Olympian quarters compared to*: Jeffrey Trask, "'The Loft Cause' or 'Bohemia Gone Bourgeois?': Artist Housing and Private Development in Greenwich Village," *Journal of Urban History*, 2015, vol. 41(6), 2018.

Page 35: *Another critic went so far as to*: Peter Blake, "Downtown Dakota," *New York*, August 3, 1970, pp. 54–57.

Page 35, *Mike Ackerman, the chair of an*: Trask, op. cit., 1027.

Page 35, *As Davidson put it: "Is it*: Houck, "Joan Davidson," op. cit.

Page 36, *Davidson joked that they might even*: Ibid.

Page 36, *"We ran the hallways like they*: Author interview, July 12, 2020.

Page 36, *The architect Tod Williams, who worked*: Houck, "Tod Williams," op. cit., p. 11.

Page 40, *Christina Maile recalls that "in 1970*: Author interview, June 10, 2021.

Interlude: A Mirage

Page 44, *The Smithsonian beat her down to*: Alex Mar, "Was Diane Arbus the Most Radical Photographer of the Twentieth Century?" *The Cut*, July 2017,

https://www.thecut.com/2016/07/diane- https://westbeth.org/westbeth-x-files/
chapter-1/arbus-c-v-r.html.

Page 44, *Another tenant who moved in around*: Patricia Bosworth, *Diane Arbus*.
New York, Norton, 2005, p. 294.

Chapter Three

Page 49, *"A very warm welcome to all of you*: Cited in Terry Stoller, *Westbeth X
Files or How the Tenants Saved Westbeth*. https://westbeth.org/westbeth-x-files/
chapter-1/.

Page 49, *But when he applied to Westbeth*: Bob Gruen, interview, February 25,
2022.

Page 51, *"I really had to get to*: Jack Dowling, email, May 30, 2020.

Page 51, *A half mile farther downtown*: David Lehman, *The Last Avant-Garde:
The Making of the New York School of Poets*, New York: Knopf, 1999, p. 69.

Page 55, *(The Stonewall Inn, which began its*: Fiona Anderson, *Cruising the
Dead River: David Wojnarowicz and New York City's Ruined Waterfront*,
Chicago: University of Chicago Press, 2019. Created from pitt-ebooks on 2020-
09-21, p. 15

Page 56, *A pamphlet issued by the Mineshaft*: Ibid., p. 20.

Page 58, *"I never got onto the cheerleading*: Joan Hall, interviews, March 11 and
17, 2021.

Page 58, *Afterward, Hall asked him,"Why would:"Art*: Terry Stoller, "Joan Hall:
Collage and Assemblage Artist," *Portraits in Art*, 2018.

Page 59, *"The Who was performing around the*: Café Wha? hosted many famous
performers, including a yet-to-be discovered Bruce Springsteen in 1967, but
there's no evidence that the Who ever played there.

Page 61,*"You could do anything you wanted*: Stoller, *Westbeth X Files*, op. cit.

Page 65, *"So it's kind of a re-creation*: Joseph Lovett, Barton Beneš: No Secrets,
2004.

Page 68, *"The men just wanted to write*: Christina Maile, "Westbeth Art of
Community," a talk given for the Greenwich Village Historical Preservation
Society, November 12, 2020, https://www.youtube.com/watch?v=XA77Mgslgpg.

Page 69, *"It was so amazing because I*: Stoller, *Westbeth X Files*, op. cit.

Page 72, *The new novel was published by*: Joel Oppenheimer also wrote some of
these under pseudonyms that are now lost to memory. He is supposed to have

planted his name somewhere in each text, the way Vladimir Nabokov signaled his authorial presence with butterflies.

Page 73, *The actor and visual artist Jan*: Jan Harding, interview, September 27, 2020.

Page 77, *For some unknowable reason, the hustler*: David Groff, "The Curious Closets of Barton Beneš," *Poz*, August 1, 1999, https://www.poz.com/article/The-Curious-Closets-of-Barton-Beneš-11353-4477.

Page 77, *"She freaked out and she stopped*: 18 Lovett, op. cit.

Page 77, *"At the end of her act, a strobe*: McKenzie, "Bob Gruen Goes Behind the Lens." *Whalebone*, vol. 8, https://whalebonemag.com/bob-gruen-behind-punk-rock-photos/.

Page 80, *"We were all running around from*: Terry Stoller, https://westbeth.org/wordpress/profiles-in-art/jack-dowlingpainterwriter.

Page 81, *"And they had children, and the*: Jeanne Houck, "Tod Williams: An Oral History Interview Conducted for the GVSHP Westbeth Oral History Project," New York: Greenwich Village Society for Historical Preservation, 2009, p. 14.

Page 83, *We . . . sat on the waterfront*: David Wojnarowicz, *In the Shadow of the American Dream: The Diaries of David Wojnarowicz*, Amy Scholder, ed., New York: Grove, 1999, pp. 118–19.

Page 92, *Writing for the striking tenants, Joel*: Joel Oppenheimer, letter, New York, August 21, 1972, p. 5.

Page 92, *"The real issue raised by Westbeth*: Barbara Rose, letter, New York, op. cit.

Page 94, *Oppenheimer put it more elliptically in*: Joel Oppenheimer, "Poem for Soho, 8 June 1970, Westbeth Boldface, https://westbeth.org/westbeth-boldface/joel-oppenheimer/.

Chapter Four

Page 99, *Because the actor playing the boyfriend*: Casey Childs, "Black-Eyed Susan," interview, Primary Stages Oral History Project, January 13, 2016, https://primarystagesoffcenter.org/interviews/p-t/black-eyed-susan.

Page 99, *It was too modern for them*: Black-Eyed Susan, author interview, September 27, 2020.

Page 101, *"I think I'm going to call you*: Childs, op. cit.

Page 101, *"It's larger than life what we're*: Ibid.

Page 105, *A last resort was Charles Evans*: It reopened the same year under the new name of the High School of the Humanities.

Page 105, *had such a bad reputation that*: Gene I. Maeroff, "A Revamped High School Finds New Popularity," *The New York Times*, August 26, 1985, https://www.nytimes.com/1985/08/26/nyregion/a-ravamped-high-school-finds-new-popularity.html.

Page 107, *Some of the older boys were*: Nat Oppenheimer, author interview, December 18, 2023.

Page 107, *A boy Lombard's age was almost*: Lem Oppenheimer, author interview, December 15, 2023.

Page 108, *"There were swirling puppets . . . witches*: Stoller, *Westbeth X Files*, op. cit.

Page 110, *"I said, 'Everywhere I go, you're*: Dylan Foley, "Jack Dowling on His Lucrative Decade Running a Gay Erotica Mail-Order Company," *The Last Bohemians*, April 10, 2020. https://lastbohemians.blogspot.com/search?q=Dowling.

Page 112, *"Out of the blue," Brier says*: Robert Brier, author interview, March 9, 2021.

Page 113, *Lovett's physician husband is a serious*: Beneš got occasional grants, but he didn't always use them for living expenses. Of the one that was awarded to him by the Ariana Foundation for the Arts in 1982, he explained, "I asked for $2,000 to tear up, and I got it."

Page 115, *He used it, mounted above a*: *Chelsea VD Clinic*, Cottrell-Lovett Collection, https://cottrell-lovett.com/clc-569/.

Page 115, *The one possible exception is* Death: David Groff, "The Curious Closets of Barton Beneš," *POZ*, August 1, 1989, https://www.poz.com/article/The-Curious-Closets-of-Barton-Beneš-11353-4477.

Page 116, *On first reading about it in*: Quoted in Susan M. Chambré, *Fighting for Our Lives: New York's AIDS Community and the Politics of Disease*, New Brunswick, NJ: Rutgers, 2006.

Page 117, *On any given day, approximately two*: A. R. Jonsen, J. Stryker, eds. *The Social Impact of AIDS in the United States*. Washington, DC: National Academies Press, 1993. Table 9-1, https://www.ncbi.nlm.nih.gov/books/NBK234564/figure/mmm00005/?report=objectonly.

Page 117, *At one well-known hospital, an*: Randy Shilts, *And the Band Played On: Politics, People, and the AIDS Epidemic*, New York: St. Martin's, 1987, p. 507.

Page 118, *In 1967 he won an Obie*: "Tom O'Horgan, Rochelle Owens, Theodore Hoffman and Seth Allen Talk About 'Futz' and Experimental Theater,' WNYC, June 17, 1968, published by the NYPR Archive Collections, https://www.wnyc.org/story/tom-ohorganrochelle-owens-theodore-hoffman-and-seth-allen-talk-about-futz-andexperimental-theater/, 14:55–15:04.

Page 119, *"My mind was reeling with the*: Bob Gruen, *Right Place, Right Time: The Life of a Rock & Roll Photographer*, New York: Abrams, 2020, p. 318.

Page 119, *"It was a scene, people crying*: Ibid.

Page 120, *The photo was later exhibited at*: Ibid., p. 268.

Page 120, *She exclaimed, "Oh my god, you*: Ibid., p. 349.

Page 120, *He got so hip to his*: Ibid., p. 343.

Page 121, The New York Times *reported, "Two*: Joyce Purnick, "City Closes Bar Frequented by Homosexuals, Citing Sexual Activity Linked to AIDS," *The New York Times*, November 8, 1985, https://www.nytimes.com/1985/11/08/nyregion/city-closes-bar-frequented-byhomosexuals-citing-sexual-activity-linked-to-aids.html.

Page 121, *It's only in recent years that*: "Westbeth Icons," https://westbeth.org/westbethicons/#:~:text=Westbeth%20Icons%20is%20a%20project,the%20Westbeth%20Artists%20Residents%20Council.

Page 123, *Early in 1981 the New York*: Leonard Buder, "1980 Called Worst Year of Crime in City History," *The New York Times*, February 25, 1981, https://www.nytimes.com/1981/02/25/nyregion/1980-called-worst-year-of-crime-in-city-history.html.

Page 123, *Ten years later, total crimes had*: Ray Suarez, "How Crime Rates in New York City Reached Record Lows," *All Things Considered*, National Public Radio, December 30, 2017, https://www.npr.org/2017/12/30/574800001/how-crime-rates-in-new-york-cityreached-record-lows.

Page 126, *"At its most basic level," Louis*: Louis Menand, "Modern Family," *The New Yorker*, July 4, 2022, p. 68.

Page 127, *He is supposed to have sold*: Liz Fields, "5 Interesting Facts About Jean-Michel Basquiat," *American Masters*, PBS Network, February 25, 2021, https://www.pbs.org/wnet/americanmasters/5-interesting-facts-about-jean-michelbasquiat/17318/#:~:text=Basquiat%2C%20who%20was%20of%20Haitian,young%20artists%20to%20this%20day.

Page 127, *Lorraine O'Grady called him "a black*: Lorraine O'Grady, letter to Jean-Michel Basquiat dated March 10, 1983. "both/and," Brooklyn Museum of Art, March 5–July 18, 2021.

Page 127, *This made it the sixth-most-*: Robin Pogrebin and Scott Reyburn, "A Basquiat Sells for a 'Mind-Blowing' $110.5 Million at Auction," *The New York Times*, May 18, 2017, https://www.nytimes.com/2017/05/18/arts/jean-michel-basquiat-painting-is-sold-for-110-million-at-auction.html.

Page 137, *In 1979 Westbeth could pay only*: Terry Stoller, *Westbeth X Files, or How the Tenants Saved Westbeth*, Westbeth, Home for the Arts website, https://westbeth.org/westbeth-x-files/chapter-3/.

Page 138, *For anyone familiar with the New*: City Realty listings of August 6, 2022, https://www.cityrealty.com/nyc/west-village/323-west-11th-street/apartment-3E/DtSOKFRdOzB?utm_source=ActiveCampaign&utm_medium=email&utm_content=Apartments+with+recent+price+drops%21&utm_campaign=Low+Eng+E.

Page 138, *Another $1.3 million would be allocated*: William G. Blair, "Artist-Housing Tenants Are Split on Co-Op Plan," *The New York Times*, November 24, 1985, Sec. 1, p. 56, https://timesmachine.nytimes.com/timesmachine/1985/11/24/issue.html.

Page 139, *A spokesperson for the anti-co-op faction*: Blair, op. cit.

Chapter Five

Page 154, *"A photographer, usually you should have*: Interview with Terry Stoller, op. cit.

Page 154, *According to one chronicler, the first*: Stevyn Colgan, "The 'Metaphoric Rubbish' Art of Barton Lidicé Beneš," *Colganology* Blogspot, September 7, 2013, https://colganology.blogspot.com/2013/09/the-metamorphic-rubbish-art-of-barton.html.

Page 155, *Beneš's longtime assistant Nicholas Cirabisi says*: Nicholas Cirabisi, email, March 9, 2021.

Page 157, *"I always experienced my family as*: Doreen St. Félix, "Lorraine O'Grady Has Always Been a Rebel," *The New Yorker*, September 29, 2022, https://www.newyorker.com/culture/the-newyorker-interview/lorraine-ogrady-has-always-been-a-rebel.

Page 160, *"Because this show was about, you*: Andil Gosine, "Lorraine O'Grady's Nature: A Conversation About 'The Clearing,' a radio interview for National Campus and Community Radio Association, Canada, 2010, https://lorraineogrady.com/art/body-is-theground-of-my-experience/.

Page 162, *New York collectors "like to collect*: Adam Gopnik, "Fluid Dynamics: What Helen Frankenthaler Brought to the Canvas," *The New Yorker*, April 12, 2021.

Page 163, *According to a tribute in* Columbia: David J. Krajicek, "The Last Beat," *Columbia* magazine, winter 2012–13, https://magazine.columbia.edu/article/last-beat.

Page 163, *They often hinge on the theme*: Dylan Foley, "Caleb Carr Lives in a Very Dark Place," *Lithub*, August 23, 2016. https://lithub.com/caleb-carr-lives-in-a-very-dark-place/.

Page 166, *"It was a paradise," she wrote*: Christina Maile, "Regrets" (unpublished), 2017. Used by permission of the author.

Page 167, *She described them in an essay*: Ibid.

Page 173, *More vividly, the actress Jackie Hoffman*: Frank Bruni, "Genre-Bending Hangout Takes Its Final Bows," *The New York Times*, May 21, 2008, https://www.nytimes.com/2008/05/21/dining/21florent.html.

Page 174, *When Roy Lichtenstein, a longtime regular*: Jessica Loudis, "Florent Was the Most Progressive Diner in New York," *Extra Crispy*, February 13, 2018, https://www.myrecipes.com/extracrispy/florent-was-the-most-progressive-diner-in-new-york.

Page 174, *Another customer remembered the first time*: Bruni, op. cit.

Page 174, *"I thought, 'This is nuts. This*: Jad Abumrad (producer), "Blood," *Radiolab*, July 31, 2013, https://www.radiolab.org/episodes/308403-blood.

Page 175, *And when she left, she made*: Laurel Reuter, interviews, May 23 and 24, 2021.

Page 176, *Prankster that he was, Beneš enjoyed*: Abumrad, op. cit.

Page 176, *"'Mom,' he says, 'I want you*: Warren Beneš, interview, March 2, 2021.

Page 176, *The designer Isaac Mizrahi explained their*: Alex Vadukul, "Patrick O'Connell, 67, Dies; Raised Awareness of AIDS with Art," *The New York Times*, May 3, 2021.

Interlude: On the Beauty of Zero

Page 188, *It allowed her to make art*: "The 13 Portals," Nicolina Art, https://www.nicolinaart.com/portals.html.

Page 188, *The floating gallery of fishing boats*: "Art in Motion: Flutuarte," Nicolina Art, https://www.nicolinaart.com/artin-motion.html.

Chapter Six

Page 193, *"I evolved more and more into*: Liza Zapol, Peter Ruta: oral history interview conducted for the Greenwich Village Society for Historic Preservation Oral History Project, March 24, 2016, and May 9, 2016, p. 9, https://media.villagepreservation.org/wpcontent/uploads/2020/05/15034826/Ruta_PeterTranscript_FinalforWebsite.pdf.

Page 194, *"Nero, when he died . . . he said*: Ibid., p. 20.

Page 194, *Everyone smelled the stink of burned*: Ahmed F. Gohniem, "The Fires," Massachusetts Institute of Technology, https://web.mit.edu/civenv/wtc/PDFfiles/Chapter%20V%20Fire.pdf.

Page 195, *"At 8:45 a.m. on September 11, 2001*: https://www.lehman.edu/lehman/depts/depts/langlit/tbj/010ctnov/c8.pdf.

Page 195, *"There's that smell again . . . That*: "Susannah Kelly's Audio Diary, Part 5 [Archival Audio]," September 11 Digital Archive, accessed January 2, 2023, https://911digitalarchive.org/items/show/96011.

Page 196, *"All artists felt, having seen the*: All quotes from Jacqueline Casale Taylor Basker, *Aftermath: 9/11 and New York Artists*, YouTube, February 6, 2019, downloaded from https://www.youtube.com/watch?v=AU-asCoIK2w.

Page 199, *The few K8 Hardy photos I*: https://www.artsy.net/artwork/tauba-auerbach-artists-space-annual-editionportfolio-2015.

Page 199, *while a selection of Beverly Brodsky's*: "Beverly Brodsky Artworks," Saatchi Art, https://www.saatchiart.com/brodskyb.

Page 200, *The bust has been especially hard*: Zachary Small and Julia Halperin, "Young Artists Rode a $712 Million Boom. Then Came the Bust." *The New York Times*, August 18, 2024. https://www.nytimes.com/2024/08/18/arts/design/young-artists-auctions-collectors.html?searchResultPosition=10.

Page 200, *In a final coup of value-creation*: Sarah Cascone, "Are Dealers Replaceable in the Crypto Era? One Artist Is Selling Her Work via ATM at Frieze New York," *Artnet News*, May 6, 2021, https://news.artnet.com/market/agustina-woodgate-frieze-atm-1965167.

Page 202, *Isabel Borgatta, a sculptor in her*: Jillian Steinhauer, "Weathering the Storm: Hurricane Sandy's Impact at Westbeth (Part II)," *Hyperallergic*, December 20, 2012, https://hyperallergic.com/62350/weathering-the-storm-hurricane-sandys-impact-at-westbeth-parttwo/.

Page 202, *The only people allowed below ground*: Christina Maile, "A Dark and Stormy Night," Mr. Beller's Neighborhood, January 7, 2013, https://mrbellersneighborhood.com/2013/01/a-dark-andstormy-night.

Page 211, *It's probably different for Cameron Crawford*: K8 Hardy, *Untitled*, Reena Spaulings Fine Art, downloaded May 8, 2023, from http://www.reenaspaulings.com/WK.htm.

Page 212, *Supposedly, that was what made it*: Jacob Kastrenakes, "Beeple Sold an NFT for $69 Million," *The Verge*, March 11, 2021, downloaded from https://www.theverge.com/2021/3/11/22325054/beeple-christies-nft-sale-cost-everydays-69-million.

Page 212, *Even in 2009, 60 percent of*: Bonnie Rosenstock, "Westbeth Comes of Age: A Unique Artists' Complex Tries to Stay Afloat," *The Villager*, January 6, 2009. downloaded from https://www.amny.com/news/westbeth-comes-of-age-a-unique-artistscomplex-triesto-stay-afloat/.

Page 212, *The median age of the artists*: Pac Pobric and Caroline Goldstein, "The Whitney Biennial Is Growing Younger and More US-Born as Time Goes By, Our Analysis of the Data Shows," *Artnet News*, May 29, 2019, downloaded from https://news.artnet.com/exhibitions/whitney-biennial-figures-1556902#:~:text=The%20number%20has%20fallen%20again,were%20both%20born%20in%201991.

Page 214, "*My pure intention . . . has been not*: Giorgio Vasari, *Lives of the Most Eminent Painters, Sculptors & Architects*, Gaston Du C. de Vere, trans. London: MacMillan and Co., 1912. Digital ed. May 5, 2008, through Project Gutenberg, EBook #25326, downloaded from https://www.gutenberg.org/files/25326/25326-h/25326-h.htm.

Page 214, *Ogotemmêli, an elder of the Dogon*: Marcel Griaule, *Conversations with Ogotemmeli: An Introduction to Dogon Religious Ideas*, Oxford: Oxford University Press, 1970, p. 89.

Page 215, *In his essay "A Kind of*: John Berger, "A Kind of Sharing," *Keeping a Rendezvous*, New York: Pantheon, 1991, p. 111.

Page 215, *Much of the art of the*: Ibid., p. 109.

Page 215, *But it also reflected Dowling's vision*: Interview with Terry Stoller, op. cit.

Page 216, "*Jack changed the whole feeling of*: Lincoln Anderson, "Jack Dowling, 89, Artist, Writer, Westbeth Gallery Director and First Westbeth Icon," *The Village Sun*, March 13, 2021, downloaded from https://thevillagesun.com/jack-dowling-89-artist-writerwestbeth-gallery-director-westbeth-icon.

Page 216, "*I laid out my work along*: "Jack Dowling Westbeth Icon Presentation, 11/19/17," downloaded from https://www.youtube.com/watch?v=6_umnQheo48&feature=emb_title. 29:32–30:53.

Page 221, *When John introduces himself and confesses*: John Dowling, "John's Trip to Coney Island," p. 15.

Page 225, *As Gay put it in the*: Gay Milius, Box Lot, unpublished, 2005, p. 1.

ACKNOWLEDGMENTS

Every book begins with a promise. Often the writer doesn't understand the fullness of what it entails. Joshua Bodwell saw the promise and held me to it. My thanks to him. Thanks beyond thanks to Gillian Mackenzie, who brought the promise to him, and to her associate Liz Rudnick. I'm also grateful to Celia Johnson, Caroline Brink, Elizabeth Blachman, and David Allender at Godine, and to designer Tamsyn Leigh Bodwell.

Much of this book is a direct record of conversations with painters, sculptors, writers, and performers who live in Westbeth, as well as with other art-makers outside the building. I remain in debt to them for their candor and self-reflection, their deep knowledge of the building and its history and of the history of bohemian New York. So: Black-Eyed Susan, Roger Braimon, Simon Carr, George Cominskie, Edward Field, Bob Gruen, Jan Harding, Jenny Lombard, Christina Maile, who in so many ways is this book's hero. To Grace Bergere, Toi Dericotte, Joan Hall, and Howardena Pindell. To the friends and family of Barton Lidicé Beneš (1942–2012), who raised him from the dead: Warren Beneš, Robert Brier, Nicholas Cirabisi, Joe Lovett, Laurel Reuter, and Tim Teran. To Dan, Nat, and Lem Oppenheimer for their memories of their father and their Westbeth childhood. To Bayan Abdelbaree and Hugues Jacaman. Gratitude and admiration to Joe Lewis and Nicolina, who model the ingenuity, suppleness, and courage it takes to live as an artist in a late-capitalist metropolis. To Rachel and Emily Paine, Edie Vonnegut, and Carroll Huffman for remembering. To Dylan Foley, who got me started.

I thank my friends and colleagues at the University of Pittsburgh, especially Erin Anderson, David Brumble, Angie Cruz, Yona Harvey, Jeanne Marie Laskas, J. C. Lee, Bill Lychack, Diana Khoi Nguyen, and Irina Reyn. At the Bennington

Writing Seminars, I enjoyed the fellowship and artistic and moral example of Ben Anastas, April Bernard, Douglas Bauer, Susan Cheever, David Gates, Amy Hempel, Dinah Lenney, Alice Mattison, Jill McCorkle, Deirdre McNamer, Lynne Sharon Schwartz, Katy Simpson Smith, and Cliff Thompson.

I'm especially grateful to those who read and gave me invaluable notes on early versions of the manuscript.

Four people whose stories are told here are no longer living. Let this be my acknowledgment and memorial to them: Joan Davidson, Jack Dowling, Lorraine O'Grady, and Gay Milius. I also celebrate the memory of Ethan Maile and Jeff Oaks.

Thank you to my friends Jo Ann Beard, Scott Spencer, Tom Carey, Erin Clermont, Deirdre Coltrera, John Corcoran, Ho-Ming So Denduangrudee, James Green, Sheila Keenan and Kevin Duggan, Julia Juster, James McCourt and Vincent Virga, Tracy O'Neill, and Vic Rawlings and Elizabeth Witte.

And beyond everyone and everything to Mary Gaitskill. This book is for her.

A NOTE ABOUT THE AUTHOR

Peter Trachtenberg is the author of the memoir 7 *Tattoos*, *The Book of Calamities: Five Questions About Suffering and Its Meaning*, and *Another Insane Devotion*, a 2012 *New York Times* Editors' Choice. His honors include Whiting and Guggenheim Fellowships and the Nelson Algren Award for Short Fiction. He is a professor emeritus in the Writing Program of the University of Pittsburgh. He lives in the Hudson Valley of New York.

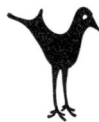

Printed March, 2025 in Hanover, Pennsylvania, for the Black Sparrow Press by Sheridan. Set in Eames Century Modern and Neue Kabel for titling. Interior design by Tamsyn Leigh Bodwell. This first edition has been bound in a jacketed hardcover.

Black Sparrow Press was founded by John and Barbara Martin in 1966 and continued by them until 2002. The iconic sparrow logo was drawn by Barbara Martin.